Can You See Me?

Can You See Me?

A Story of Surviving Alcoholic Parents with Mental Illness

By Helen Lapakko

Can You See Me?
Copyright © 2020 Helen Lapakko

Content Editor: Abigail Mechley
Copy Editor: Jessica Deapolis
Editor-in-Chief: Kristi King-Morgan
Formatting: Kristi King-Morgan
Cover Artist: Jenny Allen
Assistant Editor: Maddy Drake

Printed in the United States of America

ISBN- 9798678031174

www.dreamingbigpublications.com

Acknowledgements

I want to thank my older brother for being my go-to guy with dates and timelines. He is eight years older, and remembers some of the details of when I was very young. Also, to my husband David and my best friend Karen, who have heard many versions of this story as I wrote and rewrote, and the very valuable feedback and encouragement they gave as I wrote my story.

Author's Note

The stories in this book come from my recollections; I have retold them in a way that evokes the feelings and meanings of what was said. I have tried my best to be accurate in the timeline of stories that come from memories, photos, and journals I wrote in over the years. Memories are funny things, and when I talk with my siblings their memories may be different from mine because perceptions can be tricky things. I tried hard to find the truth in my memories.

The names of individuals and some details are changed to respect their privacy, unless I have been given permission to use their names.

Table of Contents

Prologue
Merica's Story

My husband and I park by the Augsburg theatre in Minneapolis an hour before the performance. As we walk in, I look up at him, admiring his handsome face surrounded by his rich, dark brown hair and his well-trimmed beard. He returns my look, with his quirky smile, where the left side of his mouth is a little higher than the right; his hazel eyes are warm and encouraging.

As we walk backstage to the dressing room, I touch the turtle necklace I am wearing to ground and protect me. My right hand carries a card from my Pathway Deck that assures me today is a breakout day with a foundation-shaking change. I look in the mirror, and see my colorful, long, flowing skirt, with my tunic and belt. My long brown hair is pulled behind my right ear with a small flowered barrette.

When memories of my one-year-old daughter and my four-year-old son maneuvering through life unleashed my own childhood memories from the shadows within me, I began to write songs and stories. Tonight, I am performing them for the first time: the stories I couldn't talk about as a child.

I take a deep breath, and slowly release it. I am so nervous my hands are shaking; soon I'll be performing my dramatic monologues and music. I smile at myself in the mirror and say, "You can do this." I look at the clock and see it is time to go into the theatre. My husband kisses me, wishes me good luck, and leaves to take a seat in the audience. I close my eyes and picture the audience, which is made up of friends, college students, and people from treatment centers and counseling programs. There is a group of hearing-impaired adolescents going through drug treatment across the street who provided someone to sign the performance.

As I walk out on the stage with a spotlight following my every move, I notice the grand piano set up stage right and my guitar in its stand next to it. Everything is ready. When I reach the front of the stage, I stop and look up to see a hundred faces staring at me. Merica Palen, a pen name I chose for myself, is the character in my one woman show. She is my creative alter ego. She gives me the courage to speak my truth.

I take a deep calming breath, and say, "Welcome to tonight's performance. *Merica's Story*, my story, is a one-woman show about healing and wholeness. In our life, when we have pain and hurt, we can't ignore it, avoid it, or pretend it's not there. To heal, we must go through the pain to get to the other side, where the white light of healing begins. In other words, there is a light at the end of the tunnel."

The theatre goes dark. I walk to the center of the stage, and when the spotlight shines on me again, I sing:

> *It's time to face the dragon, it's time to hear its roar*
> *It's time to face the dragon, and see what he's here for*
> *It's time to tame the dragon, it's time to make him my friend*
> *It's time to tame the dragon, and bring my fears to an end*

My parents and four siblings never came to see any of my performances. A year after my first performance of *Merica's Story*, my parents passed away, and I inherited the family slides and pictures. When I went through all those images, I saw many memories, stories, and feelings embedded in them. So, I started a scrapbook. As I put each picture on a page, more stories sprang into my mind. Pretty soon I had two scrapbooks filled to the brim, with pictures, stories, and music. People told me I should publish it. I couldn't figure out how to do that.

Years later, my three and four-year-old grandchildren came running into my house with smiles saying, "Nana I missed you, can we build a fort out of cardboard." After an hour outside cutting out windows and hauling in flashlights and blankets, the sudden rain drove us inside where they played at their tables. As I watched them, I was overcome with their innocence and vulnerability. When they turned to say something to me, their young faces were so open, trusting, and loving. An intense anger seeped to the surface at anyone who would dare hurt these precious beings. My arms itched to gather them up, hold them on my lap, protect them, and keep them safe forever.

I decided that day to give my little girl her own voice. I sat down and began writing my autobiography to let all the buried memories emerge from the little girl who had been forgotten and hidden away. I began to tell the many stories she could never tell. Asking the question I wondered about for many years . . .

Can You See Me?

Chapter 1
Daddy

When I was one, I was asleep in the crib set up in the corner of my parents' bedroom. A thundering, swirling gray energy stormed into the bedroom chasing my mother, and waking me up. I heard loud rumbling anger as my father yelled, and I started to cry. I felt the dark tornado encircle my crib, lean over me, and yell, "Be quiet!"

Then I felt a slap, the kind of slap that says don't make another sound. The bedroom was suddenly quiet, and I was suddenly afraid of my father.

**

My mother never hit me, but she also wasn't the type to cuddle or nurture. I don't think I ever heard the words "I love you" from her. She was always busy with housework, cooking, and my two older siblings.

But there was this one day in the spring, I was just over a year old, and we were sitting on a blanket in the shade of our maple tree. My mother looked so pretty with her reddish-brown hair and her smile. She sang songs to me, and I felt her eyes watch me with love as I walked around the tree. It was like she didn't have a care in the world, like all she wanted was that moment with me, laughing in the sun, her eyes full of joy. We lay down on the blanket, looking up through the leaves at the blue sky, and she pointed at the clouds floating by. I didn't want the moment to end. Later that day, I watched her practice her accordion. I loved watching her face while she played, her eyes lost in the music as her fingers walked over the keys, sometimes running over the keys so fast I couldn't keep track of them. She was lost in the music, oblivious to everything around her. She had a smile on her face.

That night, when my father came home wearing his dirty khakis after working as a foreman for his brother's company, he was angry. He drank too much, and took it out on my mother. My mother's smile disappeared, and I stayed a safe distance away.

**

A year later, the spring after I turned two, I was lying on the train table my father built for my brother William's electric train set. My mother was changing my diaper. The radio was on, and I heard the word "tornado." I watched out the windows, and saw clouds rolling by. I saw the trees bending in the wind. Suddenly the wind stopped, and I could hear Patty, four, and William, nine, playing with something on the floor. My father was pacing, and my mother was pinning a clean diaper on me, when the radio said "tornado" again, and "take cover." The windows turned dark, and there was a loud roaring that sounded like a train.

My mother grabbed me; William, Patty, and my father dove under the train table with my mother and me. Voices sounded far away, and muffled. I held on tight to my mother, and buried my head in her chest. A siren was splitting through the air, the wind howling louder and louder. My fingers gripped her blouse so hard I popped off a button. Suddenly, everything was quiet again; the voices around me sounded normal and close by. The windows showed snatches of blue between the fast-moving clouds blowing in the sky. My mother let me go, and I crawled out from under the table. Later I heard them saying we were lucky because the tornado traveling down our street only touched the tops of the trees. Little did I know that this was the start of chaos in my life, and this wouldn't be the last tornado that I'd live through.

The day after the tornado, William brought home a black dog with a white diamond on his chest that had followed him from the park. He was a stray dog, part lab and part mutt. We named him Skippy, and for me it was love at first sight. Skippy and I were inseparable. He became my new best friend.

One day, my mother said she thought I was old enough to sleep in a big girl's bed. I watched my father take down my crib, and carry my new bed upstairs to my new bedroom with Patty. I loved being out of the crib and having my own bed. The first night I slept upstairs, I noticed a small door between the beds. I lay awake imagining what was behind it, and I thought I saw it open a crack, an old wrinkled hand reaching out. I closed my eyes, my heart beating fast, and felt Skippy lying behind me. I opened my eyes, and the door was closed, so I rolled over. I put my arm around Skippy, and finally fell asleep.

A couple of weeks later, William was at the park with his friends, Patty was playing with her dolls on the couch, and I was playing tug of war in the living room with Skippy when the doorbell rang. My cousin, who lived up the block, was babysitting because my parents were going out to a fancy dinner party.

11

I didn't recognize my mother when she walked out of her bedroom to answer the door. Her brownish red hair was done up in a French roll, and on top of it she wore a sparkling rhinestone tiara with a purple scarf draped around her neck. She wore high heels, and a pretty dress. She looked so tall. I sighed as I watched her; she looked exactly like a princess in my storybook. I wished I could wear her tiara and purple scarf. My father walked into the living room behind her with a smile on his face; his blond hair was short, and he looked uncomfortable in his shirt and tie. Next to my mother, elegant and tall in her high heels, he looked like a short and stocky frog. I giggled to myself, and wondered if my mother kissed him, would he turn into a handsome prince? After they left, I kept thinking about the tiara and purple scarf.

Later that night my parents woke me up arguing; my father was drunk, and my mother was crying and saying three children was enough. She didn't want any more, and talked about a baby born dead, a baby named Diana, who was born with water on her brain, and only lived a week. The stories scared me, and felt like dark fairy tales being told late at night. I felt Skippy by me, and I hugged him. Burying my face in his fur, I fell back to sleep.

When I woke up the next morning, I ran downstairs for breakfast, and asked my mother if I could play with her tiara and purple scarf. I was so excited when she said yes, because now I could look like a princess, too. When she gave them to me, I put them on, and Skippy and I went to the big picture window in the living room. I became a princess looking out the tower window at my kingdom below, Skippy as my faithful companion. I saw my reflection in the picture window: freckles across my nose, my long brown hair flowing from under the sparkling tiara, the soft purple scarf settled around my neck, and a big smile on my face. Skippy sat proudly next to me as we watched the world through our magical window.

A little while later, I heard Mrs. Galle, who lived next door with her husband, walk into our kitchen and ask my mother if she could borrow a cup of brown sugar. Skippy and I ran in to see her. Mrs. Galle was so cuddly, and was always smiling. When she saw me and Skippy, she invited us over to her house. We followed her home, and sat in her safe, sunny, yellow kitchen. She took the cup of brown sugar, and added it to her mixing bowl. It was the final ingredient for her chocolate chip cookies. She asked if I wanted to help her spoon cookie dough onto a pan.

I took a spoon, and as I worked, I asked her a million "why" questions. Why do we have to wash our hands before we eat? Why do all the good cookies have chocolate in them? Why do the birds sing loudest in the mornings? She thoughtfully answered every question while we worked.

When we were done, she put the cookie sheet in the hot oven, and asked if I wanted her to read me a story. I looked at Skippy and we both said, "Yes!" She took a book from a bookshelf in the kitchen. It was a story of three little kittens who lost their mittens. Just as the story ended, the timer went off. The cookies were done. Skippy and I watched as she took out the pan. The cookies were hot, and the chocolate was all melted. She filled a plate with cookies, and suggested we go outside and sit on her back steps to eat them.

It was nice sitting there in the warm sunlight, hearing birds singing, smelling the grass from a fresh mown lawn. The warm cookie and chocolate covered the inside of my mouth.

I heard sounds around me and asked, "What's that?"

Mrs. Galle listened really hard, and said, "That's a bee buzzing," or, "Someone is raking leaves."

I loved sitting with her on the back step, her face wearing a smile, her blue eyes sparkling with laughter as she listened to me.

**

One night after I turned three, Patty, now six, and I were upstairs asleep. Ten-year-old William woke me up when he ran up the stairs to our bedroom. When he reached out to tap Patty's shoulder to wake her up, he was trembling. He looked scared, and his face was covered in something powdery white, like my mother's flour. Patty startled awake, and saw his white face. She screamed.

William said, "Patty, it's me."

Patty asked, "What happened to your face?"

He said he didn't know, but a loud bang woke him up and there was all this white stuff on him. He thought the loud noise was up here in our bedroom, so he came to make sure we were OK. He told her our parents were out, and he couldn't find them. I watched Patty get out of bed, and walk downstairs with William. I didn't quite understand what was going on, so I rolled over, hugged Skippy, and fell back to sleep.

When I woke up in the morning, Patty was lying in bed watching me. When she saw me open my eyes, she started talking a mile a minute about finding bullet holes in the walls downstairs. That there was a bullet under my parents' bed, that went through William's bedroom walls, the bathroom walls, and landed in our parents' room. The white stuff on William's face was the plaster exploding when the bullet went through the wall.

13

Patty took a deep breath and said, "The bullet went in the wall, right where William's head had been before he laid down to sleep. If he hadn't laid down the bullet would have gone through his head."

Then she told me when our parents came home, they called the police. The police found the bullet under my parents' bed. Then she said something about a stolen car, a guy running, and a stray bullet. I didn't understand all of it.

When she was finally done talking, I asked her what a bullet was. She told me it came out of a gun, like we saw on *The Lone Ranger* and *Roy Rogers*. She reminded me that on *Superman,* they said he was faster than a speeding bullet.

Curious I climbed out of bed, and said, "Show me."

We ran downstairs, and she showed me the holes. There were four of them. At the breakfast table, everyone talked at once about the bullet. Pretty soon the whole neighborhood knew.

I loved when my mother tucked us in at night and read us a story. Her face looked peaceful as she read to us. But after that night, no matter how cozy and safe it felt when my mother put us to bed, I felt uneasy reciting the prayer so many of us heard growing up — *Now I lay me down to sleep, I pray the Lord my soul to keep; if I should die before I wake, I pray the Lord my soul to take* — because nighttime now felt dangerous somehow, and the thought of dying before I woke up made it hard to fall asleep.

A couple of days later, Patty and I found some of William's old toy guns, and started playing cowboys and shooting at each other. We pretended to make bullet holes in the tree trunks. We didn't understand what bullets really were and what they could do. People who were shot in cartoons always got up and walked away. My parents plastered over the bullet holes in the house, and found paint to match the walls. The holes disappeared from our house but not our memories.

Later in the summer, my sister and I forgot about the guns, and started playing dress up with our four girl cousins who lived up the block. We used our mothers' discarded clothes, purses, and jewelry; later we built houses out of discarded boxes complete with a living room, hallway, and bedroom. We cut out windows, brought in small rugs, flashlights, and food. Skippy and I spent many evenings there looking out the windows at the stars in the night sky. Guns and bullets soon faded away into the shadows.

I loved running around the neighborhood barefoot, feeling the warm concrete and cool grass under my feet, the warm sun on my face. Skippy and I loved to race around the yard of our house. Sometimes, I'd find a stick, and we'd play fetch until we ran out of energy. Then, we would flop on the cool, green, grass, and watch the clouds float by.

We ate supper every weeknight in our kitchen sitting at our red formica table. Skippy sat by my legs hoping for food. My father always sat at the head of the table. He was the president of the "clean plate club," and would tell us we had to eat everything on our plates to be a member. On Sundays, we ate dinner in the dining room. After church, we set the table with a tablecloth and cloth napkins. When dinner was ready, my father sat at the head of the table, and my mother sat near the kitchen so she could get food for the table easily. After dinner, William and Patty cleared the table, and I helped carry small things to the kitchen. It always felt so serious and formal on Sundays.

Sometimes on Sunday, we visited my grandparents from my father's side. They were from Sweden, and moved here with their eight children a year before my father was born. They had thick Swedish accents, so I had trouble understanding them when they talked. My small, thin grandpa would smile, and put me on his foot, take hold of my hands, kick his leg out again and again, bouncing me up and down. I laughed, and kept saying "more."

My grandmother was big and round with breasts that rested on her large stomach. Her face was soft and squishy, and she had hairs that grew out of her chin. I didn't like her because one time, when I slept over at her house, we went to the neighborhood park where there was a pool. I didn't have a bathing suit, and I swam in my underwear. I was having fun being alone with my grandmother, until we got home, and she discovered my mother hadn't packed any clean underwear. She told me I had to wear a diaper made from a dishtowel. I threw a fit, saying I was too old for diapers. She physically put me on the floor, and sat on me while she pinned on the dish towel. I was furious. When my parents came the next day, I ran outside, and sat in the car, refusing to be there another minute.

When I was four, something happened. Looking back at that time, I picture myself as a little girl running through a field, stopping to smell the wildflowers. Holding a butterfly on my finger, I dance in the warm sunshine. Birds are singing, squirrels are chattering as they chase up and down the trees, and chipmunks chitter away in the green grass. I feel safe, content, and happy as someone's loving eyes watch me playing. Suddenly the clouds cover the sun, and there is a cold breeze. The birds stop singing, I can't see any chipmunks or squirrels, and the petals are falling off the wildflowers. I start to shiver from the cold, and turn around, realizing I am alone. I am abandoned. No one is watching me. I feel like Hansel and Gretel, who were taken out and left alone in a forest. Only I didn't leave any breadcrumbs to find my way back home.

Chapter 2
Mama, where are you?

It all started that morning in 1953 when William, now eleven, got sick. It was the first day of school. My mother called the doctor, who said it was probably the flu. Later that week, I watched him take a bite of his hamburger. He kept trying to swallow it but couldn't. He grabbed his glass of milk, and finally got it down. He drank two glasses of milk to get the rest down. The next morning, we were sitting at the kitchen table eating breakfast before school. When he took a drink of his orange juice, he had trouble swallowing it, and it came out of his nose. He tried to carry his breakfast plate to the sink with his right hand, but he couldn't lift his arm to put the plate in the sink. The dish fell, and shattered on the floor. My mother called the doctor, and my parents left with him right away. Mrs. Galle came to watch Patty and me.

My brother had polio in his right arm, throat, and part of his lung. He was quarantined, and my parents couldn't visit him. I had never seen my father and mother cry before. It scared me. Skippy and I sat by the picture window in the evenings, hearing my parents talking quietly in the kitchen. My father was worried about William, and was having trouble sleeping. My parents were afraid my brother would be crippled for life. I could hear Patty crying. I cuddled with Skippy, and waited.

It wasn't until I was an adult that I finally remembered all the details of the next day: "The Day I Became Invisible."

I was taking a nap upstairs. My mother and Patty were at the grocery store when I woke up. Skippy wasn't with me, so I walked downstairs in my white tee shirt and underwear looking for him. I didn't find anyone in the living room or the kitchen, and I didn't see Skippy anywhere. It was so quiet; I could hear the clock ticking in the kitchen.

I got scared because I seemed to be home alone.

Then I heard a faint sound from my parents' bedroom. I walked down the hall, and looked into the darkened room. I saw my father lying on the bed in his mud stained khakis and tee shirt from work. I was afraid of my father, thinking of his face twisted in anger, sounding like an enraged bear, and the night he slapped me.

I started to turn away, but he heard me and looked up. His blue eyes connected with mine. He looked different, he looked somehow smaller, tears pouring down his cheeks, as he worried about his oldest son, William, the reason he got married. He patted the bed, and asked me to lay with him. Looking into his eyes, I slowly walked to the bed. He looked so gentle lying there, like the blonde prince from Cinderella. I crawled up, and lay down next to him. One of his tears splashed onto my arm. I looked at his face again, and felt his sadness, his need. I reached up, and my fingers played in his tears. He started to smile, and his eyes took on a softness I'd never seen before.

His eyes stared into mine, and he seemed to be pleading with me as his hand moved down my back to my underwear. His hand traveled to the warm place between my legs, and his fingers wormed their way under the elastic, playing in the folds of my vagina. Still looking at me, he moved them out slowly, and took my hand. His eyes searching my face, his own face looking so open, vulnerable, and loving, I saw his hurt and wanting. He was almost pleading with me to help him. I felt his love — he needed me, and I was important to him. At that moment, we formed an unspoken, intimate bond. He placed my hand on his pants and began to unbutton them. I heard him start to lower the zipper. I looked into his blue eyes and his helplessness and pain. I felt his trust, and I was making him happy. I didn't understand what he was doing, but he seemed to need it.

Suddenly, I heard my mother yell, "Frank!"

Then she yanked me off the bed, her face twisted in anger. She wouldn't look at me, and she demanded that I leave the room. I was so confused at her reaction. I didn't know why she was so mad, and she never told me. After that, I heard my mother telling my father he had to see a counselor. No one ever came and talked to me.

All I felt was confusion because for the first time I really saw my father. He opened up an intimate part of himself to me. There was no anger, and I cared about him. The special moment was gone, and all that was left was guilt, confusion, and anger. My father wouldn't look at me after that. I became invisible to my parents because if they saw me, it could break up their marriage. To pretend it didn't happen was easier.

No one ever talked about what happened the day I became invisible. I learned from my father that love involved letting men touch my body. I was four; I didn't know about physical boundaries. All I knew is what I learned from the world around me. I felt my mother's anger, but didn't know why she was angry.

I learned it must have been something I did wrong. I didn't feel any anger like I did at my grandmother when she forced me to wear diapers because my father didn't force me to do anything. He was gentle and loving. I was four, open, and wanting love and to belong. I felt a sense of being special somehow, separate, not like the others. At four, I was groomed to be a mistress, and it forever changed my life. It shaped my future and who I became.

My father didn't touch me like that again, but he treated me differently than my siblings, an unspoken intimacy between us that I didn't understand. It became my first lesson in tolerating and understanding aberrant behavior.

Chapter 3
Alone and Afraid

The doctors released William from the hospital the next day. We all went in the car to pick him up. I kept looking at my father to see if I'd see the father I saw yesterday, the one with the kind eyes. But he was gone, and my dark, angry father was driving the car. I disappeared into the cracks. When William got into the car, he talked about the other children who had polio in his hospital ward. He said their legs didn't work, and some children couldn't even sit up; he felt like he was one of the lucky ones.

The next day my mother started a rigorous exercise program with my brother. Three times every day, she laid him on the kitchen table, exercising his arms and legs. My mother didn't want my brother to be a cripple. I watched her, lifting his arms, then his legs, over and over; my eyes were just level with the kitchen table. When I started asking questions, she sent me away, looking angry, and still not looking at me. I felt scared because my mother couldn't see me and only loved William. (The exercises paid off, and a year later, William looked like a normal twelve-year old boy.) I walked away with Skippy following me, and went upstairs to my bedroom. A couple of tears were drying on my cheeks.

When I saw the books on the bookshelf, I felt better. I took refuge in *Cinderella, Snow White, Sleeping Beauty,* and *Rapunzel.* They showed me other places and realities in their pictures. I felt so many feelings I didn't understand. I was so confused and scared. I felt so alone. Skippy pushed his nose under my hand so I'd pet him. I smiled at him through my tears as I petted his ears and his head. He sighed, and laid his head in my lap. After a while, I laid down next to him, and wrapped my body around his, laying my head next to his. He licked my tears away.

We laid there for a long time, and I told him what happened. He was a good listener. I looked into his eyes, and I could tell he loved me. I went to a special place inside me where the world was different than the one around me, and I was content to be surrounded by my books and my dog.

**

19

Thanksgiving night, Patty and I had just put on our pajamas, and were sitting on her bed. She was going to read me *Cinderella*. When she turned a page, I read some of the words to her.

She dropped the book, and ran downstairs yelling, "Helen can read! Mom, Helen can read!"

I ran down after her. Patty, at seven, was learning to read at school, and she couldn't understand how I knew the words. But I just did. My mother just shrugged, and said that's nice. Then she looked out the front window, and told Patty and me to look outside. We all watched big, fluffy snowflakes coming down and landing on the grass and the trees until my mother said it was time for bed. The next day, Patty and I built a snowman, and a snow horse we could ride on. Skippy ran around in the snow, sticking his nose in piles of white, powdery flakes, and sneezed. I loved being outside. We went in after a while, and had some hot chocolate while my mother asked us what we wanted for Christmas.

When Christmas Eve came, we went to my father's parents' house with my aunts, uncles, and cousins. My grandma made Christmas cookies with funny names like Swedish pepparkakor and lingonberry hearts. I was the youngest one there, and my older cousin, Joanie, took me under her wing. I sat with her and her fiancé, Bill. I loved Joanie's blonde curly hair, blue eyes, and dimples when she smiled. She made me laugh, and we talked. She even snuck me cookies.

I wanted my mother's attention back, and I was always volunteering to help her. I wanted to please her, and see her smile. She said I did everything too fast and was always breaking something. She complained she couldn't keep up with me mentally or physically and wished I could start kindergarten a year earlier. I felt sad because the harder I tried to win her love back, the further I seemed to push her away.

**

The first day of summer, I walked by my mother's bedroom, and saw her sitting at her dressing table, putting on makeup, smiling. I watched as she put on her eye shadow, mascara, and lipstick. She looked so pretty. I looked in that same mirror when I was three, and had the red measles. I saw a scary monster with red blotches on my face that made my skin look like strawberry revel ice cream. I couldn't look in the mirror again for quite a while. When I had the mumps ten months later, I snuck a look in that mirror, and saw a face with bumps or sacks on my neck and jaw like a chipmunk that had filled his cheeks. It made me laugh, and Skippy seemed to smile too. I looked in the mirror when I wore my mother's purple scarf and tiara and saw a princess. But nothing made me happier than seeing my mother smiling that day in the mirror. For some reason, her smile made everything alright in the world.

When she was done putting on her makeup, she saw me, and reminded me we were leaving for a resort the next day. She told me to put any books that I wanted to bring on my bed, and she would pack them.

We left for the resort the next morning. After we unpacked at the cabin, my parents started drinking. I went to the lake, and found a deserted spot next to the dock. I was really into minnows, and when I waded into the water, I saw minnows swimming around me. I stood real still, and scooped them into my net. Then I released them, and watched them swim away. I loved being alone, in the quiet.

An hour later, Patty came, and got me for lunch. I started walking out of the lake, and Patty screamed. My legs were covered from the top of my thighs to my feet with leeches — little baby leeches with a big huge leech wrapped around my ankle. Patty ran to get my mother, and I stood there, paralyzed with fear. All the kids came running when they heard Patty scream. William saw me, and laughed. Then he took a stick, and worked the big leech off from around my ankle. It bled from the spot where it was attached. William started teasing me with the leech on the end of the stick. I was crying by the time my mother got there. She brought a container of salt and shook it on my legs. I stopped crying when the little leeches started to fall off. When I found the large leech, William had been teasing me with lying on the ground, I took the salt and poured it on him. I liked watching the leech shrivel up, but I was afraid to go in the water after that. After lunch, I brought Skippy to the beach with me, and I threw a stick in the water. He ran in, put it in his mouth, and swam back, dropping the stick at my feet. We did that over and over until I forgot about the leeches.

When we got home from the resort, there was an invitation for my cousin Joanie's wedding in the mail. She was getting married in August. The day before the wedding, my mother took me clothes shopping for school. I bought some new red tennis shoes I thought were the fastest shoes I ever had. With them on my feet, I ran like the wind, and when I jumped on my bed, I bounced higher. I didn't want to take them off when I went to bed, so I wore them all night. The next morning, I got up right away, and ran around the house. When it was time to get dressed for the wedding, my mother got frustrated because I kept running around. When she finally got my dress on, she told me to take off "those god awful shoes" and put on my black patent leather shoes. I was devastated. Why didn't she see the magic in them? Tears welled up in my eyes, and I said I wanted to wear my red shoes. We had a power struggle; I won and wore my red tennis shoes. For once, I didn't care what my mother thought or that she didn't like me.

Image was everything to my mother, so to her chagrin, my picture was taken standing on my tiptoes kissing the bride after the wedding. Everyone thought I was so cute with the bow in my hair, my pretty dress, and my red tennis shoes. The professional photographer captured it with his camera, and an 8x10 picture was put in the official wedding book. Years later at a Carlson family reunion, people asked about that picture, wondering who the little girl with the red tennis shoes was. I said with pride it was me.

Chapter 4
Why Did you Leave Me?

I was so excited when the first day of kindergarten finally arrived. I was going to school! Skippy watched me as I put on my green dress and red tennis shoes. After I was dressed, I sat down with him. I told him I'd be gone all morning, but I would be home at lunchtime to play. He licked my face, so I thought he was OK. But when I started walking with Patty and my cousins, Skippy started following us. I told him to go home, but he just kept following. When we got to my friend Jodie's house, I asked her parents to keep him inside until we left. I heard Skippy whining and scratching at the door as I walked away.

I loved my first day of school. My classroom had a toy kitchen with dishes, pots, and pans. I loved the books and dress up clothes, and at naptime, we laid on mats for twenty minutes. After twenty minutes, a student took a wand, and woke everyone up by tapping our shoulder. I wanted to be the fairy with the wand. I loved the sparkling silver stars with thin ribbons dancing from its points.

I couldn't wait to tell Skippy. After school, I ran all the way home, anxious to see him and tell him about my day. I felt bad about leaving him at Jody's house.

But when I got home, Skippy wasn't there. My mother said she hadn't seen him all morning. She reassured me he'd turn up. When my father came home, he drove around the neighborhood looking for Skippy, but there was no Skippy when I went to bed. My bedroom had more shadows that night, and I couldn't sleep.

When the sun came up in the morning, I raced downstairs, and looked out the front door and the back door. There was still no Skippy. After my neighbor let him out, he disappeared. We put up flyers, posted ads in the paper, and called the pound every single day.

I kept asking my mother, "Where could he be?"

She said maybe he found a new family, maybe he wandered off too far and got lost, or maybe someone took him. The scariest maybe was: maybe he got hit by a car, and was lying on the side of the road. I asked how we would find him then. She said Skippy didn't have a collar or an

ID tag, so a road maintenance truck would pick him up and dispose of him.

I cried and prayed for days that I would see him again. The sadness moved into the pit of my stomach, and nestled in with a constant aching. Sometimes the aching crept into my eyes, and tears flowed down my cheeks. When I went to bed at night, I could smell him: his doggy smell mixed with earth, grass, and flowers.

I yearned to see his face and the way he looked at me when he listened patiently to all my stories. When I was sad, he licked the side of my neck, like he was giving me a kiss.

The third day, the pound called because they had a dog fitting Skippy's description. I was so excited and relieved I'd see him again. I could tell him I was sorry for leaving him at Jody's. I could tell him how much I loved him. I couldn't wait to hold him in my arms and pet him. I ran to the car, and bounced on the seat all the way there. But the dog looked nothing like Skippy. I cried all the way home, and felt like I was going to throw up. I cried myself to sleep. It was my fault he left because I had abandoned him at my neighbor's house. He must've thought I didn't love him anymore. I wanted so much to see him and reassure him. Every time the phone rang, my heart beat faster, hoping for news of Skippy.

My sleep became filled with nightmares. Days went by, and we didn't find Skippy. My house felt empty and scary with him gone. I had no one to talk to. I lost trust in the world around me, and learned that someone I loved could suddenly disappear, abandoning me. I had a knot in my stomach, and felt like there was a hole inside.

A couple weeks later, I went to Mrs. Galle's for lunch after school. She sensed my mood the minute I walked in the door. It seemed that my smile had disappeared, my eyelids always felt heavy, and my feet dragged. But when I sat down in her yellow kitchen, I started to feel lighter. I smelled my favorite lunch, creamed tuna fish, cooking on the stove.

Mrs. Galle sat down across from me, and held my hand. She told me about losing her own dog when she was a little girl. She talked about how it felt to lose something so precious. Tears trickled down her cheeks, and my tears began to tickle the corners of my eyes. I got up and sat on her lap, and we cried together about our dogs. I told her stories about Skippy, and she listened. She looked at me, and said when I smell that doggy odor of the earthy outside and I remember the feeling of Skippy's kisses on the side of my neck or the love in his eyes, then Skippy was there visiting me.

Sitting there with the smell of creamed tuna fish in the air, I knew I wasn't alone; Mrs. Galle understood. I sat there cuddled in her lap, and began to feel my heart beat again. A smile appeared on my face. I imagined Skippy standing there, wagging his tail.

After the day in Mrs. Galle's kitchen, I felt like myself again. The next day, I put on my purple scarf and tiara, and became a princess. I started playing with my friends and making them laugh. But late at night, I still shed a few tears thinking about Skippy. I fell asleep cuddling my pillow and pretending it was him. I could almost smell his doggy smell of outdoors and dirt.

A couple weeks later, my mother found out she was pregnant, and my parents started talking about moving. With the prospect of needing a bigger house, my father's drinking got worse. I could hear my parents arguing late at night. My father didn't know how he was going to afford a bigger house.

**

In June, my baby sister, Becca, was born, and in July, we spent a weekend up north with Eileen and her family. My mother's cousin, Eileen, was the only relative of my mother's who lived in Minneapolis. My mother told me she lived with Eileen until she was eight years old, so they were more like sisters. I was glad Eileen came to the resort because she taught me five different solitaire games with a deck of cards like Klondike, Pyramid, and Osmosis.

When we got back, my mother's father called, and invited us to come out to the state of Washington for a visit. So in August, we took a train to Washington to see my mother's parents, whom I'd never met. I loved the train ride. I was six, and my little sister was just a baby. Every evening, my mother sent me to the dining car to warm up a bottle for my sister. My father was in the club car drinking. I felt so big going by myself. The waiters in the dining car fascinated me; I had never seen skin that dark. The waiters sat me at a table and brought me a free ice cream sundae with chocolate sauce, whipped cream, and a maraschino cherry while they warmed the milk. They told me funny stories while I waited. I thought they were so handsome with their dark skin, bright white smiles, and warm, friendly voices. Their eyes danced with humor and fun. They liked me. As I walked back with the bottle of milk, I pretended Skippy was with me, and I talked to him all the way back to our train car. His tail wagged the whole time.

A couple of weeks after we got home, I started first grade. My parents announced a week after school started that they found a new house. I started crying. It had been a year since Skippy disappeared, and I wanted to be there when he came home. But on October 1st, we moved to a new house five miles away. It was still located in Minneapolis, but in the new house, we had to walk six blocks to school.

Chapter 5
The Room with the Darkened Window

Our new house was on a corner with a big kitchen, dining room, living room, a bathroom, and a den. The upstairs had four bedrooms, but William, almost fifteen, had to walk through the bedroom I shared with Patty to get to his room. My mother didn't like that because she thought it would bother Patty and me, but William only used his bedroom to sleep.

The Monday after we moved in, Patty and I walked to our new school. I felt shy that first day, walking into the first-grade classroom with everyone looking at me. When I found my seat, the boy in front of me kept turning around to talk to me. I didn't like him, and tried to ignore him. But he kept turning around, so I picked my nose, and wiped my green, crusty, gooey boogers on the back of his shirt. A week later, he turned around, and told me his mother couldn't figure out what was on the back of his shirts. Whatever it was didn't wash out in the washing machine. I just shrugged, and when he turned back around, I smiled.

I liked my new school. I finished my work way ahead of the other students, and I felt seen and heard. When I asked questions, the teacher patiently answered every one of them.

But at home, it was a different story. A week after we moved in, my father was acting strange, shaking and talking fast, drinking a lot, and he couldn't relax or settle down. He paced back and forth, and sounded scared and out of control. My mother brought him to the doctor, who said he was having a nervous breakdown and put him in the hospital.

A couple of days later, I heard the words *manic/depressive* and *bipolar* for the first time. I asked my mother what they meant. She said they meant sometimes, my father had too much energy, and other times, he had too little energy. My father was in the hospital for three weeks receiving shock treatments. Over the years, I experienced the roller coaster of my father's moods.

The night he left, I sat in the living room, and stared out the picture window. I felt so alone, sad, and afraid, and when I looked out the dark window, my tears came and got tangled in my hair. It was so lonely in this house; my father and Skippy were gone, my mother was overwhelmed with four kids to take care of alone, and Mrs. Galle didn't live next door anymore.

I sighed, and went upstairs, and put myself to bed.

When my father came home three weeks later, he looked different. He walked around the house like a zombie with empty blank eyes, living in his own world. He walked around, mumbling angrily to himself. If I came home from school and my mother wasn't there, I was scared to be alone with him. One day he was crying, and asked me to come into his bedroom. His eyes looked sad, so I sat on the end of the bed, and listened while he talked and cried. When he eventually fell asleep, I tiptoed out the door, and ran upstairs to my bedroom.

I didn't relax until I heard my mother's voice downstairs. She was telling Eileen, as they walked in the back door, that my father's doctor said he should never have had children.

**

My father continued to drink a lot, and my parents argued. I stayed in my room, or I ran around the neighborhood trying to find a friend or another Mrs. Galle.

My father was still struggling, so he went back to see his doctor, who encouraged him to take his medication and go on a vacation. A week later, my parents and William flew to California for two weeks. A woman my parents found, Mrs. Travis, took care of Patty, Becca, and me. Mrs. Travis was short and stocky and wore lots of makeup with red lipstick that leaked into the wrinkles around her mouth. She was nice, and seemed to like baking a lot. She made delicious homemade cinnamon rolls. The dark presence of my father and his anger was gone, and our house was calm for two weeks. No yelling late at night.

When my father returned from California, he was happier. I actually saw him smiling, and he even cracked a few jokes at the dinner table, which made us all laugh. A couple of nights later, we were sitting at the kitchen table eating supper, and I told my father to shut up. I wouldn't apologize, and was sent away from the table. I went into the living room, saw my father's cigarettes, took them, and then hid under the dining room table. After my family was done eating, he started looking for his cigarettes. Finally, he found me with his cigarettes.

When I crawled out, he called me, "a little pixie."

I was surprised because I thought he was angry with me, but his words sounded nice. Then I smelled alcohol on his breath. When I sat on the living room couch, he sat next to me, put his arm around me, and sang "You Are My Sunshine." I felt my stomach tighten up because he was really drunk, slurring his words as he sang to me. When my mother found us, she seemed angry, and told me it was time for bed.

Later that night, I heard my parents arguing because my father didn't want to take the medicine the doctor prescribed. He said it took away his energy. My mother yelled back that he had to do something. I lay in bed thinking about how Little Red Riding Hood felt when she realized her grandmother was really a wolf. Lying there in the shadows of my bedroom, I felt the wolf. I felt danger, and saw his long sharp teeth. I pulled up my covers to protect myself from the angry voices swirling through my house like the howling of a wolf.

**

I was so happy when the weather finally turned warm again. I loved being outside, feeling the sun on my skin and the breeze tickle through my hair. I could get away from the darkness in our house.

On one spring day, I was playing outside in our backyard, and I heard my father calling me. I ran to the front yard, and saw him standing next to a new two-wheel bike with a light blue frame and silver fenders. I couldn't believe it. He had bought me a bike. He told me to get on, and held the bike up. I climbed on, felt the pedals under my feet, and then he told me to pedal. When I was going fast enough, he let go. I was flying, but because I didn't know how to use the brakes, I just jumped off when I wanted to stop. My bike traveled another few feet, and fell over, which was hard on the bike. I looked at my father, and he was smiling and clapping. He patiently explained to me how to use the brakes. I looked into his blue eyes, and saw the gentle man lying on the bed, crying, with his dirty khakis and Tee shirt. I remembered playing with his tears.

With my new bike, I was always outside where it felt safe in the warm sunlight with the blue sky overhead, and I rode my bike, feeling free. A week later, I met some boys my age who lived on the block across the street. We all started riding bikes together. Soon, we found trees that were good for climbing, seeing who could climb the highest. One day, one of the boys shimmied up a clothesline pole with his bare feet and hands. Pretty soon, we were all doing it. When we got to the top, we reached over to the "T" on the pole, and swung like monkeys. We played every day after school and on Saturdays.

One Saturday in late May, my brother put the car in the garage, and drove over my bike. I was devastated. My bike was my freedom. We brought it to a bike shop, and left it there to be fixed. The next day the boys came with their bikes, and I told them my bike was in the shop, so I couldn't ride with them. Later that day, four of the boys came over, and asked me to come with them. They brought me between two garages, and asked me to stand under the apple tree, behind a low wooden crate. I was puzzled; I couldn't figure out what they were doing. Then, one of the boys picked up a green, rotten apple that was lying on the ground. He said if my bike didn't come back from the shop by Friday, they would pull down my pants and throw rotten apples at my private parts. I turned around, and ran home with tears in my eyes and a knot in my stomach. I thought they were my friends.

Later, I sat at the dinner table, and ate supper. I felt invisible, like a ghost sitting there, watching them talk. I had all these feelings inside, being betrayed by the boys I thought liked me, suddenly turning on me. One minute looking at me with kind eyes, and the next looking mean and angry. I looked around the dinner table; my family seemed normal and unconcerned while I felt the turmoil and fear I couldn't talk about. After dinner I drifted away from the table to get ready for bed.

At seven years old, I learned to keep my secrets, and only trust myself. I was so scared that week, I couldn't sleep. Luckily, my bike came back from the shop on Thursday, but I stayed away from the boys and rode by myself, pretending everything was Ok.

Towards the end of the school year, my parents were drinking, and talking in the kitchen. My mother told my father that she hated this house and convinced him to put it up for sale. We lived in that house for nine months. It was a dark house, and I was glad to be moving, hoping the next one would be better.

Chapter 6
What Is She Looking For?

In July, we moved eight blocks to our new home, and the next day, I was climbing the apple tree in the backyard. I was a fearless seven-year-old. A strange looking, tall, large, lumpy man with blonde hair suddenly appeared under the tree watching me. He had a funny smile on his face. I kept climbing, trying to ignore him, and a minute later, my mother came out when she saw him through the kitchen window. Just then, our neighbors Alfred and Doris Stevens walked into our backyard to introduce themselves. The strange looking man with blonde hair was their son, Gordie, who was 30 years old. He had "sleeping sickness" from a bug bite in Africa. It caused a bacterial infection, affecting his neurological functioning. He slept a lot, got confused, and was mentally delayed. He acted more like he was five. At times, it was unsettling because he just wandered into our house uninvited. My mother might be upstairs making the beds, and when she turned around, he was standing there watching her. Some nights, he walked into our house while we were eating supper, looked at us, surprised, then turned around, and walked back out the door. He was harmless, but his behavior gave my family the creeps.

My mother liked our new house because it had a sunken living room, and *my* favorite was the screened-in porch off the living room. There were four bedrooms upstairs, and a finished basement.

A couple weeks after we moved in, my father, who was in a happy mood, decided we should wallpaper the kitchen and the kitchen nook. He went out, and bought wallpaper and paste. He mixed the paste while my mother told us what to do with the wallpaper. It took us all day, but we did it. It was fun because William made us laugh, and at one time, we even got into a water fight. After we finished, we took a step back, and looked at the beautiful wallpaper. We were proud of ourselves and went out for dinner to celebrate.

The next morning, we rushed downstairs to see our handiwork. But when we stepped through the door, we couldn't believe it: the wallpaper was curling off the wall. Some places the wallpaper was gone and lying in the middle of the floor. We stood there in shock, all our hours of work sitting in ruins on the kitchen floor. My mother shook her head and said, "Never again." It turned out my father had added too much water to the paste.

A couple days later, my mother hired someone to wallpaper our kitchen.

That night, my father's yelling woke me up. My parents were in their bedroom, and he was angry my mother hired someone to do the wallpapering because we couldn't afford it. My mother calmed him down. I heard them go downstairs, and I went back to sleep.

The next day, I decided to explore the neighborhood. I found my bike in the garage, and rode around looking for someone to play with. The lonely place in the pit of my stomach was back, and I missed Skippy. There was no one around, and I ended up playing in the front yard, trying to catch a bird for a pet. The birds were too fast, and I went to bed empty handed. But the next morning, when I woke up, I couldn't believe it: there was a bird flying around my room. I was so excited. I tried to catch it, but it flew into the corner of the ceiling where I couldn't reach. I ran into my parents' bedroom, and woke up my mother. I told her I had a bird flying around my bedroom, and asked if I could keep it. She told me I was just dreaming, and to go back to bed. I went back into my bedroom, and the bird started flying around again. After ten minutes of trying to catch it, I ran back in, and told my mother there really was a bird. She sat up, looked at me, and asked me what it looked like.

When I described the wings, she screamed, "Fran!! Wake up! there is a bat in Helen's bedroom!"

My hung-over father flew out of bed, and went into my bedroom.

When he came back, he said, "Yup, it's a bat. I better dress up in my battle gear."

He put on his old army jacket, which was too small so he couldn't button it, and his potbelly was exposed hanging out over his pants. He put on his dark green army helmet with the chinstrap hanging down, grabbed a broom, and marched into my bedroom. He looked so funny, I started laughing. Suddenly, the bat was in the hallway, and my father was chasing it. William and Patty were awake, watching from their bedroom doors. We all started laughing at my father chasing the bat. He finally caught him, smashed him with the broom, and threw him out on the flat garage roof.

I loved jumping off that garage roof to the grass in our backyard. For a few seconds, I felt like I was flying, and I did it over and over again. But after the bat incident, whenever I jumped off the roof, I saw the remains of the bat, and felt sad.

**

One rainy day, when I was bored and looking for something to do, I found shelves of books in our basement. One of the books was about World War II, and I started paging through it, looking at the pictures.

There was one especially sad picture of a baby, dirty, crying, and sitting on the railroad tracks alone. When I looked at it, the knot in my stomach came back, and I could feel his loneliness, his hunger, and his fear of being abandoned.

I found a photo of a bombing: it was a woman lying face down, and her clothes had been blown off her body. I could see her naked bottom. I felt a sense of death. I wondered if she was the mother of the baby on the railroad tracks. A couple of tears trickled down my cheeks; he missed his mommy like I did.

My mother saw me looking at the book, yanked it out of my hands, and put it on a top shelf. I wasn't afraid of my tears or sadness like my mother was.

My mother didn't like it when I started crying at commercials about starving children dressed in rags, their eyes sad, the ad asking for donations. I wanted to reach out to them; I begged my mother to send money. She said the money didn't really go to the children, and then she wouldn't talk about it anymore.

A couple of days later, I couldn't believe it; my father came home with a little black, curly-haired puppy he found at a construction site. There was a whole litter, and all the workers took one home. I was smiling again. I named the puppy Snoopy. Snoopy and I cuddled under the desk in the kitchen, we played on the screened porch, and we watched people walk by. He slept with me at night. We were always together, and I told him my secrets. I spent hours with him in our backyard, throwing a ball for him to retrieve or playing tug of war with a piece of rope. I loved the smell of his puppy breath when he playfully bit at my fingers.

A month later, I noticed his nose looked crusty with mucous. My mother brought him to the vet, where he had to stay for a couple of days. She said he was being well taken care of. I hardly slept for those two days.

Finally, it was the day we were supposed to pick him up. I woke up, and ran downstairs, calling my mother.

When I saw her, I said, "Mom, today we pick up Snoopy."

My mother's face had a funny look.

I asked her, "What's wrong?"

Then, my mother told me Snoopy had died. He had distemper, which was like pneumonia in dogs. I was shocked, my mind totally confused because my mother told me Snoopy was being well taken care of and would be home today. I ran upstairs, and flung myself on my bed, crying. I'd never see Snoopy again.

I didn't understand why the animals I loved suddenly left me. I felt so alone. My mother tricked me because she said Snoopy would be home in two days. She never told me he was really sick. I found out later that the vet told my mother the first day that he had to put Snoopy asleep. *So, she knew all along.*

I was jealous when I saw children holding their parents' hands, trusting their parents to keep them safe. I learned my parents didn't make me safe, they tricked me. I always had to be on guard. The next day, I was back outside with tears in my eyes, trying to catch birds. I'd lost another dog. When I was hurt and angry, I tried to figure out why. Why would my mother lie to me? If I could come up with an answer, it would ease the hurt and anger I held inside. It wouldn't be so bad if I could think of a reason I could understand, but I couldn't.

The next day was Sunday, and I loved Sundays. We got up early, went to church. Afterwards, we came home, and my mother started cooking while Patty and I set the table and put on plates of pickles. I loved sneaking pickles off the plate while the dinner was cooking. Finally, at 1:00, we all sat down for our Sunday dinner of roast, chicken, or ham. After dinner, we piled into the car, and we drove along the river, around the lakes, or went to the pony rides my father heard about by Minnehaha Falls. Sunday was my favorite day because my parents didn't drink.

Summer was winding down, and soon I'd be in second grade. A week before school started, I was riding my bike around the neighborhood, and I met Geraldine, who had red hair, freckles, and blue eyes, and Pam, who had dark brown hair and brown eyes. They were best friends, but they made a little room for me. It became the three of us. My world opened up, and I went to Saturday matinees with my new friends at the Parkway theatre. Geraldine's father owned the lunch counter in the bowling alley next door, and after a movie we went there, got a snack, and sometimes bowled. I was excited and happy to have friends again.

Chapter 7
Memories of a Child

My mother treated me differently than Patty. She and Patty seemed to be buddies, laughing together in the kitchen while they cooked. I always felt like I was an annoying mosquito my mother batted away from her head. I tried to help in the kitchen, but I never did it quite right.

A couple of weeks before school, I looked forward to our traditional shopping for school clothes and going out for lunch. My mother took us each individually. Patty, who was in fifth grade, went first. Then, it was my turn. Even though my mother didn't seem to like me, I still looked forward to having time alone with her, hoping it would be better this year. But when we went to stores, and I tried on clothes, I had trouble finding clothes that fit. I was too short from the knee down, so the dresses and skirts that fit me were always too long and she had to hem them. My mother hated to sew.

When we bought shoes, the salesman joked and said, "You could just wear the shoebox."

I had small, wide feet with a high instep. By the time we finished shopping, my mother was frustrated. I felt sad, but I kept a smile on my face.

Finally, my dresses and skirts were hemmed, and I was ready for the second grade. Geraldine and Pam picked me up the first day, and we walked together. At school, I made a new friend, Colby, who sat next to me in class. Colby had big brown eyes, a round face, and when she smiled, she had dimples. Her black hair was short and curly, and her skin was way darker than mine. The only other person I knew who had dimples was Joannie, my favorite cousin. Colby made me smile inside. When we had reading time, we sat, and read out loud to each other. She liked the same books I did. When we lined up to go to the gym, the library, or outside for recess, we always held hands. We started talking about playing at each other's houses. She became my best friend at school. One day, she brought me an invitation to her birthday party — a sleepover. I was excited because I loved sleepovers.

When I got home, I showed the invitation to my mother. She looked at the address and then at me. She asked me if my new friend was black.

I thought for a minute and said, "No, her skin was darker than mine, but she wasn't black... She was more of a brown color."

My parents wouldn't let me go. They said she was black, and if people saw me there, then no white boy would want me.

I didn't understand what they meant. I was devastated. I begged and I cried, but they would not let me go. I was sad when I told Colby I couldn't come. I didn't understand my parents' attitudes. I didn't know what racism was, and I really liked my best friend. Colby and I stayed friends at school, until the next year when she was in a different classroom from mine. We only saw each other passing in the hallway. We didn't even have the same recess.

**

The drinking continued, and some nights my parents argued in their bedroom, waking us all up. One night, the phone rang, and my father's older brother was drunk and in jail. My father was angry because he had to bail him out. I laid in bed, and listened to the angry words. Pulling my covers up under my chin, trying to picture the apple tree in the backyard or the large pine tree in the front yard, I eventually fell asleep.

The next day was Saturday, and I was sitting on the living room couch, reading a book. My father came in with a drink in his hand, and sat down in the chair by the window. My body tensed up, and I pretended to keep reading. I could feel his eyes on me.

Then, he asked, "What are you reading?"

After I told him the title, he started telling me he didn't like to read. Suddenly, he was talking about his brothers, and how they could speak Swedish, but he couldn't. He told me being the youngest in a family with eight children was hard. He always felt lost, and helpless. He talked about working for his brothers, how much he hated it, and his brothers drank too much. He stopped talking, and swallowed down the rest of his drink. When he got up and went into the kitchen, he seemed so sad. I was afraid he'd come back, so I brought my book to my bedroom and closed the door.

I found myself spending more and more time in my room when I was home. I always felt better if I was alone, and didn't have to deal with the things happening outside my bedroom door. I was content to play the five games Eileen taught me. I brought food to my room: cookies stolen from the cookie jar, a bag of chips from the cupboard, a chocolate bar my mother had in the drawer. The food felt good in my mouth, the chocolate opened my taste buds, and the salt soared through my bloodstream. I fed the emptiness inside me.

**

In early December, my family piled in the car, drove to the "Y's Men" lot, and picked out a Christmas tree. We went home, and set it up in front of the living room windows. My favorite was putting tinsel on the tree and seeing it sparkle in the lights while listening to Christmas carols. As the days went by, presents started piling under the tree, waiting for Christmas Eve. I found seven boxes with my name on them. I asked Santa for a Ginny Doll, and my older sister asked for Chatty Kathy. A week before Christmas, I heard my mother crying in the kitchen. I went and asked her why she was crying; she said she was sad because no one believed in Santa that year. I was in second grade, and my younger sister was only a year and a half. Feeling my mother's sadness, I pretended to believe in Santa, but she kept crying. It made my Christmas feel sad.

One day, after Christmas, I was playing with my Ginny Doll when William walked by and wanted to teach me a new game. I had a love/hate relationship with him. When I was first toilet trained and sitting on the toilet, he came in sometimes, and pulled me off the toilet because he needed to use it. He threw me on the floor. As I got older, he chased, and tackled me, dangling a gob of spit just above my nose, slurping it up just before it fell on my face. Or he gave me an Indian burn, where he grabbed my arm with both hands, and then twisted his hands in opposite directions, which made my skin really hot. But for some reason, I loved his attention, and went back for more. I was excited when he walked by and asked if I wanted to learn a new card game called The Captain and the Crew.

He took the cards in his hand, and acted like he was going to shuffle them.

Instead he threw them all over the floor, saying, "I'm the captain, you're the crew, so clean up the deck."

He walked away laughing. Disappointed, I slowly picked up the cards and put them away.

A week later, it was my eighth birthday. I gave out birthday invitations to my friends, except Colby, since my parents wouldn't let me invite her. My mother made Patty help me decorate the basement with streamers. We had sloppy joes, and, of course, a birthday cake. That night I had a birthday dinner. I chose lobster tails.

My presents from my family were two decks of cards with a birthday card addressed to "the card shark." I felt really sad, and tried to hide the tears in my eyes. I know my mother had trouble being around me, and she was relieved when I stayed in my room and played cards. She always told me I was too emotional, too sensitive, and had too much energy like those were bad things. Sometimes, she told me she had trouble keeping up with me. So, I guess she liked me in my room playing cards. I began to feel better when I could just be with myself, and I started feeling deep inside me that I was special somehow.

**

Later that month, my father went to the hospital for hemorrhoids, a word I'd never heard before. He had surgery, and when he came home, he sat on a white donut shaped cushion. One day, I heard him yelling for my mother. He'd lost control while he was taking a bath, and there was poop floating everywhere. My brother and sisters and I thought it was funny.

A couple of weeks later, I was in school, and suddenly I had to go to the bathroom in the worst way, so my hand shot up in the air. I was excused, and ran to the bathroom where I had a case of diarrhea. I'd never had something like that before, and I remembered my father saying he couldn't control his bowels because of his hemorrhoids. I was sure I had hemorrhoids. I was scared, and told my teacher I had the stomach flu. My mother came to get me, and when I got home, I went to bed, pulling my covers up to my chin, shaking inside. I didn't want to have surgery like my father. When my mother came in, she caught me crying. I blurted out that I had hemorrhoids, and I didn't want to go to the hospital. My mother laughed, and told me I had the flu. My body relaxed. I fell asleep dreaming of sitting in the bathtub with things floating around me.

**

I began to notice my father's mood swings. Sometimes, he was so happy, like he was on the top of the world, and other times, he struggled just to get out of bed. One day, when I got home from school, my father was home from work early, pacing with a smile on his face. When everyone was home, except William who was out with friends, he told us all to sit down. He said, with excitement, that he was quitting his job, and we were moving to California because his brother there offered him a job.

My mother looked shocked, and us kids just sat looking at each other. Later that night, I heard my parents arguing after we went to bed.

My father was a wheeler-dealer, and was always saying he knew a guy who could get him a good deal. A couple of weeks after the California job offer, he came home from work all excited, and told us all to climb in the car. We drove to the Minnesota River Valley, where there was a house he said he was going to buy. A customer at work was offering a good deal. My father went on to say when we moved in, Patty could have a horse, and keep it at the horse ranch down the road. He said we could get an in-ground swimming pool in the backyard. When we drove home, my mother looked really upset. That night, I heard her yelling at my father, telling him to take his medication. Instead, he got really drunk, and later, I heard my mother helping him up to bed. We never heard another thing about moving to California or the house in Minnesota Valley. It was just a manic dream, floating around the whispers in the house.

When summer came, Pam and Geraldine both moved out of the neighborhood. So, I was alone again. When we tried another resort up north, my mother hated it. I felt confused and lost, always looking for a friend or a pet to fill my loneliness. But I realized that summer, my whole family seemed lost, always looking for something: the right resort in the summer, the house that was big enough, a good job, or a happy peaceful way to live.

When we got back from the resort, I rode my bike, and saw a girl playing in her front yard with braids that were wrapped around her head and fastened with bobby pins. I stopped, and told her I liked her hair. She said thanks, and told me her name was Heather. She lived two blocks from me, and we started playing at each other's houses. Her mother was a heavy woman with flyaway hair that seemed to wisp around her face; she was very friendly and happy. When I slept over, she made bacon sandwiches for breakfast. At her house, we couldn't say, "gosh, darn, golly, or gee whiz" because it was too close to using the Lord's name in vain. My parents said words that would never be allowed in their house.

Heather said she was a Baptist. Her church services were Saturday nights at a big barn of a church. I loved going there because the people were friendly, and after the service we had skin-on hot dogs with potato chips. When Heather turned eight in August, she was baptized, and I was invited to her baptism. There was a large tub-like structure at the front of the church filled with water. I watched as Heather climbed into the tub, and the minister dunked her head while saying words of baptism. Afterwards, there was food and gifts in the church's dining hall. I went to church with her almost every Saturday evening. My mother didn't seem to like Heather's family. She said they reminded her of poor white trash. But at least she let me play with her.

Chapter 8
Death You Do Linger

The first week of third grade, I was playing hopscotch by myself on the front sidewalk after school on a sunny, fall day. Suddenly, I heard a loud crash up the block, and a few minutes later, I heard sirens. I ran up the sidewalk with other neighbors who heard the crash.

I saw the car when I got to the corner, its front end wrapped around the thick trunk of a tall tree. The squad car lights flashed as an ambulance pulled up next to the car. Two people were trapped inside.

"Teenagers," I heard someone say.

We all stood on the street corner, watching the tragedy unfold; two bodies soon occupied two gurneys. On one gurney, I saw the face of a teenage boy, cuts oozing blood all over his face as he was loaded into the ambulance. The other gurney carried a body whose face was covered with a sheet.

I stood there, watching, a knot in my stomach. I was seeing things I didn't really want to see, but I couldn't look away.

The ambulance took off, sirens blaring, and I looked at the mangled car that just moments ago, carried two laughing, smiling students on their way home from school, two students who were driving too fast and couldn't make the curve in the road, two students who wouldn't be home for supper, two students with two mothers waiting at home, looking forward to their sons' stories of their school day.

I started crying standing there, staring at the accident while my neighbors walked away. I felt haunted by the two lives trapped in the car. I felt empty inside, like something was missing. I never forgot how it felt to be there on that street corner on a crisp, fall day, colorful leaves dropping around me with a hint of death in the air.

I turned to walk home, and saw Gordie, my neighbor, rocking back and forth, talking to himself, his eyes staring at the car wrapped around the tree. He looked scared, so I took his hand, and I walked him home.

When I walked in the door, I tried to tell my mother what I saw. But she was busy with Becca and seemed overwhelmed, so I went upstairs to my bedroom and played solitaire until dinner was ready. At the dinner table, the accident up the block was all anyone could talk about. Everyone was talking at once, and I never got to tell them what I saw.

**

I looked forward to Sunday and hearing stories about Jesus. My father's father helped build the church we went to, and my father and his siblings were expected to attend with my grandparents. My mother went because my father did. My sister Patty was very involved in the youth program, choir, and volunteered for the youth center projects. William loved church, and was very involved in the youth leadership program and choir. That fall, I started singing in the girls' choir. I loved singing, and discovered how much I loved music. For my father, it was just a family obligation, and years later, when my grandparents passed away, my family quit going to church, except William, who continued going on his own.

I was usually happy after church, until the Sunday I got home, changed my clothes, and watched a movie on TV about a boy who found out, when he was eight years old, he was adopted. My heart started beating fast as I watched.

That's why I felt so different from my family, I thought. I was adopted.

When the movie was over, I walked downstairs, and asked my mother if I was adopted.

She looked at me, and said, "Yes."

I was devastated. I ran upstairs, hid in my closet, crying, feeling lost and betrayed. For the next few minutes, my reality was shattered. My family had been lying to me, I thought. I was adopted, and that's why I always felt so different and never fit in. I cried tears that erupted from deep within my loneliness. My family suddenly felt like strangers to me.

Then, I heard my mother calling my name.

When she eventually found me, she looked at me, and said, "Helen, you weren't adopted."

I didn't believe her, so I asked her why she said I was.

She said, "It was just a joke. Because you look so much like Patty, I thought you knew deep down you couldn't be adopted."

She had teased me. I never forgot the feeling I had, and I never forgave her for teasing me. She was my mother. I expected to be teased by my brother and sister, but not by my mother. She was no longer the mother I saw in the mirror when I was younger.

**

At school, I was in a split classroom with third and fourth graders. Rick Olson was a fourth grader who sat next to me. He had reddish blonde hair, freckles across his nose, and his two front teeth overlapped, making his smile cute. He wrote me notes in class, and kissed me when we were in the cloakroom. He was my first boyfriend.

I was happy at school; I loved going to the library once a week and checking out books. I discovered *Anne of Green Gables, Robin Hood, Rebecca of Sunnybrook farms,* and *Huck Finn.* The characters brought me sunshine, smiles, and wonderful adventures in places I'd never been. They filled the emptiness inside me. I loved being in my room or sitting on the screened-in porch, reading, being transported into the pages of the book. As an adult, I heard once we find out about ourselves by having mirrors that show us who we are. My family mirror reflected that I was invisible and different. But books gave me characters I could see myself in. They had feelings and thoughts like mine.

One night, my mother picked me up from choir, and dropped me home, saying she and Patty were going to Eileen's. She told me William was on a date, Becca was in bed, and my father was home watching TV. I felt tense as I walked into the living room and sat down. I didn't feel safe being alone with my father. He didn't notice me walk in. I kept stealing looks at him, sitting in his chair, a drink in his hand, lost in the characters on the television with his head turned to the side as he watched the screen. This is how he spent most nights when he was home, comatose, eyes never seeing his family, only the people on the screen. I felt so torn. He gave me the creeps, and yet, looking at him there, I felt sorry for him. When I was four, I felt the vulnerability and gentleness hidden inside this haunted man I watched in the chair. He sat there alone, imprisoned in his own dark, mysterious, tormented, inner world.

I sighed, and quietly walked upstairs and put myself to bed. I lay in bed, and wondered if I would always be able to find something good in the monsters around me.

**

The weather started getting colder, and soon, fluffy, white snowflakes filled the air, it meant Christmas was coming. At the beginning of December, our family began a tradition of going downtown to see the Dayton's department store windows decorated with magical Christmas adventures. I stood looking at each window. One had children looking up the fireplace for Santa. Another had children tucked in their beds waiting for Santa. The next window had Santa standing in a living room, a Christmas tree next to him, and a bag full of presents to fill the stockings. Some windows had life size nutcrackers or children skating on a snow-dusted pond. The windows were filled with Christmas magic. Afterwards, we saw Santa, sat on his lap, and filled his ears with the dreams and wishes we had for Christmas. The night filled me with hope.

This year at Christmas, Eileen gave me my very first book by Maud Hart Lovelace, *Betsy-Tacy*. I loved the book because I was Betsy: I had freckles, I was chubby, I had brown hair, and I wanted to be a writer. Betsy became my mirror because I saw myself in her, and I loved the world I saw through her eyes. Her family loved and understood her; she had what I dreamed for.

For my birthday she gave me *Betsy-Tacy and Tib*. I felt their friendship wrap around me, and I loved going on adventures with them. I couldn't wait to have friends like Tacy and Tib. Their world was a place I ran away to. Every year for my birthday and Christmas, I received the next book in the *Betsy-Tacy* collection from Eileen. They were always my favorite presents. Besides the stories, I loved the feeling of a brand-new book in my hands, being the first to open its crisp, clean pages, turning them one by one. The smell of the paper surrounded me, comforted me, and I was home.

**

One night in March, my parents were sitting in the kitchen drinking their whiskey and ginger ale earlier than usual. William, now sixteen, was out; Becca, who was three, was in bed; and nothing was on TV, so Patty and I went and sat in the kitchen with my parents. When we sat down, Patty, now twelve, asked my mother how she met our father. My mother rarely talked about herself, but because she'd had a few drinks, she opened up.

She told us she grew up in Glendive, Montana, where her father was a railroad man. When she graduated from high school, she left there, and moved to Minneapolis to live with Eileen and her family. One night, she and Eileen went bowling, and on the lane next to them were my father and his friend. My father asked my mother out, swept her off her feet, and a week later, proposed to her.

When my mother stopped talking, Patty and I said, "Tell us more."

The story changed to after they were married, and my father was in the service. He was stationed in Colorado Springs. My mother, father, and baby William had trouble finding an apartment, and finally found one on the first floor of an apartment building. The first night, they didn't get much sleep because people were going up and down the hallway stairs all night. The second night, my mother got up and went outside to see what was going on. She looked at the upper floors of the apartment building, and there were red lights in all the windows. They had moved into the "red light" district. "Johns" were traipsing up and down the stairs all night. They moved out the next morning, and found a one-room apartment in a better area. I asked what a "red light" district was. My mother quickly said it's a place where people have parties. Then, she suggested it was our bedtime.

We begged for one more story, and she told us a sad story in a funny way. William was three years old and napping. My father was gone, training for the army. My mother needed some groceries, and left William home alone to go to the store a block away. On the way home, she saw William standing on the sidewalk crying so hard he had the hiccups.

When he saw her, he asked, through his hiccups, "Where were you, Mommy? Where did you go?"

When my mother told the story, she said those words just like him with the hiccups, which made us laugh. But the story made me feel like crying. My mother told us it was time for bed, and we reluctantly got up.

A couple of weeks later, my father came home from work early; he was having terrible pains in his stomach. He ended up in the hospital, having his gallbladder and part of his stomach removed because of a bleeding ulcer. The doctor thought he might have diabetes. He told my father his excessive drinking could be the cause of his health problems, and he needed to cut back. Plus, he shouldn't mix his medication with alcohol.

Patty babysat when my mother went to the hospital to visit my father. One night, she got so angry at me, she slammed the kitchen cupboard door open, and it broke in half and fell to the floor. I laughed. The harder I laughed, the angrier she got. When my father came home a week later, he had two scars on his stomach, one from having his gallbladder removed and one from having half his stomach removed.

**

I was so glad when the weather started getting warmer. I could get out of the house, and go outside to climb my apple tree in the backyard. I could ride my bike. I always felt better outdoors. My house, except my bedroom, always held tension in its walls, and fear and uneasiness lingered in the shadows.

The first week of summer vacation, I wandered around the neighborhood looking for something that I couldn't find at home, hoping to find a friend, someone who understood me, or a place I belonged and didn't feel so different. I looked for a place I could feel safe like I did in Mrs. Galle's kitchen.

I went to Heather's house, and on the way back, I cut through someone's yard across the alley when I heard a woman's voice from the back porch say, "Hi, I've seen you around the neighborhood, what's your name?"

After I told her, she invited me onto her porch to have some freshly baked cookies. She and her husband were sitting with a pot of coffee and cookies on a plate.

"Hi, I'm Lucy, and this is Al. Grab a cookie, and have a seat," Lucy said. I found out as we talked they had two teenage sons. I told her about my sisters, my brother, and what school I went to. After that day, I stopped at their house whenever I heard them on their porch. I thought maybe she could be like Mrs. Galle.

A couple weeks later, she noticed I bit my nails, and challenged me to quit biting them. She promised me a manicure set if I did. I loved the thought of my own manicure set and getting Lucy's attention, and I loved a new challenge, so I stopped biting them. A couple of weeks later, I showed her my nails. She went in, and brought out a brand-new manicure set with emery boards, a little nail scissor, a metal nail file, and a tool to push back cuticles. I never bit my nails again.

One day, after I'd been visiting Lucy and Al, I walked in the back door, and asked my mother if we could get another dog. She came up with a long list of reasons why we couldn't: she didn't have time to housebreak the puppy, there was enough chaos with four children, she didn't need to listen to a barking dog, and didn't have time to take it for walks. I started crying, and said I missed Skippy. I begged her please, but she said no. I was so hurt and angry, I walked upstairs, packed my overnight bag with clothes and my favorite book, walked downstairs, and announced, as I walked through the kitchen, I was running away. My mother didn't stop me or ask me why. I slammed the back door, and walked rapidly away and down the block.

I stopped on the corner at the other end of the block, and realized no one was coming to find me. I sat on my suitcase, tense and angry, wanting to run away, not wanting to go back to my house. I sat, and read my book until the sun started to get lower in the sky. A wind started to pick up, and I felt a raindrop. When I looked up from my book, I noticed the tree with a scar on its trunk from the accident where two teenagers had crashed. I felt sad and lonely. So, I sighed, got up, and walked back home in the warm rain; I had nowhere else to go. When I walked in the door, I walked up to my room, put my clothes away, and changed into dry clothes. When I went back downstairs, I asked my mother and father why they didn't come looking for me. My mother said she knew I'd come home when I was hungry.

My parents drinking habits changed in the summer, and when I got home from my outside adventures in the neighborhood, my parents were already in the kitchen drinking and smoking. I could smell the cigarette smoke and the pungent sweet smell of alcohol mixed with ginger ale. In fact, most of my family hung around in there with them. I didn't like the smell or the conversation. But every once in a while, I heard them laughing, and I went in and joined them. On those nights, we usually ended up going out to dinner somewhere. One night, when we were out to dinner, my parents announced they found a new resort, and had a brochure we could look at. It looked like the perfect place, and my father called the next day, reserving it for a week in July.

It was on Round Lake, and on the way to the resort, we drove by a deserted house that looked haunted. We begged my father to stop, so he pulled over. We walked up the wooden stairs to the front door, and went in. It was really spooky to walk through the empty rooms because each room looked like someone had just suddenly got up and left. One room had a chair pulled out from the table, a man's shoe lying on its side next to it, and a dirty plate and cup on the table. Another room had a single mattress, a little girl's faded, yellow, sundress hung over a broken chair, and a teddy bear on the floor that was missing an eye. In the living room was an old stuffed couch, green and faded, missing a cushion. There was an open book lying upside down on the arm of the couch. I was glad to leave that house and get in the car because images of who lived there were hidden in the shadows and the things they'd left behind. I felt a knot in my stomach, a sadness washed over me, and I felt the emptiness.

As we drove away, I looked back, and a shiver ran down my spine. I thought I saw movement in the kitchen window.

Fifteen minutes later, we arrived at the resort. We got out of the car, and ran into the cabin to claim our bedrooms. It was a nice cabin and a nice lake. There was a store in a shack down a dirt road, where we bought treats, milk, or bread. We walked there every day. I loved the push-ups with orange and vanilla ice cream. Every morning, there was a jeep that went through the woods, collecting garbage we could jump on and ride along. It was fun whipping through the woods. The lake was great for swimming with a nice beach and floating dock. It was a perfect week with sun every day, and lots of kids to play with. I was sad when we had to leave. My family needed a week like this now and then, so we could regenerate our batteries for future battles. It also calmed my father's anger, and he relaxed for a couple of days.

When we got back from the resort, my sister and I were bored and trying to figure out something to do.

I said, "Let's put on a play."

I ran in the house and got a pencil and paper, and wrote a script called "Murder at Midnight." It was a murder mystery/comedy. Patty, Heather, and Patty's friends were in the play, too. Everyone had a part. We had fun rehearsing, walking around the neighborhood, and selling tickets we made out of cardboard for fifty cents. The day before the play, we set out folding chairs, lawn chairs, and picnic table benches for the audience. We cleared off the back patio, and set up our stage.

Finally, Saturday arrived, and the neighborhood kids came with their parents. Patty stood at the gate, and took the tickets. My mother made snacks for intermission, which we sold for a nickel. It was a big success; everyone loved the play. Neighbors talked about it for weeks afterwards. It was really special to have Patty and our friends work on the play with me. It was a really exciting day. I realized then that it was up to me to find happiness. That I had the ability to give myself what I needed, and I loved writing, acting in the play, and making people laugh. It was a release I needed for myself.

**

I was feeling happy, busy, and full inside all of August. The weekend before Labor Day, I was singing to myself as I walked home from Heather's and I cut through Lucy and Al's yard to get home. Al was sitting by himself on his back porch, heard me, and invited me in. I sat next to him on the couch, and we started talking.

He quietly put his arm around me, and began to tickle my thigh. I was wearing shorts. Suddenly, his fingers moved up from my thigh, and he was rubbing his thumb on the outside of my underwear. The sensation felt kind of good, but I wasn't sure what he was doing. I felt uncomfortable and said I had to leave. I felt sick to my stomach.

After that, I avoided their house. I never told anyone. I thought I had done something wrong because I felt ugly, like I did the time my mother caught me with my father and got angry. A darkness settled inside; I felt empty again, alone. I threw away the manicure set Lucy gave me, and I stayed in my room, nurtured myself with food, and played solitaire. I seemed to have so many things happen I had to hide deep inside. They became buried so far down that soon, I could hardly see me anymore.

Then, I found out Heather was moving. My mother said she was glad school was starting because she would get a break from seeing me moping around the house.

Chapter 9
Horses, No One Can See

I walked in the door after my first day of school, and mother told me a new family, with a girl in fourth grade, moved into a house on our block. The girl's name was Lisa. I ran up the block to meet her, and introduce myself. When I got there, she was carrying a box from her car into the house. She was tall and thin, with long brown hair, a nose that was a little too big, and her upper lip didn't quite touch her lower lip because of her teeth.

When she saw me, she gave me a huge smile. I introduced myself, and started telling her all about the neighborhood. She was a good listener, and we hit it off right away. It was like a dream come true because Lisa became the Tacy to my Betsy, and we told each other everything. When she stood next to me, I joked that we looked like Mutt and Jeff, the cartoon characters, because she was tall and thin, and I was short and stocky. We laughed together, and talked about our families. I told her about my parents arguing, and she talked about her parents' divorce. We walked to school, and played together every day.

We played on my screened-in porch, where we created imaginary worlds with imaginary people. Sometimes, we were pirates, and the porch was our ship. Or we were sisters, and the porch was our bedroom. Or it was our ranch house, and we had our horses tied up outside. Once in a while we brought our Ginny dolls. When her mother called and said it was time for her to go home, I would hide Lisa's shoes because I didn't want her to leave.

On the weekends, we played at her house or packed a lunch and rode our bikes to the Minnehaha Creek two blocks away. We loved the creek because there were dirt trails that led through the trees and large rocks we could sit on where no one could see us. It was a magical place. Sometimes, we were cowgirls and we rode our "horses" along the paths. Mine was a brown Arabian, and hers was a black and white pinto. Some days, we were explorers in a jungle looking for wild animals. We were inseparable.

On Saturdays, we went to matinee movies at the Parkway Theatre. The two movies I remember the most because they made me cry were *Imitation of life*, where a black woman had a daughter who could pass for white, and the daughter became famous. She was ashamed of her black mother. I cried so hard when the daughter rejected her mother. Why was she bothered that her mother looked black? Her mother was loving and nurturing. It upset me that she couldn't love her if she were black, like there was something wrong with it. The other one was *Miracle at St. Michael's*. The boy in the movie went to church, and saw Jesus hanging on the cross. He talked to Jesus about his problems, his hurts, and his pains, and Jesus answered back. He went to visit Jesus every day, sometimes just telling Him his little boy stories of catching lizards or playing stickball. With Jesus, he felt heard and loved.

So I started to write letters to Jesus when my parents were arguing and drinking too much and when I felt lonely and afraid. I put the letter behind a picture in my brother's bedroom of Jesus walking on water. It was the first time, other than my dogs, that I told someone what was happening in my life, a place I shared my feelings.

I wrote a letter to Jesus one night in late October, after my parents woke me up arguing in their bedroom. My mother was crying because she was pregnant. The baby was due in May or June. She was so angry because she thought four children was enough, and now she was having a fifth. This baby would be eighteen years younger than my older brother. She did not want to go to my older brother's graduation pregnant. Those arguments were almost weekly. She cried a lot at night.

A couple of months later, my mother woke me up because she was yelling at my father, saying he had to hire a cleaning woman to come in once a week because being pregnant with four kids was exhausting. She had heard about Sheila from a friend, who did a great job at a reasonable price. The next day she hired Sheila, and now the yelling in the middle of the night was my father, who was anxious because my mother was spending money we didn't have.

Lying in bed, listening to my parents arguing, I realized in a month it would be my tenth birthday. When I mentioned it to Lisa the next day, she told me about a friend in her old neighborhood who had *The Cisco Kid* at her birthday party. I was in love with Wyatt Earp, so I wrote him a letter inviting him to my party. At the end of his TV show, Wyatt Earp wished happy birthday to boys and girls who wrote in. I kept watching hoping he'd say my name.

Then, one day, I missed the show because I was downstairs playing on the train table with my ranches and horses with Lisa.

Suddenly, my mother and my sister started yelling "Helen, come quick!"

Lisa and I ran upstairs, and they said I just missed Wyatt Earp saying happy birthday to me. I was so disappointed. But Lisa was excited because he'd said my name, so he must have seen my invitation, and that meant he might come to my birthday.

I couldn't wait for my party. I kept telling my mother that maybe Wyatt Earp would be at my birthday because he said my name on TV, so I knew he got my invitation. On the Friday, before my birthday, my mother confessed that she and my sister made it up about him wishing me a happy birthday.

She explained, "He just gets so much mail from fans that he couldn't possibly read all the names he gets."

Those words deflated me, and my hopes were shattered. My birthday, the next day, was fun, and all my friends came. But secretly, inside I held on to a flicker of hope that Wyatt Earp might still surprise me at my party. If he came, then I'd know I was special. Maybe, my parents would see me. Every time I heard the back gate open, I looked, hoping, then feeling disappointed when it wasn't him. I shed a few tears in bed that night. I realized that dreams didn't really come true, and my dreams and my believing in magical moments began to fade away.

**

School was always my safe place. I felt seen, valued, and understood there. I finished my schoolwork way ahead of everyone else, and would ask my teacher each year if there was something else I could do. They smiled, and assigned me projects to research and write reports on. I felt seen and understood by my teachers, who seemed to love my energy, patiently answering all my questions and encouraging me.

But one day, at the end of March, in fourth grade, I was teased at school. Because it was snowing, I was waiting outside for a ride home. Two boys were waiting for a ride, too. They looked at my legs, and started whispering.

One of the boys looked me in the eye, with a smile on his face, and said, "Did you know you have fat legs?"

Then they both started laughing.

My mother pulled up while they were laughing, and I jumped into the back seat of the car. My face was red, and I had tears running down my cheeks. I didn't know I was fat. They made me feel ugly. I went home, and hid in my room.

I felt better the next day when I saw the sun out and the snow starting to melt. Finally, spring was coming and it was getting warmer. When I saw Lisa, I told her what the boys said. She said not to listen to them, because boys were stupid. I shoved the teasing comments to the back of my mind, and decided I was fine.

**

One day in late April, when I got home from school, my mother was in the basement, standing in front of the wash tubs with a bunch of little fish in buckets. I asked her what she was doing. My mother told me William went smelt fishing with his friends, and they caught these smelt as they swam upstream to lay eggs.

My mother taught me how to slice open the belly of the fish, clean out the orange eggs, and rinse the fish in the water. Then they were ready for deep-frying. It was a little sad to think of all the fish's eggs being tossed away. But I felt so happy working alongside my mother, in the basement by the wash tubs. I can still smell the fish, feel the cold water on my hands, and hear my mother's voice as she was talking to me. It was rare moments like these I felt maybe my mother could like me. We had smelt for supper that night. I must admit, it was pretty good for fish. Lisa called after supper, and invited me to go see *Journey to the Center of the Earth* on Saturday afternoon.

Lisa's mother brought us to the Boulevard Theatre on Saturday. When Lisa and I walked into the lobby, we noticed a table was set up by the concession stand. They wanted us to fill out a questionnaire about accordions. I thought of my mother and her accordion, and I took a questionnaire to answer the questions. Lisa and I walked into the theater, and saw what was to be my new favorite movie. As I got older my favorite movies changed to *"The Music Man* and *Helen Keller."*

A couple of weeks later, when I came home from school, there was a strange man in our living room. My mother asked me if I really liked accordions. I was confused; I couldn't figure out why she was asking me that. She said I filled out a form at the movie theatre that said I was interested in taking accordion lessons. I didn't remember the part on the form that talked about taking lessons, but I shrugged and said I guess I did. I realized my mother wanted me to take lessons, and when the man took out an accordion, I got excited.

Suddenly, I owned an accordion, and was signed up to take lessons at a music studio by Lake Calhoun with Gary Palstrom. I started my lessons the following week. My teacher was nice, but he kept sucking on his dentures. They kept clacking. I was also in his accordion band. After lessons, my mother and I stopped at Abdullah's Candy store across the street to get a banana ice cream cone. It was delicious. It became our Saturday routine; I had my mother to myself once a week until the third week of May.

On May 23rd, a Saturday, my mother went to the hospital. When I came home from Lisa's, my mother wasn't there, my father said that she was in the hospital and I panicked. My first thought was she had a nervous breakdown like my father had a couple of years before. I was relieved when I found out she was having the baby. Edna, Sheila's daughter, came and stayed with us while my mother was gone. She was kind and soft-spoken. My little brother, Derek, was born Monday, May 25th.

I was excited the day my mother came home with the new baby. She was sitting in the living room when I got home from school. I went in, hugged her, and told her I was glad she was back. The house never felt right when my mother was gone. She laughed, and said I was the first person to greet her. Everyone else just went to Derek. With a new baby in the house, we all took turns patting him on his bottom to help him go to sleep. William graduated from high school in June.

**

June was a busy month. I went to Bible school with Lisa, I took accordion lessons to get ready for a contest in July, and I played with Becca so my mother could take care of baby Derek. Petite, blonde, curly-haired Becca was now four, and loved to play catch. One day, I set up a run and jump game, where I had a pile of pillows and she'd run across the living room and dive into them. She was laughing and having so much fun. Then, I don't know why I did it, I moved the pillows at the last minute. She hit the floor face first, and got a bloody nose. I felt terrible, and got a cold wet washcloth to put on her nose. Soon, I had her laughing again, telling her stories about falling in dog poop. After, we went outside and drew a hopscotch, and I tried to teach her how to play. Some days, Lisa came over with Charlie, her four-year-old brother, and the four of us played catch or hide-and-seek in our yard. There were nights where my father didn't come home until I was in bed. My mother didn't seem to know where he was. I heard them arguing downstairs late at night.

The third week of July, I played my accordion in a contest the Aquatennial held at the Calhoun Beach Club. I performed a solo in front of judges, who were nice but not very friendly. I tried to say something funny to relax the atmosphere, but I just got a blank stare from them, which made me more nervous. I thought I was going to throw up. My accordion band also performed, and qualified for a contest in St. Louis. The band members took a Greyhound bus to and from St. Louis at the end of July. My mother came as a chaperone. It was nice walking around downtown St. Louis with her and eating lunch at a restaurant where I ordered a turkey sandwich made with real turkey and a toothpick stuck in the middle with colored cellophane curled around it. It was the best turkey sandwich I'd ever had. I competed in the Aquatennial every summer.

When we got back from St. Louis, my mother told me she was concerned about how much weight I gained in the last year.

I guess the boys in fourth grade were right. I was fat. I felt fine with who I was until my mother said that. I started to feel self-conscious about my weight and how I looked. I didn't know I was fat. Now, when I picked up M&Ms or chocolate chip cookies and put them in my mouth, I felt guilty.

Food usually gave me comfort, made me feel safe, and nurtured me. But now I only felt shame. I wasn't any heavier than my older brother and sister, so why did I have to go on a diet? I felt singled out, like the time I wore my red tennis shoes to the wedding.

My mother brought me to a diet doctor downtown. He put me on thyroid pills, saying I had low thyroid, which meant I had a slow metabolism and had to exercise twice as much as other people to burn off calories. It was another reason I was different than everyone else. Lisa and her mom couldn't believe what good willpower I had because I didn't cheat on the diet. The only snack I was allowed was Lifesavers. No more ice cream.

I found out later in my life I didn't have low thyroid. It was a doctor's scam. But I lost 15 pounds by the end of fifth grade. A year after I stopped seeing him, his office closed in the Foshay Tower Medical Bldg. I continued to struggle with weight issues, not wanting to gain weight and feeling uncomfortable if other people were heavy. I was always careful of eating sugar, and felt guilty if I did. It was important to my self-image to have a small waist, but I never really thought I was pretty or attractive, no matter how hard I tried.

Chapter 10
Why Must I Say Goodbye

One August night in the summer, Lisa and I had a sleepover at my house. It was a nice warm evening, and we laid out on the front lawn, looking up at the sky. First, we tried to count the stars, then we tried to find pictures in them. Then, we just laid there looking up past the stars close to us, to the ones further away, and then into the vastness that lay beyond.

My heart started to beat fast. I started to feel weightless. There was too much space up there with nothing to hang on to. I got lost in the darkness that went on forever. I felt like I was floating. I panicked and sat up, shaking my head, taking a couple of deep breaths and blowing them out slowly.

I began to feel the warm, firm earth caressing me. My heart started to beat normally. It scared me to not be able to feel my body grounded to the earth. It felt like I was inside infinity. I didn't look up into the night sky for a while after that.

On Monday, our first day of fifth grade, Lisa and I walked to school. School was easy and I was bored, always looking for something to do. At the beginning of fifth grade the teacher had a special conference with my parents, the principal, and me. She wanted to skip me a grade, because I needed more of a challenge. My mother said no, because she had skipped a couple of grades and felt like a social outcast. I never knew my mother skipped a grade until that day.

When we got home, I started asking questions. She told me it was hard being two years younger than her peers. My mother also told me she played French horn, was first chair in the band, and loved to play tennis. I saw tears glisten in the corner of her eyes when she told me her dream to be a physical education or music teacher. I asked her why she didn't become a teacher. She looked at me and said because she met my father, got married, and had William.

That was the first time I saw the real person that hid inside my mother. I felt sad. But I was still upset that I had no say in the decision to skip a grade. Sometimes I wondered if she saw herself in me. I was smart like she was. I was independent and wanted to do things my way, which I think she was like before she got married to my father. She seemed jealous of me somehow; she didn't want me to be better than her.

In fifth grade, Craig was my boyfriend. But one day he ignored me, and started talking to Marcy. I was hurt. A couple of days later, Marcy was sitting next to me, and when the teacher left the room, she said something that made me angry. I slapped her across the face. Marcy looked surprised with her hand on her cheek. I was shocked and embarrassed. I could hear the slap echo through the classroom and down the hallway. I knew everyone was looking at me. After class, I apologized to Marcy, but I'll never forget feeling the shame and hearing the slap echoing through the room.

We had a music class every Wednesday in school, and had to audition to determine where our seats would be. The best singers were picked to sit in the back row of the desks because they were strong singers and kept a good pitch. I was in the back row. I was so excited because I loved to sing.

A couple of days later I was pulled out of class to be part of a special group of kids who did research in the library on a topic of their choice. It was for the "gifted" students, I heard the teacher say. After we completed the research, we wrote a paper, and presented it to our class, the principal, and our parents. I wrote about dinosaurs. I learned about all the different dinosaurs, what they ate, where they lived, theories of where the dinosaurs came from, and why they became extinct. I learned all the names. I got a perfect score on my project.

That night, I heard my parents in their bedroom. My father seemed to be freaking out and started ranting about pressures at work, worrying that his brothers were going to fire him. My father's bipolar issues were getting worse and he was paranoid, fearful, and drinking more. He was afraid he was having another nervous breakdown.

He called his doctor the next day and the doctor recommended taking a vacation without kids. My father came home the next day, told my mother he got time off from work, and scheduled a trip to the Virgin Islands to relax. My mother got Edna to take care of us while they were gone. A week later, my parents left, and Edna moved in. I loved Edna, who was patient and kind. We had our first snowfall while they were gone. My father was more relaxed when they came back home two weeks later, and he took us sledding on our favorite hill.

By the first week of December, a tree was put up, and it, along with our house, were decorated with all the colors of Christmas. Two nights before Christmas, my parents were having cocktails in the living room before dinner. William was off with friends from college, and Derek, only seven months old, was upstairs asleep. Patty, Becca, and I sat in the living room with my parents. My father told us a story about my grandfather, who was a carpenter and a legend at Mount Olivet Church. He said that one day, while my grandfather was working, a wall of the church fell on him, and broke his back. His recovery was long, and his five sons all helped him monetarily until he could work full time again. My father was in high school, working three jobs to help out at home, and ended up having a nervous breakdown when he was a junior. My grandfather eventually recovered, and helped finish the church. So, Mount Olivet Church was very important to my grandparents. Everyone was expected to go to church on Christmas Eve, and afterwards, go to my grandma and grandpa's house across the street. Knowing the story about my grandfather made Christmas Eve a little more special this year. We opened presents from our grandparents and godparents that were under the tree, and I got to see my cousin Joanie and her husband.

After Christmas, my mother got a call that her brother would have a layover in Minneapolis at the beginning of February. I was excited to meet him. Uncle Daniel was an airplane pilot for a major airline, and he spent a night at our home. I thought he was so handsome with his dark hair and mustache. My uncle told me that my mother was always like a mother to him growing up. My mother's eyes were filled with love and pride whenever she looked at him; I could tell he was her favorite. I wished she looked at me like that. It felt like my mother liked boys more than girls — and me least of all.

I liked my Uncle Daniel, and wished he lived closer, so my mother and our family could see him more. But he lived in the state of Washington, and rarely flew into Minneapolis, so we saw him only a few times growing up. She seemed depressed after he left.

A couple of days later, my parents got a letter in the mail saying there was a freeway being built to go downtown and would run right through our block, which meant after four years, we had to move again. My parents told us that night at supper. We all moaned and complained, and then my father announced he got us free tickets for the Shrine Circus.

My parents started looking at houses. A couple of nights later, I had trouble falling asleep, and then I heard my father. He was very drunk and angry. He didn't want to move again. They couldn't afford a bigger house to fit five children in. He didn't want any more change; he wished life would settle down. He went on about work and all the pressures there. My mother was crying. I felt like my parents were teetering on the edge. I hoped we could survive another move.

A week later, my father, Patty, Becca, Lisa and I went to the circus. I loved the smell of the sawdust and peanuts. I loved the roar of the lions, the beautiful girls, and the handsome men on the flying trapeze. They looked so magical to me. I loved the clowns and the monkeys, the dogs doing tricks, and the horses parading with their costumed riders. I loved the bang of the cannon as the man flew out and the elephants with their trunks curling up and their ears flapping back and forth. I loved eating peanuts and cotton candy. Mostly, I loved that Lisa got to sleep over after the circus.

We started having sleepovers almost every weekend, sometimes her house and sometimes mine. I felt like we were sisters, and we felt sad knowing we each had to move. In May, when Lisa told me her family found a house and they were moving at the beginning of June, I cried. I couldn't believe my best friend was moving away in a few weeks. I had finally felt happy and safe for a short time, and now it was ending. So many changes and so much moving; I just wanted things to stay the same.

Pretty soon it was June, and I was waving goodbye as Lisa's family drove away. I sat on the screened porch, and watched the world outside. I realized I was alone again. I had to face the crisis and the chaos with my parents' lives alone. I felt fine when I was busy, but now, I felt loneliness and something was missing. The secret I held inside about Al, the neighbor across the alley, made me feel even lonelier. I missed his wife Lucy. It reminded me of how I lost my mother after what happened with my father. I felt jinxed somehow, causing these bad things to happen. It haunted me to not know what ever happened to Skippy. When Lisa moved, I was so lost. I took refuge in my room, and played cards, read my books, and created fantasy worlds where I knew things would get better. I loved my books because they helped me realize that there was the possibility of something more.

I saw my father's pain in this house and his dark, lonely world. His drinking was worse and affecting his health. His brothers were alcoholics he didn't get along with, but he took care of them and their DWI's.

I watched my mother deal with my father's operations and his drinking. She had five children to take care of. Sometimes, I felt sorry for her. My mother was the closest thing to normal I had, and my father was dark and scary. But I noticed my mother's drinking was almost as bad as my father's. My mother showed love to William, connected with Patty, doted over Becca, and was excited to have another son, Derek. But for some reason I didn't fit anywhere, there wasn't any room for me. I yearned deep inside to belong, be loved, and cherished like my siblings.

A couple weeks after Lisa moved, a couple came who wanted to buy our house and move it by the falls. We found a house, and moved eight blocks away where I went to a new grade school.

Chapter 11
Peaceful Waters

We moved to Tarrymore Avenue, which was a service road off Minnehaha Parkway and only a block long. It was the last house on the top of the hill, and Page School was across the street. When I sat in the living room or the formal dining room, I could see the Minnehaha Creek through our windows. My mother loved this house with its five bedrooms and three bathrooms. On the main floor was a living room, formal dining room with bay windows, a kitchen nook for our regular informal meals, a kitchen, a bathroom, and a den.

My bedroom was at the back of the house on the second floor. When I looked out the windows, all I saw were trees. Right outside my back window was the roof of the attached garage, surrounded by a wooden railing that was perfect for sunbathing and slumber parties. There wasn't a door, so we had to climb through my window to get out there. There was a two-car garage, and our backyard had a large private patio that was surrounded with apple trees, plum trees, rose bushes, and peonies. But best of all, there was a tree house. I loved to climb up, sit in the tree house, and spy on people walking by in the alley. I liked to play at the creek across the street with its footbridges, walking paths, and swimming hole.

I couldn't believe my father in this house. He was happy, and smiled. I don't think I ever saw him cook or wash a dish. His attitude was men worked and women took care of the house and kids. My father wouldn't let my mother work, saying it reflected badly on him. I could tell she was frustrated. When my siblings and I got older she wanted to get a part time job, but he wouldn't let her. We all thought my father's attitude was ridiculous.

But in this house, he became our outdoor chef. He loved to man the outdoor grill, and cook up barbecue chicken, religiously basting it with a tangy sauce while it was grilling. He loved to put a rolled roast on the spit, which he basted like it was a delicate flower needing watering every ten minutes. He stood out there wearing only a pair of summer shorts, his bare belly exposed, looking like he was eight months pregnant, sipping on his bourbon concoction, and overseeing the grill. He loved his patio, cooking out there, and eating at our picnic table. It was his therapeutic getaway.

On the weekend, he was always outside spraying down the driveway or the patio. We could hear the water running, and see the spray from the hose for hours. My mother called him "hose happy." But he said if we were going to eat outside, it should be nice and clean.

In the evening, he and my mother sat out on the patio, and had a few drinks with the neighbors. Some nights my siblings and I went out, and sat with them. My mother loved the flowers and the hummingbirds that came, their fast fluttering wings holding them in one place while they drank the nectar from the plants. There was always a nice summer breeze whispering through the trees. It was so peaceful. It was the eye of the storm that enveloped our lives, and I was aware that it was only temporary. I cherished these moments, like when we went up to a resort on a lake or took a road trip and my parents smiled more, drank less, and life was free of tension. It made me feel like my family was "normal."

I made a lot of friends. I was now thin enough for my mother, and boys seemed to like me. Patty was in junior high, and she had friends who lived in the neighborhood with siblings my age. One was Kate, who was tall and gangly with a large mouth that always had a big smile. She and I became close friends. Her father resembled Ward Cleaver from *Leave it to Beaver,* and her mother was short, petite, and blonde. I loved eating dinner at their house because it seemed so normal, like a Norman Rockwell painting. I thought her parents were good-looking.

When I saw them I'd say, "Hi, beautiful. Hi, handsome."

Later, Kate pulled me aside, and told me her parents didn't want me calling them that. So, I stopped.

At the end of June, Dani moved in down the block with her parents, the Rowens. She had a sister Becca's age and a brother Derek's age. My mother and father liked to drink and party with the new neighbors. Some Saturday nights, they had all-nighters at our house, and other Saturdays, they were gone all night at the Rowens. At our house, my father and Howie started singing, "How dry I am" and "Show Me the Way to Go Home" at 3:00 o'clock in the morning, waking everyone up except Derek.

Our new house was only five blocks from Eileen, Frank, and their three girls, who were close to William and Patty's age. We started having supper at their house one Sunday a month. Usually, after supper, Frank fell asleep on the couch, and the rest of us sat on their screened porch. One time, Eileen started talking about when my mother, as a baby, came and lived with her family.

She said they were like sisters, and then suddenly, eight years later, my mother's dad appeared on the doorstep to bring his daughter home to Montana because his new wife was pregnant.

I asked my mother, "Why did you live with Eileen and not your dad?"

She explained that her mother died when she was a baby. Her dad didn't know what to do with her and asked his sister, Eileen's mother, to take her. That story reminded me of Cinderella, but in my mother's case it was stepbrothers and stepsisters she took care of. It made me sad that she had to leave her best friend and her childhood behind. I was haunted by her story, and stared outside of the screened porch feeling lost.

A squirrel caught my attention; then, I saw a smaller squirrel following behind the bigger squirrel. I watched their journey into a nearby maple tree. I couldn't believe how vibrant the colors were; orange, red, and yellow, which meant fall. Fall meant school was starting.

Suddenly I blurted out loud "School starts in a week!"

I loved school, and was excited for the first day. Dani and Kate were in my class, and the school was right across the street from my house. The first week, a couple of boys in the class had a "best legs" contest for the girls. I was nervous because in my old school, I was teased for having fat legs. The boys met during recess, and voted. When recess was over and we were in the classroom, — the teacher wasn't there — the results were announced. I won first prize, and Vicki came in second. I knew in that instant my life had changed.

I met Ally the first day on the playground. She wore Spanish blouses that billowed out, and she wore a bra. Then, I realized her blouse wasn't billowing out. She had boobs. In sixth grade, girls didn't have boobs. They mesmerized me. We started talking, and I found out she lived across the creek from me in a large house. There were so many rooms, I got lost the first time I went there.

I met AJ in gym class. We were playing baseball and she said "faoul" ball, instead of foul ball. I asked her why she talked like that, and she said because she was from Missouri. AJ had two brothers and a sister. Her parents were strict. I didn't really like AJ's father, who was always teasing me and flirting in a sleazy grown-up way. He was definitely the head of the household. AJ and I became close friends, and I could tell her everything. We loved playing double solitaire and jacks. I liked her older sister, who was a beatnik and wrote poetry. AJ and I played at Ally's house after school fairly often because she had a pool table.

One day in early October, we were shooting pool at Ally's, and decided to go across the street to the creek and sit by the footbridge. While we were there, a man with black hair and a trench coat was walking toward us by the creek. When he saw us, he stopped, opened his trench coat, and started to pee on the ground. Then, he left his private part hanging out, and kept walking toward us. Ally just stared at him. AJ and I grabbed her arms, and we took off dragging Ally with us.

At the end of October, when we went trick or treating, we walked up to a house by the creek, and rang the doorbell. The man who answered was the man with the trench coat. I hung back, and didn't get a treat from him.

The next day at recess, we talked about whether it was really him, and if we should tell someone what he did. But the bell rang, and we went inside, soon forgetting about it.

I loved my new school, and when the teacher said someone turned in a perfect paper or got a perfect score on the test, I knew she was talking about me. A new boy, Geoff, joined our class. One day, the teacher was talking about the person with the best paper. I, of course, expected to hear my name, but it was Geoff. I was surprised, but from then on, I was more humble. My teacher assigned a report about the American Indians in Minnesota. I went home, pulled out a book from our set of encyclopedias in the den, and wrote about the Chippewa and the Ojibwe.

I loved sitting in our den with its wood paneling and bookshelves crammed with books. When I got bored, I found a book to read from those shelves. I read all the Somerset Maugham books: *Of Human Bondage*, *The Razor's Edge*, *The Painted Veil*, and *The Moon and Sixpence*. No one else ever read those books, so it felt like they were mine. I loved being tucked away in the den reading. There were also books that were in Swedish. When my father was in a rare good mood, he opened a book, and began to talk in "fake silly Swedish." Sometimes, my mother joined in, and we all laughed. There was a photo of me on the shelf, playing my accordion. My hair is in a ponytail, and I'm smiling a big toothy grin. It was a photo of me performing at one of my Aquatennial solo competitions.

On Saturdays, when my siblings and I woke up, we watched cartoons in the den. Patty, who started sucking her thumb as a baby, still sucked her thumb in ninth grade. She would sit on the couch, pillow in her lap, take a corner of the pillowcase between her thumb and first finger, put her thumb in her mouth, and her finger held the pillowcase against her nose. My mother kept trying to break the habit, suggesting putting something on her thumbnail that tasted bad. My sister refused, but when she started high school the next year, the fear of peer ridicule finally got her to quit. A couple years later, she developed an eating disorder. Another word I'd never heard before: bulimia.

**

One day after school, I was sitting in the den because I wasn't feeling well. Then, Kate called, and invited me to her house. I told my mother where I was going, and left. Kate and I were in her room, and I was coughing and sneezing.

Her mom came in, placed her hand on my forehead, and said, "You are burning up. You need to go home and tell your mother to take your temperature."

When I went home, my mother took my temperature, and it was 102. When she brought me to the doctor, he said I had walking pneumonia. I missed a week of school. I thought it was weird my mother didn't realize I was sick, and it took my friend's mom to notice. I suppose with five kids it's hard to keep track, but I always seemed to be falling through the cracks.

The day I went back to school, there were big flakes of snow falling and melting when they landed on the street. Winter was coming, and soon I could go ice-skating again.

Pearl Park was close by, and it had a great rink and warming house. I ice skated with my friends and some nights with my family. I loved skating backwards and racing around the rink as fast as I could go. My friends and I played tag, or we created the whip, where the last person in the line just flew around when the whip got going. One night, everyone was calling me to go ice-skating, so I made a comment that I felt popular. My mother heard me, and got angry because she said I was bragging. The big bubble filled with good feelings popped, and I felt shame. I never called attention to myself again.

Andy, a boy in my class, started teasing me. When he had a skating party, he invited me as his date. After skating for an hour, we all went to his house for hot chocolate and snacks.

**

The Tarrymore house felt lighter than the other houses we lived in. For a while, I didn't see or feel the darkness that had haunted my life. My parents were still drinking a lot with neighbors on the weekends, but there were no late-night anger filled arguments. Plus, my father was involved in the family, grilling outdoors, and that winter, my father decided to flood the backyard patio and make a skating rink. It was fun to just walk out the back door, and skate on our own rink. I had skating parties. We skated for a couple of hours, and then went into the house for hot chocolate with large marshmallows floating in it.

I kept waiting for the other shoe to drop, knowing this wasn't going to last forever.

My favorite winter sport was sledding. I dressed up in my winter uniform of snow pants, a thick winter jacket, a scarf around my face, a thick stocking cap on my head, and warm, lined winter boots. All of *that* was worn over long underwear, a thick sweater, pants, and thick, wool socks on my feet. I grabbed a sled or toboggan, and found a nice hill with friends at a park nearby. I was gone for hours, sliding down long hills, and trudging back up, dressed in layers of warmth, pulling my sled, sweat dripping down my face and into my eyes. The best part of all was going home afterward, taking off the outer layer of clothes, sitting down at the kitchen table, and eating cinnamon toast dipped in hot chocolate, marshmallows floating on top. I always slept well after a day of sliding.

Christmas felt magical this year because my parents were in good moods. I hadn't believed in Santa since I was seven, but for now, I enjoyed the thought of a mystical Santa finding the perfect present for me. I had hope which is what the birth of Jesus represented every Christmas, so this year, I felt the birth of baby Jesus and the hope He brought with Him. I felt like miracles could come true. Our family tradition was unwrapping presents on Christmas Eve and sitting around the tree singing carols. Patty, fourteen, and I, now eleven, stood in front of the tree, and sang and harmonized to a couple of carols. Then Becca, five, and Derek, two, stood up, sang, and performed hand motions, to *Up on The Housetop*. They were so cute. The next day we stayed in our pajamas, and played with our new gifts — or in my case *read* my new gifts. I felt so happy.

My father was promoted in his family-owned construction company. He worked on the bids for job sites, which meant more money. In early February, he came home excited because he'd met a guy from work who told him about a dude ranch in Arizona, and told him he could get a good deal for him. In two weeks, our car was packed up and we headed to Tucson. I missed two weeks of school. My father was happy, and he did silly voices, like having a slipped palate and pretending he had "desert sickness." We all laughed, and begged for him to do it again. This was a part of my father I rarely saw. We drove through the country traveling the backroads of Texas and New Mexico, and saw adobe homes that were more like shacks with air conditioners in one window. I remember looking out the window, laughing at my father, wondering if my father was so happy because he was *manic*, and I wondered when the depression would hit, and everything would fall down around us.

The scary part of the trip was the huge blizzard we drove through in the mountains outside of Albuquerque. Visibility was bad. My mother was so scared, she made me trade places with her. I rode shotgun. There were semi-trucks and cars in the ditch by the side of the road, but my father kept going. My mother kept her eyes closed. We drove with the big flakes coming at our window.

I thought it was exciting as I watched a car ahead of us slip into a ditch, but my father kept going. A semi-truck started to jackknife just after we drove by. The semi blocked all the other cars behind us. We finally got through the blizzard, and when we checked into the motel that night, we went to bed early because we were exhausted.

Saddleback Ranch was surrounded by desert and rolling hills adorned with cactuses of all kinds, like the saguaro and prickly pear. I felt like I was on a *Gunsmoke* episode with all the cowboys and horses. I couldn't believe I was actually on a ranch like I'd built on the train table in our basement. Every morning, we rode horses out into the desert to collect Indian pottery or arrowheads. In the afternoon, we swam in the pool, and after supper, we went for another horseback ride.

We took a side trip to Nogales, and crossed into Mexico to buy souvenirs. My father bought a cheap watch that looked expensive, and it broke the first week. I bought some kind of statue.

Driving home, my parents seemed happy and relaxed. I loved the drive home and getting up at the crack of dawn to watch the sun rise as we drove. Each motel had a pool, and my father threw us off his shoulders or we swam through his legs. He actually played with us. I wished this could be our life forever. We arrived home, relaxed and with the best tan ever. I wondered how long my parents' good mood would last.

**

When I went back to school on Monday, a new boy, Terry, was in my class. He was the cutest boy I'd ever seen. I thought he was sexy. He had black hair with blue eyes, and his lips were full and pouty. He had this way of licking his lips that made you want to watch his tongue the whole time. Every girl had the hots for him, but it turned out, he liked me. He came over every day after school, and we played four square. We sat on our rock wall, that was waist high along our driveway, and talked. When he put his arm around me, I felt a sensation I'd never felt before. He was soooo exciting.

One Friday night, he came over when my parents were out, and I was babysitting my little brother and sister. I wasn't supposed to have boys

65

over when my parents were gone. Derek was in his crib asleep, and I was outside in the driveway with Becca and Terry. Becca liked Terry's bike, and kept asking for a ride. When he put her on his handlebars, she laughed, and they started riding down Tarrymore, which was a hill. He lost control of his bike, and Becca slid down the pavement on the right side of her face, which became scraped-up and bloody. We brought her home, and I cleaned the scrapes, while Terry teased and got her laughing and smiling. My mother was angry when she saw Becca's face, and Terry couldn't come over for a week.

Our sixth grade class started having boy and girl parties at my house where we played "spin the bottle," which involved one person going off and making out with another. I was always with Terry.

After one of the parties, Mrs. Olson, our teacher, asked me to stay after class. She started quizzing me about our class having parties with boys and girls, and wanted to know if we were playing "spin the bottle." Then, she commented about Terry hanging out at my house after school and having boys at my house. I left her classroom with her words ringing in my ears. Living across the street from school had its disadvantages. I liked it better when school was at least a couple of blocks away.

At the end of the school year picnic, we had a field day with a ball throw and relay races. I won the ball throw. When we had a picnic, Terry gave me an engraved friendship bracelet with his name and my name, and a straw hat. It was such a magical night, walking with Terry, wearing my engraved bracelet, and holding his hand. I didn't want it to ever end.

One day that summer, I was at Ally's when Terry and his friend came over. I had an accordion lesson later that day. The four of us walked up to the drug store, and I lost track of time. My mother was furious because I missed my lesson. A couple of months later, I decided to stop taking lessons. I never had time to practice, and my mother didn't seem to want to take me.

A couple of weeks later, Terry moved.

I spent the summer riding bikes with my friends to Lake Nokomis, where we existed on nice buttery popcorn and cold sodas from the concession stand. I had a great tan that summer, and my body started to develop some curves in just the right places. A thinner waist, a chest starting to bud, and my legs were developing nice muscles from all the exercise.

**

The *best* day of the summer was the morning my parents said we could get another dog. We looked at ads in the paper, and found one for springer spaniels and beagles. We all piled into the car, and drove to a farmhouse in the country. When we got out of the car, we saw puppies in two different pens. I saw a white puppy with black spots wagging his tail and ran over to play with him. It was unanimous that the white puppy with spots was the one we wanted. He was a springer spaniel, and because of all the spots, we called him Freckles. As we drove home, my mother said we had to keep him in the back hall until he was house broken.

The first night he sat downstairs and whined, so I got out of bed, grabbed my pillow, and went down to lay on the floor with him. He quieted down, and went to sleep cuddled in my arms. A couple of weeks later, he was trained, and he had the free reign of the house. At bedtime, he lay with me, and I talked to him about everything that was happening in my life until I fell asleep. I was so happy to have a dog again.

Freckles was amazing and friendly, except with the mailman. Every time the mailman came, he charged the front door, barking his head off. One day, the front door was open, and there was just the outer glass door. Freckles was in the back hall when the mailman walked up to our front door. When Freckles heard him, he started barking, and charged the front door. He ran so fast he went through the glass door, almost giving the mailman a heart attack. Freckles was stunned as he sat on the ground surrounded by broken glass. After that, we made sure the inside front door was always closed when we knew the mailman was coming. Dani saw the glass on the sidewalk when she came over, and asked what happened. She laughed when I told her, and asked if I wanted to go for a walk along the creek.

As we were walking a boy, who was a year younger, started walking with us, and we tried to ignore him because he was annoying. Suddenly he dropped his jeans — he had no underwear on. We started running away, and he chased us with his penis flopping in the breeze. I felt guilty, wondering if we made him do it by ignoring him.

Dani's mom found out the boy's name, and told my mother. We went to the boy's house and sat in his living room. I had to tell his mom what he did while he was sitting there looking at me. The mother and her son apologized. I wondered how to protect myself from men and boys exposing me to their body parts. I always wondered if I was doing something to cause it.

In the summer, Kate and I went to the swimming hole at the creek. The creek was really high and over the banks, so it was really fun to run, grab the rope, swing out over the water, and drop into the creek. It was a thrill to fly over the deep water and let go at the center of the rushing water. We swam and jumped over and over until we heard some people yelling to each other by the walking bridge.

We walked along the curving path of the creek, until we saw a couple of men on the bridge and one in the water with a diving tank, and asked what happened. They said a dog jumped into the creek, and because the creek was so high, he got trapped under the bridge. We watched the divers going under the bridge for a couple of minutes, and then I left because I got a bad feeling. I was afraid to find out what happened to the dog.

**

Weather in Minnesota was unpredictable in the summer, with severe storms and occasional tornadoes. One night was especially scary because there were reports of tornadoes on all sides of the Twin Cities. They all seemed to be heading our way, and my parents and William weren't home. I looked out the windows, and saw black skies with thick thunderheads rolling around that looked like black, growling bears wrestling.

Then, the sirens went off. I yelled to my siblings, and we headed downstairs with flashlights to sit in Derek's plastic cabin he got for Christmas because it was away from the windows in the basement and provided extra protection. I brought my transistor radio so we could listen to what was going on. We heard thunder and pouring rain, then an angry wind was blowing and whistling through our windows. Suddenly, it was quiet, and I heard a couple of planes flying over our house. I felt safe, because if the planes were flying, then the weather couldn't be that bad. Soon the sirens stopped blowing, and we could go upstairs.

The quiet family hiatus ended that night when my father came home drunk and angry. I was asleep, and he woke me up yelling at my mother, saying she spent too much money, buying clothes or groceries. My mother tried to say it was the trip to Arizona that caused the money shortage. He interrupted, and said no, it was her fault, spending too much on us kids.

The words came out hard and fast, and I felt like he was beating my mother with his words. Her voice got quieter and quieter. I knew my father's other personality would appear, and here it was. He was the true Jekyll and Hyde.

I woke up the next day with a knot in my stomach. Later that day, my father came home from work with a smile on his face, and a new car to make up for last night. The car was an Electra 225. It was a white convertible with red interior.

Eventually, my mother began an ongoing battle with my father, and tried to line us kids up behind her, using us like a weapon. I never bought in, and I wouldn't line up. I knew that both my parents were at fault for the arguments and the drinking. I had an unexplained bond with my father that was created when I was young, and for some reason, I needed to take care of him, so I became his silent advocate.

I was glad I had many friends because it helped me escape from the drinking at home. When the hole inside me ached, I called my friends, and planned a slumber party. I learned if I stayed busy, it kept me from feeling the loneliness and frustration of my parents drinking behavior. I could pretend when I was with friends that everything was okay.

One Saturday, my friends and I were on the sundeck, under the stars, in our sleeping bags. We raided the icebox at midnight, and found sandwiches on a plate, a bag of chips, and cupcakes my mother left for us. We woke up at five in the morning when the sun was first peeking over the horizon, and decided to go down to Pearl Park and play on the tennis courts. We got rowdy, and sang all the way there at the top of our lungs:

"Wake up, wake up, you sleepy heads, get up, get out of bed, you've been in bed too long . . ."

We sang it over and over, louder and louder, until someone yelled out their window to stop the racket or they'd call the police. We laughed but stopped singing.

**

Later that summer I went to my church camp, The Cathedral of the Pines. I was so nervous. I didn't know anyone else on the bus. Some familiar faces from Sunday school, but no one I knew well.

There was a chapel service every morning. The chapel looked out over Caribou Lake with a hill across the way. It was so pretty. The whole front of the church was a large glass window. For one of the morning services, I was asked to sing "Beautiful Savior". After I sang, I sat down, and looked out the window. The whole church started singing "The Old Rugged Cross" and suddenly, as I was looking out the window, I felt myself being pulled across the water to the top of the hill. I was suddenly standing on the green hill far away, while everyone continued to sing.

When the song ended, I felt myself pulled back into the church. It felt very spiritual, and I started sobbing. I walked out of the church, and sat on the wooden steps. No one came to ask me if I was OK. I didn't really know why I was crying, but there was just something about the feeling of being pulled over the water and being outside of myself. Camp had been very eventful for me, and I loved all the lanyards I brought home. But the experience in the chapel stayed with me forever.

When I got back from camp, I tried to tell my mother about my experience in the chapel, but she didn't understand. She told me I was just daydreaming, which didn't explain my tears.

The next morning was Sunday. My father's yelling scared me late at night, but on Sunday mornings, he was funny. He talked about seeing pink or blue polka dot elephants. Everyone joined in, and laughed. And his story got wilder and funnier, which kept us laughing. I realized, as I got older that he talked like that because he drank too much and woke up with a terrible hangover. So, he came down, and had a few Bloody Mary's with breakfast. Everyone laughed at his humor, but eventually it made me sad.

Things at home got more intense, and darkness moved back in. My parents started having neighbors over, or relatives and longtime friends. They camped out in our kitchen nook. There were many Saturday afternoons when Eileen, Marie, Uncle Ed, my mother, and my father sat in the smoked-filled kitchen drinking, telling stories, laughing, and arguing. Soon, my mother threw some dinner together, and the drinking fest went on all night to the wee hours of the morning.

Once in a while, when they had these get-togethers, I sat on the kitchen floor around the corner from the kitchen nook, where they couldn't see me, but I could see and hear them. I sat and listened to their conversations. I realized how manipulative my mother was, and I heard her sidewise anger directed at my father. I heard her making fun of my father and trying to gain support and pity from those around her. I started to feel she was just as bad as my father. They were both at fault for the late nights and crazy behavior. She put up with it, and accepted his guilt "gifts." My father seemed oblivious to what she was doing, playing his role of "Goodtime Charlie."

At first it was kind of fun, then I got bored and went to a friend's house. Eventually, my parents' drinking continued into the weekdays, and we heard our father's anger and drunkenness, beating my mother with his words almost every night.

When their arguing woke me up, I read my Betsy-Tacy books. I read about Betsy's family having friends over on a Sunday evening for a sing-along around the piano. Betsy's father made onion sandwiches, and there was rich, hot soup for anyone who stopped by. Their home was filled with laughter and singing with a warm caring father who went for walks with his daughter. They talked, and her father imparted his loving wisdom. I felt safe reading those words, filling myself with their home. It was a world where dads weren't scary, and people didn't get drunk.

One night, at the end of the summer, Ally slept over. My parents were gone for the evening, and we went to bed around eleven. At midnight, when my parents came home, my mother walked into my bedroom to check on us. My father, who was angry, followed her into the room, and his yelling woke us up. Then, he slapped her across the face.

I could see that Ally was awake and watching. I got a stomach ache, and pretended to be asleep. The next morning, it was like it never happened. Ally didn't say anything, and neither did I.

After Ally left, I walked into the kitchen, and saw my mother sitting at the kitchen table. She looked up at me, and I could feel the bruises I saw in her eyes. It was almost a year before I invited someone to sleep over again.

Chapter 12
Love and Life Go On

I was excited for the first day of seventh grade and walking to the junior high. But when my friends and I walked into the building, we felt intimidated with three floors of classrooms. I went from being one of fifteen girls in a classroom, to being one of 200 girls in the seventh grade. It felt strange to change classrooms every hour and have seven teachers.

In sixth grade I was popular, smart, and seen. In seventh grade I felt lost, confused, and invisible. There were so many kids. I learned about cliques: "eggheads," "jocks," "popular clique," and the "nerdy clique." We had sock hops, a dance right after school for each grade.

Being the best student was important in grade school because that was how I got my positive attention. My teachers saw me. But in seventh grade, I became invisible at school, too. I became closer to my sixth-grade friends to fill in the void, and I found a couple of teachers who saw me. There were more students, and therefore more students who were smart. There were more teachers as well. So, I struggled, and soon, I started getting into trouble for talking, but not in Ms. Lauenstein's class because she saw me. She was my gym teacher, and I became her helper. She and I talked when I worked in the gym.

Our first sock hop was the third Friday in October. Ally, who was five feet tall and wore a triple E bra, was walking to meet us by the gymnasium. Three boys cornered her in the hallway, made fun of her large chest, and started pinching her nipples. She got away from them, and came to us crying. Through her tears, she said she couldn't take it anymore. The next day, she withdrew from Ramsey, and started attending Northrup, a private school for girls. We all felt sad.

The weekend after the sock hop, I got my first period. My mother wasn't home, and I didn't know what to do, so I went to Dani's mom, who gave me the equipment I needed. When I told my mother later that day, we went and bought supplies for me. Later in the week, I had terrible cramps, felt my period gush out when I coughed, and felt dizzy. It was a new sensation that made me anxious, so I told a teacher I had the stomach flu and wanted to go home. My mother came to get me, and I told her why I really came home. Then she explained what to expect from my period with all the hormonal changes. I wished someone had told me about it ahead of time, so I wouldn't have felt so freaked out.

That week my girlfriends started talking about going shopping downtown on Saturday. I didn't have any money, and had already shopped in the fall for school clothes with my mother, plus my father's angry words late at night about spending too much money on clothes kept me from asking for money to go with my friends. So, I didn't go with them when they took a bus to Dayton's on Saturday. I felt left out when I heard them talk about the Gant shirts or Capezio shoes they bought. Appearances were important to my mother and father; they wanted to look like we had money, but we were poor.

**

At home, weird things happened. One night I had a sleepover with AJ, and we slept in Becca's bedroom because she had twin beds, and Becca, now six, slept in my room. The next morning, she came down for breakfast, and said she had a strange dream that a man was stuck with his body halfway through the window, looking at her.

AJ, Becca, and I ran upstairs to look. The window she was talking about was open part way, stuck, and wouldn't go up any further. There was no screen on the outside of the window, and it was lying on the sundeck. We ran, and got my mother. A man had tried to get in but couldn't because the window stuck, or maybe he was surprised when Becca looked at him

I slept in Becca's room for a week after that. We got the screen fixed, and when I slept in my room again, I made sure the window was locked and the shade pulled. Feeling afraid was part of me now.

Another time, I was the first one home from school. I opened the back door, called out, and no one answered. Freckles was shut in the back hall, which meant my mother was gone. I walked into the living room, and the table drawers were pulled out and open. Derek was two, so I thought, "Boy, Derek was hyper today." I went upstairs to change clothes before I went to Kate's house. I noticed my piggy bank was broken on the floor, and the money was gone. I went into Becca's room to get a book, and noticed her piggy bank was broken, too. As I walked past my parents' bedroom, I noticed the drawers in their dresser were pulled out.

I shook my head on the way out the front door, wondering what had gotten into Derek because he'd never broken anything before.

An hour and a half later, I walked home from Kate's, and as I turned the corner, I noticed two police cars outside my house. I hurried up the block, walked in the front door, and heard my mother talking about a robbery. When I came in, they turned and looked at me.

I said, "Did I hear you say robbery?

Then, I told them what I saw when I got home from school.

One of the policemen said, "You were lucky. The burglar could have been in the house, hiding, while you were changing your clothes. It's a good thing you left shortly after."

It turned out that a couple of other houses along the creek were broken into that week.

A couple of nights later, I woke up because I heard my father crying in pain. My mother was talking on the phone. Pretty soon there were flashing lights and a siren. It turned out my father's appendix had burst, and he was full of peritonitis, which is a very serious infection. He was rushed to the hospital in an ambulance. The doctor said he could have died if he had waited any longer to call. William took care of us while my father and mother went to the hospital.

William was in general college at the University of Minnesota, studying business, and still lived at home. His friends nicknamed him Melvin Crudley after some comic book character with a big nose. They teased him about being the only one they knew who could smoke in the shower and needing Roto Rooter to clean his nose. He liked to party and drink with his friends. He had a serious girlfriend, Connie, whom he dated in high school. And when he was home, he was now Mr. Responsible, and taught us how to play catch or make us eat our vegetables when he was babysitting. He was very strict, and acted more like a dad than our father did.

He taught me how to throw a softball, baseball, and football. We went out after dinner or on weekend afternoons and played catch. He threw fly balls, sliders, and line drives. It was fun and because of my brother, I usually won the Ball Throw at field day events for school, being told I threw like a boy. One night, in the winter, he was in his bedroom next to mine doing his homework late at night. When my parents were too loud in the kitchen, he got fed up with their drinking and arguing, so he went downstairs, took their liquor, and poured it out, telling them to knock off all the drinking and go to bed. I could hear him yelling downstairs through the floorboards in my bedroom. It made me feel safer knowing he was home.

74

**

Winter this year was unusually cold, and girls couldn't wear pants to school. We had to walk a mile to school, and on very cold days, even with the freezing wind blowing snow in the air, my parents refused to give us a ride. We heard stories of their childhood, how they had to walk five miles down a dirt road to school, and *they* didn't get a ride.

Every morning my sister and I begged, "Just this one day. Please?"

But they just answered, "Walking in the snow builds character."

By the end of the winter, I felt like I had enough character to last a lifetime.

In the winter, my parents' drinking got worse. There were many nights my father wouldn't be home for supper. When he came home drunk a couple of hours later, he sat at the kitchen table, demanded supper, and yelled that he was the breadwinner so he should be served his supper.

One night, I was sitting on the stairs by the kitchen, and I could hear my mother banging pots and mumbling to herself, getting really angry while she made him a supper of corned beef hash. He sat at the kitchen table with his glasses sliding down his greasy nose, slurring his words about no one respecting him and what was taking her so long. She lost it, took his supper, dumped it over his head, and left the kitchen. My father sat there with egg yolk dripping down his nose, pieces of corned beef stuck in his hair and on his ear lobe, and pieces of potato and green pepper sliding down his cheek. He didn't say a word. He pushed his glasses up, stood with the food dripping on the floor, walked by me, and went upstairs. He went to bed without changing clothes or washing off the food.

On the weekends, my parents and their friends kept us up all night with their drunken singing or sometimes drunken arguments about religion and politics. During the weeknights, my parents woke us with their loud drunken arguments. One of my father's favorites was: we kids loved my mother more than him. He said she poisoned us against him, and she spent too much money. My mother always yelled back that he just had a persecution complex and was paranoid. He yelled louder, calling her names, and I could hear my mother's voice grow quieter. She was crying.

When their late night battles woke me up, I felt a knot in my stomach, buried my head under the covers, and dreamed of a handsome prince or a handsome social worker I saw in a TV show to come, fall in love with me, and save me. I got up the next morning, blurry eyed, and walked to school. It's hard to concentrate in school with only four hours of sleep. I was always in trouble for talking because I was hyper from the adrenaline that kicked in from lack of sleep.

After one of their drunken arguments, my father brought home a mink stole for my mother. It was his way of saying he was sorry for the abuse the night before. My mother put it on with a big smile on her face, and went to look in the mirror. When my parents went out on Saturday night, she wore it.

I remember thinking she had paid a high price to get that mink. It was blood money, and I hated that mink stole. My mother was changing, and getting weaker. The hope of anything getting better was gone. I always held out hope that she would again be that strong, proud woman I saw wearing a smile on her face when I was little. Instead, she seemed to be joining my father in his drinking behavior, and getting farther and farther away from the mother she was. I wanted so much to belong in a family where I felt love and was seen.

**

The people in our family used teasing in varying ways. At the resort that summer, I swam out to the floating dock to sunbathe. William and Connie were there sunbathing. I spread out my towel, put on suntan lotion, and laid down in the sun.

Suddenly William says "Helen, what's that on your towel? It looks like a leech."

I stood up screaming and checking my legs.

Then, William says, "Oh, never mind. It's just a wet pretzel."

For the rest of the week they kept teasing me about being afraid of wet pretzels. There was no place I could go and feel like I could relax and not be on guard.

The teasing continued, and when Derek was two, he had these stick-out ears that William would pull out and say "Eek—a mouse" to make us all laugh. Patty and I picked Derek up by his ears. When he was a baby, we dragged him around on a blanket. One day my mother took him to the doctor because she thought he had impetigo. But it was just a rug burn from being dragged around.

Once Derek and Becca were outside, and Becca took an Oreo cookie and filled it with dog poop. She gave it to Derek, telling him it was a chocolate Oreo cookie. He took one bite, and Becca started to laugh and took it away from him.

As Derek grew older, he became one of those kids who couldn't keep still. He was always jumping on my parents' bed, and had a couple of scars on his forehead from falling and hitting the foot of their bed. In the car, he sat in the back seat, and put his hands on the seat in front of him, bouncing the whole time. When it was warm outside, he was out on the patio riding around on his big wheel. He was the youngest in a family that teased; I think that would make anyone hyper. I wonder if he ever felt safe.

**

Very often, I'd walk by the living room, and my mother would be sitting in the armchair, staring out the window, not looking at anything. On very rare occasions, when she saw me, she would invite me to sit down and have my back tickled. I sat on the front of her chair, she tickled my back, and she would tell me I was the prettiest one in the family with my fine features or I was different from my brothers and sisters. Once, she told me that William said I was the smartest one in the family. Another time, she told me I was more sensitive and vulnerable than my siblings, so she worried about me out in the world. And one time, she told me I was getting fat. The back-rub time was when she focused on each one of us kids. When I was younger, my mother was tall, proud, and loved to visit with people she didn't know. I don't remember getting hugs or her saying, "I love you." But once in a great while, she saw me for those twenty minutes, sitting in the living room, tickling my back. But then, she would disappear back down the rabbit hole, and drink.

Growing up, I often found her sitting in the chair, in the corner of our living room, and staring out the two big windows. In those moments, I knew she wasn't there in the house with us, that she went to a place she'd always wanted to be. I could almost see her dreams of being a musician or a physical education teacher dancing around outside those windows.

I learned early my mother loved my older brother differently than the rest of us, and he was the apple of her eye. When he had polio, she worked hard so he wouldn't be a cripple. I found out when I was older my mother and father weren't married when William was born. My father was in the service when she found out she was pregnant, and he couldn't get a leave until after William's birth. They were married a month after he was born. My mother always wanted boys, and Derek also became another apple of her eye. I think girls scared her because of our vulnerability.

Years later, I wondered if she'd been sexually abused. I tried to talk to her about it, but she always shut down. But because of her talk about her older sexually promiscuous sister who had to leave their small town because she was pregnant and her talk about a father who was a philanderer with mistresses, I thought she probably had been. Years later, when she went through alcohol treatment, the counselor said she wouldn't open up to anyone about her past, holding tight to a secret she wouldn't reveal.

**

77

In August, I was sitting in the den with Patty, and my mother came in and told us our grandfather died. A couple months later my grandmother passed away from a broken heart, they said. We no longer had Christmas Eve with my aunts, uncles, cousins, and grandparents. My family quit going to church on Sunday, only going on special holidays like Christmas and Easter. I went to church every Sunday because I sang in the choir. My father's sadness and grief surrounded him, and he was like a ghost in our house. He had trouble getting the energy to get to work along with his brothers. Their business started to suffer for a couple of weeks, things falling through the cracks. My grandparents were the center and the glue that held the Carlson clan together.

Chapter 13
Three O'clock in the Morning

I loved fall because it always gave me a cozy feeling inside. The air outside was cool and crisp, the leaves full of vibrant colors, and I yearned to be home curled up with a good book and a sweet, crunchy, red apple, Freckles was lying by my side, waiting to be petted. I discovered new books about animals by Jack London: *The Call of the Wild, White Fang,* and *The Sea Wolf.* I continued reading the latest Betsy-Tacy books. Eileen gave me my all-time favorite, *A Tree Grows in Brooklyn,* by Betty Smith. I read *Lord of the Flies, Animal Farm, Catcher in the Rye, Little Women, Diary of Anne Frank* and *To Kill a Mockingbird.* I had so many feelings reading the different books. I identified with Francie in *A Tree Grows in Brooklyn,* who had an alcoholic father and sat on her fire escape to read and write in her diary. Anne Frank wrote in a journal about living inside of someone's walls and hiding for her life. I lived with these girls for a short time every day, experiencing their lives. No one else in my family read books. My bedroom was filled with books. Reading developed my curiosity, my fascination with people, and the desire to write about what I saw and experienced. It helped me escape to a different world, away from my family.

Fall also meant school was starting. The first week of eighth grade, AJ and I were walking along 50th street, and saw a man exposing himself on the new freeway bridge. We crossed the street to avoid him, and when we got to school, we reported it to the school counselor. Later that day, my mother and I went to the police station to look at mugshots, but I didn't find his picture.

Lunch time was fun in eighth grade. I was sent to the principal with a couple of friends for participating in a food fight in the cafeteria.

I looked the principal in the eye and said, "What food fight?" as I stood there with Jell-O in my hair, pudding running down my cheek, and milk all over the front of my blouse.

He wasn't happy.

Mrs. Lauenstein was my teacher again in eighth grade, and I was still her helper. I started to get into trouble for talking and doing mischief with the other kids, so she pulled me aside and talked to me about where I was heading. Then, one day she asked me if everything was all right at home and if there were any problems. I said no. I learned from an early age not to talk about my home. I was embarrassed by my parents' drunken behavior in front of my friends. Plus, my friends thought I was lucky because my parents weren't strict, and I could go out every night of the week if I wanted to. Also, there had always been drinking and yelling, so it seemed normal to me. I couldn't admit to myself things were that bad. My younger siblings and I made jokes about our parents' behavior to each other; humor became a way to cope with the tension and alcoholic behavior in our home. But as I look back now, I know the drinking was getting worse, and I was starting to act out for attention. I'll always feel grateful for Ms. Lauenstein for caring, even though I never opened up to her.

I loved my first sewing class, and enjoyed making my own clothes. We had a sewing machine at home, so I went out, and bought patterns for dresses, skirts and jumpers. I also bought one for a lined suit. I started with simple A-line skirts and dresses, and then, as I got more confident, I went to jumpers and a suit. My mother didn't sew, so if I ran into difficulties, I'd go see Kate's mom who did a lot of sewing. I made quite a few clothes in junior high and high school.

By eighth grade, sock hops changed — we actually danced. I had my first slow dance with a boy. For days, I talked with my friends about it. I relived every moment and how it felt while I sat waiting at a bus stop or alone in my bedroom. I pictured the boy and the dance, and heard the music playing. I felt the slow dance over and over, dancing so close, feeling the warmth of his body, his hands holding me.

I met Logan Peters in my home economics class, and we started hanging out in eighth grade. I often went to her house after school, and helped her make supper for her family. When I was there, I got to choose what we fixed. I usually chose skin-on hot dogs from the butcher and chocolate chip bars for dessert. Logan also had an older brother and sister and a younger brother and sister like me. Her father was six feet tall, weighed 300 pounds, and was bossy. After dinner, when Logan and I were in the living room, her dad, who was still at the kitchen table, told Logan to get his beer, which was in the refrigerator right behind him. She did it without questioning him.

Lisa and I still kept in touch by phone. She called one day, and told me she gave a guy my phone number. His name was Tim. He started calling me every night, and we talked for an hour. After about a month, we decided to meet. I slept over at Lisa's house, and we met him at the park. He was cute with dirty blonde hair that hung over one eye and a teasing smile that made me want to know him better. We hung out for the evening. He continued to call, and when Kathy had a boy-girl party, I asked him to go with me. The night of the party, Tim's parents brought him to Kathy's house, and I met him there. I introduced him to people, and we ate a few snacks and talked. Then, we started playing spin the bottle. Eventually, couples broke off, and started making out. We went to another party later in the fall that was a hayride through a forest of colored leaves, with apple cider and snacks. He stopped calling after school started.

**

At home, fear and danger appeared again with the feeling of never knowing what to expect. One night in the fall, Patty, Becca, Derek, and I were home alone. My parents went out for the evening, William was out on a date, and Patty was in charge. We were all upstairs in our bedrooms and suddenly Freckles started barking frantically at the back door. We went into William's bedroom to look down at the back door. There was a man standing there starting to turn the doorknob. We started screaming, and told Patty to get the phone and call someone. When she ran to call our parents, the man looked up at us, turned, and ran away. We went downstairs, locked the back door, then checked the front door to make sure it was locked. Freckles calmed down, his tail wagging; it seemed we were safe now. But we were all glad to hear our parents' car pull into the driveway.

When I was in eighth grade, William had beer parties at our house. Our basement had a wet bar, and was a perfect place for a party. If people had too much to drink, they spent the night on the couches downstairs. Sometimes at breakfast, there were a few boys and an occasional girl who joined us. Those breakfasts were fun. Two of William's friends, Crouch and Crack, would regale us with colorful stories that made us laugh, filled with vivid images of their escapades after school dances in high school. They still seemed a little drunk.

Whenever my parents went out of town, they left William in charge. William was very strict, and when we had dinner, he expected us to clean our plates. One night, I refused to eat my green beans. He told me to eat them right now! I told him he couldn't make me; he stood up so quickly, he knocked his plate over. Suddenly, he was behind me. I stood up, he put me in a headlock, and his arm tightened around my neck. Patty started yelling at him to stop, that I was turning blue. He seemed to come to, and loosened his grip around my neck. I ran out the back door crying and screaming. After I calmed myself down, I walked back into the house, and got my supper. I went down to the basement to eat; everyone else was still at the kitchen table.

When I was done eating, I brought my plate up to put it in the dishwasher. William was the only one left in the kitchen.

He looked at me a minute, then quietly, almost whispering, he said, "I'm sorry."

I was shocked. My brother never apologized; my brother was never wrong; my brother was never soft. I couldn't speak. I didn't know what to say. So I just put my dish in the dishwasher, and walked out of the kitchen. Things changed between my brother and me that night. He couldn't bully me anymore. He realized he couldn't control me. My other siblings always did what they were told. My behavior caused him to be physically abusive, he lost control, and I think it scared him. He left me alone after that.

My father was a Shriner, and went to events with his Shriner buddies, where he drank too much. Our phone would ring late at night, and my mother left to go to get him. One time, we got a call in the middle of the night, and I heard my parents arguing. Then, I heard them say William's name. It turned out William was at a party, and had too much to drink. He laid down in the back seat of his car, and passed out. His friend, Bill, took the keys, and drove. But his friend was drunk, too, and had a head-on collision with a car. It wasn't just any car; it was a police car. Bill was arrested for drunk driving, and the car was left on the side of the road. William was brought to the police station, where my father went to pick him up.

After that night, I realized our beautiful house off the creek in our upper middle-class neighborhood was very isolated. On one side was a grade school that was closed at night. The area across from the front door was the Minnehaha Creek. On the other side was an empty lot with trees and trees surrounded our backyard. The isolation made our house a target for many different kinds of invasions over the years. It was a place where I felt safe at first, but now, fear crept in at all levels. Our house was like our family: it looked good to the outside world, big and beautiful at the top of the hill, but inside it was chaotic, scary, and unpredictable.

**

My family's biennial trip to Arizona was in March this year. It was for three weeks. I was excited because for those three weeks my father would be relaxed and happy, and there would be no more fights in the middle of the night. I could get some sleep.

The beginning of March, we hopped into our Electra 225, and drove to Arizona for a week at the Paradise Inn in Phoenix. I loved these vacations because life was like one of my books; it was fun to pretend our family was normal.

The Paradise Inn was at the foot of Camelback Mountain. It was a luxurious resort with private two-bedroom adobe houses with a bathroom. At the resort, our parents went their way with Derek, who was three, and my sisters and I went ours. We hung out at a large pool where we laid in the sun and ordered food and drinks from our lounge chair. We spent our mornings by the pool, and after lunch, we went horseback riding. One morning, we rode horses to the top of Camelback Mountain where there were pancakes, eggs, bacon, and toast for breakfast, and one night, there was a steak fry. Patty and I hung out with the bartenders from the resort in the evening, shooting pool. They were funny, and told us some great stories.

After a week at Paradise Inn, we drove to Los Angeles to visit my father's brother, Uncle Edward, who lived with his family. Uncle Edward was tall with dark hair, and my Aunt Winnie had reddish blonde hair and a pretty smile. I met my four boy cousins who were older, and we swam in their pool while my father and his brother got fairly inebriated and started bragging about all the scars on their stomachs. My father called his a roadmap, and said his were bigger and better than my uncle's. Of course, their scars were not really roadmaps, but battle scars left by years of drinking too much. While we were in Los Angeles, my parents drank the whole time with my aunt and uncle.

We went to Disneyland and took a day trip to the San Diego Zoo. On our last day, we went to the Santa Anita racetrack. My uncle brought a newspaper about the races and the horses' names. I studied the names while we drove to Anaheim. I was drawn to a horse in the third race. His name was Ozzie's Boy; he was a long shot, my father said. My father bet two dollars on Ozzie's Boy for me. Ozzie's Boy came in first, so I won $125.

We left the next day, and drove up the coast to the outskirts of San Francisco where my father's sister, Aunt Anna, lived with her husband, Uncle Cecil, by the ocean. Uncle Cecil was a sailor, and he took us out on the ocean in his large sailboat that had a cabin for sleeping. When we drove back home a couple of days later, everyone was relaxed, tan, and tired.

But when we got back home, my parents' drinking and arguing started up again. One night, when I went to a movie with my friends, my parents were supposed to pick us up from the theatre. They weren't there when the movie was over. We waited twenty minutes, and they still weren't there. I searched for a pay phone, and called them to find out where they were. They were drunk, and said they forgot. It was embarrassing. I couldn't wait to get my own driver's license, or date a boy who could drive. We never had that problem when other parents drove. I started taking refuge at AJ's house.

Saturday mornings in the summer were my alone time. My chore was ironing. My mother sprinkled clothes with water, and rolled them up to get them ready. Then I'd take over the basement and iron, listening to Joe and Eddie, the Chad Mitchell Trio, Peter, Paul and Mary, and the Righteous Brothers on the stereo, singing at the top of my lungs. Joe and Eddie's song, "Crawfish", was my favorite. It was a soulful song about a world I knew nothing about. It carried the same emotion as "Porgy and Bess" by Ella Fitzgerald and Louis Armstrong. I loved the rhythm. I loved the freedom I felt in my body when I heard it. It made my body move and feel. I smiled as the notes filled the room.

**

In eighth grade, Kate liked Steve. When I went to her house after supper, Steve came over with Dan, a friend of his from church who liked me. On Saturdays, we played basketball at their church. That summer, when Kate and I took a bus to her church camp, we talked a lot about Steve and Dan. When we got to the camp, we hiked, swam, and played softball. The third day, Kate and I were in our cabin thinking about our boyfriends, and we decided to pretend that I was Steve and she was Dan. We started making out, the kind where it's just lips pressing on lips. After a while we pulled apart, our faces were red from hormones.

We took one look at each other, and both said, "Maybe we should go out and join the other campers."

I had never heard of anyone doing what we just did, and it felt weird that we got turned on. We never did that again or talked about it.

When I got home from camp, my mother's father came to visit. I had met him a couple of times when we visited him in Washington, but he'd never been to our home. After he left, I learned that my grandfather was a philanderer, and it was rumored he had a girlfriend in every city when he was married to my mother's mother. In fact, one day, when my mother was nine, he brought her to a malt shop for ice cream, then excused himself while he headed upstairs to spend an hour with his mistress.

A few days after my grandfather left, my father brought home a new motorboat, and said he got a deal for a new resort. We left a couple of days later, and drove to Lake Vermillion, pulling the boat behind us. Patty, now a junior in high school, had a serious boyfriend. Parker was six-feet-four and a star basketball player. He came up to the lake with us.

The first day, we went out on the lake to water-ski. I rode in the boat; I'd never water-skied and wasn't sure I ever wanted to. After everyone skied and we were out in the middle of the lake, my siblings picked me up, and threw me into the water. They wouldn't let me back in the boat. They said I had to ski back. They were serious, so I put on the ski belt and the skis, grumbling the whole time, angry that they just threw me in. I got up the first time and skied back, wondering the whole time how I would stop. When they swung by the resort, they motioned for me to just let go of the rope. I slowly sank into the lake and swam to shore. I have to say it felt great, like I had really accomplished something. I didn't like the way they got me to do it, but I skied every day we were there and loved it.

Chapter 14
Lord Hear Our Voices

In late summer, just before the start of ninth grade, there was a huge change in our family. William, now twenty-two, was getting married. Patty was a bridesmaid, Derek was a ring bearer, and Becca was a flower girl. My mother, father, and I sat in the first row right behind William and Connie while they were saying their wedding vows.

I started sobbing, and I couldn't stop. I embarrassed my brother, and was teased for years because I cried at his wedding. I cried because William was leaving our house, and I felt scared. Who was going to pour out the liquor now? Who was going to try to keep my parents in line? He was more of a dad to me than my father, and he was abandoning us.

When we got home after the reception, I felt the void in our house; all of William's stuff was gone. His room looked empty. Who was going to fill the space he left behind? Patty was busy with her boyfriend and high school activities. Quiet little me, who used to hide in her bedroom or behind chairs reading books, somehow inherited his role. My younger brother and sister started coming to me for answers and comfort, and I kept vigil over my parents' drinking. When my father was drunk and his anger was out of control, I was the one who calmed him down. My mother started sitting me next to him at the dinner table. When she went out shopping with my two sisters, she left me home to do something with my father.

I was supposed to be the strong one, the confrontive one, the truth seeker, and the problem solver. I could never go someplace right after school because I always felt the need to check in at the house to see if everything was OK. If it was, then I went to a friend's house. I began carrying around an extra backpack full of my family secrets and pain.

I was no longer invisible. Now, I was responsible. I became hyper-vigilant. I could never really hide in my books or my room again. I had to be in control, in charge.

A week after William moved out, we had a new occupant for his room.

Patty's boyfriend Parker moved in. His father was transferred to California, and Parker wanted to graduate from Washburn, so he asked my parents if he could move in with us for his senior year. Parker, being a star basketball player, was busy with school and sports, so he was rarely around. Patty was ecstatic to have him there. Sometimes, Becca, who was seven, wanted him to put her to bed and read her a book. Years later, Becca had memories of him touching her inappropriately during bedtime.

A couple of weeks after Parker moved in, we got a phone call. My favorite cousin Joanie passed away from complications from her diabetes. She was only thirty-four. I was devastated, and the day of her funeral, I told my mother I couldn't go because I wanted to remember Joanie as the person I saw at the last family gathering, laughing and smiling with her blue eyes twinkling and her blonde curls bouncing. I was afraid of death. I was afraid of the permanence of it. I couldn't face another loss. I didn't want to see her in a casket. I went to school instead.

**

This year, kids at school started going on adventures in the middle of the night. One night, I slept over at Logan's house, and we planned to meet friends at a park at 1:00 am. We waited for her parents to go to sleep, climbed out her bedroom window, walked across the roof, and went down the ladder she'd put there earlier. We took off running, and when we got to 50th St, we started walking. A squad car came around the corner, and saw us. We took off down the alley, and hid. The police parked their car, and came down the alley with their flashlights, looking for us. When they found us, they asked us where we were going. We told them we were meeting friends at the park. They asked where we lived, and we told them I was sleeping over at Logan's house around the corner. They stood there a minute, looking at us, trying to decide what to do. I guess they decided we were not delinquents because they told us to go home and go to bed or they'd call our parents.

We walked back to Logan's house, climbed up the ladder, went in the window, put our pajamas on, and went to bed. We lay there a minute staring at the ceiling.

Finally, Logan said, "Whew, we were lucky."

I answered, "You can say that again."

I must admit, though, I enjoyed the adrenaline rush and excitement. I started to realize the feeling of adrenaline rushing through my body was familiar because I awoke in the morning with the same feeling after a night of listening to my drunken parents and getting no sleep.

As I got older, it was how I learned to live; chaos, excitement, and unpredictability were "highs" I sought. They became normal to me.

One night, a few weeks later, I was doing my homework in my bedroom when I heard yelling downstairs, and I went to investigate. My father was drunk and upset because my cousin was getting married to a Catholic. I asked what he was so angry about. He said his sister didn't want a Catholic son-in-law. His anger felt so real. I couldn't figure out what he was so concerned about. So what if someone is Jewish or Catholic, didn't they all believe in God?

But my father, for some reason, didn't like Jewish people, Catholics, or people of color. As I got older, there were many arguments because I just didn't understand. I don't know what he was afraid of. He seemed threatened by anything that was different. I read books by Chaim Potok, and loved hearing about the Jewish traditions, the Talmud, and people living with faith. When I read *Another Country* or *Native Son,* I felt the hurt of not being liked because of the color of their skin. I felt the stories inside me. I wanted to share what I knew, but there was no one in my family to talk to because they didn't know those places. They didn't experience books and different ways of living. When William said that I was the smartest one in the family, I thought *I don't know if I am the smartest, but my mind is more open to ideas and differences.* Books were my lifeline. I knew from them that my family wasn't the only way to live. My feelings for Colby in second grade told me they were wrong. I loved people, and I loved their differences. I found people intriguing; they were like little mysteries to discover. It was like reading a new book that brought me into a different world. I kept reading, hoping to make sense of the world around me. My family seemed to be afraid of anything different.

**

On November 22nd, I was walking with my English class to the library. As we passed through the lunchroom, the loudspeaker went on throughout the school.

We all stood still as we listened to the words, "President Kennedy has just been shot."

The rest of the day, we got updates on his condition. School felt like we were going through the motions of going to class, but no teaching was happening that day. We were all in shock. It was the first time in my life a president had been assassinated. I walked home alone, feeling lost and disconnected. The world around me didn't make sense; people didn't kill presidents.

When I walked in the house, I heard the TV set and a newscaster speaking in newspeak, recounting the day again and again. I watched the president being shot over and over. I watched his wife trying to crawl out of the car. I felt the fear of being so close to someone you loved being killed. I think every house in the country had their TV sets on for the next few days, watching the coverage, then the national mourning of our assassinated President. The televised funeral procession of cars was on every screen.

The next week, in my history class, we had an assignment to study an aspect of World War II. I checked out books about Hiroshima and Nagasaki from the library, and went home to my bedroom and began to read. There were eight personal stories of people who survived the nuclear bombing. The more I read, the more horrified I became. I couldn't believe anyone would drop a bomb that could do such damage.

I read stories about people walking down the street, miles away from where the bomb dropped, and suddenly their clothes were imprinted into their skin. There was a story of a man being knocked over by the power of the blast, and when he came to, he looked for his family. While he was looking, he reached up to scratch his ear, and it came off in his hand. A woman was carrying groceries, and was knocked over by the blast while she was walking up the front walk to her house. When she stood up, her skin started falling off her arm. Young children were crying; all their hair was gone. I had to put the book down.

I felt the terror and anguish, confusion and pain. I started bawling my eyes out. My mother walked by, opened my bedroom door, and asked me what was wrong. I told her what I'd been reading.

Her only response was a disgusted and impatient, "Then, just stop reading the book."

She turned around and walked away.

She didn't comfort my horror or acknowledge the pain I was feeling. This was a true story, and those images stayed with me. I would never forget what nuclear weapons were capable of. I felt death. I couldn't believe what people did to each other. The more I felt and experienced the world around me, the more confused and alone I became. I wanted to live in the world of Betsy and Tacy. I wanted to feel loved, protected, and understood. I was full of love, and didn't have anywhere to express it. My parents never said words like "love."

**

School used to be my safe refuge. Now it became a place for me to act out some buried angst, a place where I challenged the authority around me. I had Mr. Patrick, a little man who wore bow ties and round horned-rimmed glasses, and took life seriously, for civics. I liked to upset him. One day, the TV set was on when we came into the classroom. Mr.

Patrick turned it off, making some joke that the other class got to watch TV because they were good kids.

I raised my hand, and said "Mr. Patrick, we don't like you either."

He got flustered, and left the classroom.

I had Mr. Champlin for Typing. He was very persnickety about using the typewriter. We were supposed to carefully remove the paper and not just rip it out of the machine. One day, I was talking to my neighbor, and he told me to stop talking and type. I ignored him, and kept talking. He came over, and ripped the paper out from the machine. He told me I got a zero for the assignment, and I had to come in after school to make it up.

I also had Mr. Andrews. In his class, I turned around, and talked to the person behind me. When he told me to face front and be quiet, I did for a minute or two, then I turned around again. Angrily, he sent me out in the hall. I wandered the halls distracting my friends in their classrooms. When he came to bring me back in the class, I was gone. One day, I made him so mad, he threw a piece of chalk at me, which missed and hit the blackboard and broke into pieces. Then, he stormed out of the classroom. I liked the attention, even if it was negative. I wasn't invisible. I hurt inside; I ached for a loving home where people hugged, cuddled, and talked. A place I could feel safe.

My report cards read A3 or B3. The numbers were citizenship grades to acknowledge my behavior in school. A 3 meant I was a troublemaker and disruptive in classes. I was nervous to bring my card home to have signed. But my parents never noticed the 3's. They just signed the card, and gave it back to me.

Eventually, I was called to the office because of these issues. The school counselor told me I should be getting straight A's without even trying. She said because of my age, the school couldn't expel me, but if I continued my behavior in high school, they could kick me out, so I needed to get my act together.

I know I puzzled the teachers because my grades were good but not my behavior. I don't think I ever realized how much my brother's getting married and moving out affected me. He was the only male figure at home who gave me attention. He could be strict, and I fought with him when he set limits. But I liked that he cared enough to set them. I think I wanted my male teachers to replace my brother. I wanted someone to care enough to set limits.

I don't know why the school never contacted my parents about my behavior. I think deep down, I wanted them to. I wanted someone who cared enough to see me and notice my pain. I was no longer the smartest girl in my class, now, I was the class clown, trying to deflect my inner struggles, getting energy from the adrenaline running through my bloodstream.

**

In ninth grade, I started coming out of my shell. I realized for the first time I was short. When I walked out of my typing class, I could see my reflection in the trophy case across the hall. I saw how much taller everyone was. I was just under five feet, and I had a small waist. So, I was starting to get a desirable shape. My long hair was brown with blonde streaks from the sun. I was surprised to see how small I was, because I always felt big inside.

The sock hop was fun this spring. I had a crush on Matthew Peters, who was tall, dark, and kind of sexy. When the music started, I usually just sat, and waited for someone to ask me to dance. But for some reason, that day, I decided I could be in charge of my own fun, and, I got up to ask Matt to dance. We were the first ones dancing, and soon, the dance floor was full. I had so much fun just being myself and not worrying what people thought. I took a risk. I opened up this shy, timid place inside, and it worked. There was still the part of me that hid in her room reading books — the part that wasn't sure the world was safe enough to show my real self.

And when there was a talent show in the spring, I auditioned for it. Kate and I decided to sing as a comedy act. We found some silly songs to perform. One of them was "Oh, I With I Were a Wittle Thugar Bun". We sang with a lisp. Kate dressed as up Raggedy Ann, and I dressed up as Little Lord Fauntleroy. After the talent show, we were asked to perform at churches and nursing homes with other acts. We even got paid once.

I started going to dance places with Jennifer, a fast girl from our group. She scared me a little, and I didn't quite trust her. But I slept over at her house one night, and we went to the Marion to see The Gestures, a band from Mankato. Her sister drove us to the Marion, and we danced all night. Jennifer was flirting with the lead singer, and when the night ended, Jennifer told me her sister couldn't pick us up, so she arranged for the lead singer to give us a ride home. I didn't like the idea because we didn't know these guys. Jennifer sat in the front of the car with the singer, and I sat in the back with the drummer. We parked in front of Jennifer's house, and Jennifer and her guy laid down in the front seat, going at it. I wasn't attracted to the guy who was with me. But it was a two-door car, and I was trapped in the back seat. Until Jennifer came up for air, and opened the car door, I couldn't get out. So, the drummer and I started making out. Finally, Jennifer sat up, and opened the door. I was angry with her for putting me in that position. Then, to make matters worse, the next morning, I realized the guy had given me a hickey.

When I got home from Jennifer's, I saw a new piano sitting in our living room. I was surprised, and I asked where it came from. My mother said my father brought it home. I sat down, and played that piano for hours, figuring out the notes. I could read the right-hand notes from choir and accordion lessons. The left hand was a little harder, but I worked it out. I learned songs from a folk song book: songs by Peter, Paul and Mary or simple folk songs like "Kumbaya". I learned a Frank Sinatra song called "When I was Seventeen". I played, and sang.

Later that night, after I'd been asleep for about an hour, my father was drunk and ranting about the Mafia. He woke me up, and I listened to him yelling about how Frank Sinatra, Dean Martin, and Joey Bishop were all part of the Mob. Also, his construction company had a fleet of trucks. So, he had to deal with the Teamsters Union, which was known to be "connected." He was so angry, my mother tried to get him to quiet down, but then he started yelling that she was just like them. Always lying, spending too much money for groceries. I took my latest Betsy story, and read until I fell asleep.

The next day, in our civics class, we had to do a research paper about something that had been in the news. My father's anger gave me the idea to do mine on organized crime — the "Costa Nostra," "The Syndicate," "The Mob," "The Mafia" — there were so many names for it. I read articles from newspapers and magazines and books. I found out my father was right: there were connections with the Mafia and entertainers in Vegas. I was attracted to and fascinated by "the Family" and all the far-reaching connections it had. I was surprised how an organization like that could exist so openly in our society without ever getting caught.

**

My father was a Shriner, and proud of it. He loved wearing his red Fez with the tassel dangling on the side, and went to many Shriner affairs where liquor flowed freely. This year, my parents were given a great honor: they were chosen as the next Matron and Patron of the Eastern Star, which, was affiliated with the Shriners, was a charity based organization with some loose connection to the Bible. There was an installation ceremony to name the new Matron and Patron at the Zurah Temple downtown. It was a big deal, and my parents asked me to perform a couple of songs at the ceremony. That was my first solo performance in the general public, not counting one time at church camp. There were maybe one hundred people there. Food was served afterwards, and people came up to me to comment on my singing. I felt shy but thanked them. Deep down, I never felt like I was very good, so it embarrassed me when people made comments. I had learned from my family to only trust criticism, and when someone gave me a compliment, it was phony and they were just being nice. Praise was suspect. My family never said anything about how I did. It always felt like the more I tried, the harder I worked, the more I did, the more I over-functioned, I still remained invisible. My father strutted around that night with pride to be the Patron of Eastern star.

My father loved attention, prestige, and being someone important. My mother loved to cook, and was proud of her meals, happy when we enjoyed them. The rule after supper was we took turns doing the dishes. Patty and I were always fighting about whose turn it was. As I got older, I got out of kitchen duties. I don't know if it was because my mother was sick of Patty and me fighting or if she was sick of arguing with me. The change seemed to be around the time William told my mother I was the smartest one in the family. There was now an expectation I would go to college.

**

Junior high school was ending in a couple of weeks. Next year, I'd be going to high school. I was looking forward to the freedom of summer and warm weather. At the beginning of summer, I went to my church camp, and Jennifer was in my cabin. She entertained everyone, telling us stories of her exploits with boys. One night, she started talking about French kissing. I had never heard of French kissing, so she tried to describe it to me. Then, she told me to come over by her.

She said, "Here, let me show you."

And she French kissed me; I was so surprised, having her tongue in my mouth. So my first French kiss was with a girl.

When I got home from camp, there was an above ground, chest-deep, swimming pool, complete with a ladder in our backyard. We all swam in it. There were other changes in our house. Up until now, our family's favorite restaurant was Nelson's, the home of the Mr. Big and fresh strawberry pie. My father's drinking had gotten to the point that he wouldn't go to restaurants that didn't serve alcohol. So, our family restaurant changed to Gannon's on East River Road. They served alcohol, and had a piano bar where we sat after dinner while my parents drank.

In the summer, we kept up the Sunday tradition of a big dinner after church, which meant for our Sunday night supper we ate peanut butter on toast and homemade malts my father whipped up in the mixer. We always sat in the den with our toast and malts, and watched Ed Sullivan.

One night, William and Connie came over to watch with us, and share in our toast and malt supper. The den windows and shutters were open because it was a warm summer evening. After Ed Sullivan was over, I went upstairs to call AJ.

While I was talking on the phone, I heard a scream from downstairs. I hung up, ran downstairs, and rushed into the den. Connie was the one who screamed because she saw a man's face peeping in the window at her. When she screamed, he ran away. We got up, and looked out every window in the downstairs to make sure he was gone. We called the police, and when they came, they said that window peepers usually just peep, so not to worry about a break in. For the rest of the summer, I didn't like sitting in the den at night to watch TV because I kept thinking I would see a face in the window.

Connie and William also joined us on our boat outings down the St. Croix River, where we stopped at beaches to swim. Our destination was The Steamboat Inn in Wisconsin for dinner. Those trips were fun. William would get silly, saying words like "Pequot" in a high nasal voice, or he'd stand on the front of the boat like a hood ornament, swing his arm up and down like an elephant's trunk, and trumpet like an elephant. We all laughed so hard, our stomach muscles hurt.

I realized that summer, as we rode our boat back to the marina after supper, that in my family there was light and dark, sweet and sour, up and down, and one adventure after another. My bi-polar father created a world of swinging emotions, first fun and exciting then dark and depressing. He was a man who randomly brought home large expensive gifts and wanted to suddenly run off to the Virgin Islands or Portugal. Then, the next day, he'd barely be able to get out of bed to go to work because of anxiety and nerves. At night, he continued to yell at my mother for spending too much money. When you throw in the drinking, our family became a complex, stained glass window, reflecting different colors with different lights, a jigsaw puzzle of events that were like a juggler tossing four balls in the air, trying to catch them before they hit the ground. That was my family's motto: keep moving, keep juggling, whatever you do just keep going because it could all change at a moment's notice. Sometimes at night, I looked at my father, and thought I saw a silent scream coming out of his mouth.

**

That summer, AJ came over one day, and asked if I'd heard about Barbra Streisand. When I said, no, she explained that Barbra Streisand was discovered at a club in New York and had one of the best singing voices of all time. She brought her Streisand record, and we went down to the basement to put it on the stereo, and soon the room filled with the song "People." I fell in love with her voice. I began to see her picture everywhere: on TV, billboards, and magazine covers.

A couple of weeks later, I went to Kate's house, and her mom and dad showed me a magazine.

They covered the name, and said, "Who does that look like?"

I said, "Barbra Streisand."

They said, "That's right, but who else does it look like?"

I was confused.

They laughed and said, "You! It looks just like you. Only, you're prettier."

That awakened something in me. First of all, they said I was pretty. And I'd always dreamt of being a singer. At that moment, Barbra Streisand became my idol, my mentor who encouraged me to sing even more. For years, I'd been singing along to Peter, Paul and Mary, Joe and Eddy, and the Chad Mitchell trio when I ironed. Now, when I heard Streisand on the radio, I sang along to her songs.

Later that summer, AJ invited me to her church camp. We took a camp bus from Westminster Church. The first night at camp, a boy came, and sat next to me in the camp commons. He was really cute with wavy, blonde hair, and blue eyes. He started talking to me, and when it was time for bed, he said he'd see me tomorrow. I was excited. His name was Grant, and he had just moved to Minnesota from Canada. I loved his Canadian accent and how he ended his sentences with "eh?"

The next night, he asked me to go for a walk on the camp trail.

I said, "Yes," and he held my hand as we started down the trail.

He asked things about me, and then he stopped, bent down, and kissed me. Then, we walked a little farther. When he stopped again, he kissed me longer, and he French kissed me. I had never French kissed a boy. Grant was an aggressive kisser, and his tongue was in my mouth, feeling everything I had inside there. He walked me back to my cabin when it was time for lights out.

After AJ and I were tucked in bed, I told her Grant had French kissed me. My body was wired that night from newly discovered hormones, and I didn't sleep a wink. Grant and I spent a lot of time together at camp. He asked for my phone number on the last night, and when I got home from camp, he called me to ask me out. I was excited to have a boyfriend again, and he was a grade ahead of me, had his driver's license, and his own car.

**

A couple of days before tenth grade started, I was in a strange mood, feeling unsettled inside. That night, I was sitting with my family, watching television in the den. My eyes wandered away from the screen, and I started looking out the den window at our backyard patio. The window was open, there was a warm breeze, and I could hear the crickets; they were so loud this time of year. Their song pulled me out of myself, and for some reason, I started imagining what it would be like to have all the things I was looking at outside disappear, to no longer be there.

Suddenly, I felt weightless and a deep sense of loss. I felt an empty nothingness and wondered, *Is that what death felt like?* I ceased to exist for that moment. My heart started beating fast. I felt anxious, and I tried to shake off the feeling. I turned to look at my family, who were watching TV, no idea of what I had just experienced. I felt disconnected from them. It was the first time I'd ever thought about feeling death. It was a profound moment I've always remembered vividly. I felt changed, somehow, like the meaning of my life deepened and became important. I realized how precious life was.

Chapter 15
Now I Am in High School

Starting tenth grade was exciting because I was in high school with new people and classes. My favorite class was choir. I fell in love with the albums my teacher played in class. In fact, the best album I ever bought was Bartok and Kodaly's *Hungarian Folk Songs,* performed by the Kodaly Girls choir. I loved the dissonant harmonies they sang.

When there were tryouts for the Madrigals choir, which was the elite choir, I rehearsed my song every day with Kate accompanying me on piano. I was so nervous for the audition. I walked into the choir room — my blouse wet under my arms, my heart beating like a bass drum — and I sang my songs. I waited anxiously for the list of who made it in to appear on the bulletin board. Finally, the white paper was pinned to the board, I looked through the names, heart pounding. My name wasn't there. I was stunned.

I started acting out in choir, being disruptive by talking to students around me when the teacher had his back turned, cracking jokes under my breath, making people laugh. A couple of us took rubber bands, and shot at him when his back was turned. One day, he caught me, and kicked me out of class. I had to write him a letter, go in, and apologize personally to convince him to let me back in the choir. He let me back in with a warning.

He was my favorite teacher, but I was *not* his favorite student. I learned from him there were consequences to my acting out. Like they told me in ninth grade if I didn't straighten up, I could be kicked out of school in tenth grade. So, my acting out became more subtle, and I didn't get caught again. School wasn't my favorite place anymore. Having a boyfriend who drove was.

I saw Grant almost every weekend when we got back from camp. On Sundays, we visited the Minneapolis Art Institute, the Walker Art Institute, or walked the trails at Theodore Wirth Park. After, we had an early supper at Lincoln Del. A few times, we went to his house, and had dinner with his parents and his older brother. The dinners were formal. They called napkins "serviettes," and the dessert was a flaming cherry jubilee, which his father lit with a flourish. Then, after dinner, everyone loosened up, and sat on the living room floor to play Yahtzee. When the game was over, everyone went their separate ways: his father to his office, his mother to the kitchen, his brother outside to work on his car, and Grant and I went into the den, sat on the couch, and made out. It felt weird sitting in there kissing while I heard his father talking on the phone in the next room, his mother clanging pots and pans in the kitchen, and his brother outside starting his car.

Grant was a year ahead of me in school, and two years older in age. He drove a Triumph sports car, and smoked a pipe. I thought he was so exciting. Some nights, we went to a movie, and after, parked by Lake Harriet to practice French kissing. One of those nights, his hand started moving toward my breast. I wasn't sure what to do, so I stopped him.

The next day, I went over to AJ's to talk to her sister, Ruth. I told her what happened, and asked her what was OK to do with boys.

Her advice to me was, "If it feels good, do it."

So, the next time he tried, I let him. It felt good, but I didn't know if I really wanted him to do it. I felt kind of guilty. I don't think my close girlfriends were doing things like this with their boyfriends. At least, no one talked about it.

I went with Grant all of tenth grade. I invited him to my Sadie Hawkins dance. Kate, AJ, and I had a party at my house before the dance, and we decorated the basement like a hillbilly's house with a strung-up clothesline with bras, long underwear, and shirts hanging with clothespins. We had a washtub with a washboard, we hung funky pictures of shacks and moonshine stills, and we put candles in beer bottles. Everyone came in hillbilly costumes. It was fun, and so was the dance.

AJ slept over after the dance. We lay in the dark bedroom and talked about the dance and the party, and then she told me she had started smoking cigarettes. She taught herself how to inhale, and then, taught Kate. She asked me if I wanted to learn. After we got up and had breakfast, we walked down to the Minnehaha Creek, and AJ pulled out a pack of cigarettes. She gave me one, and I put it between my lips. She lit a match, held it to the end of the cigarette, and told me to breathe in. I did, and started coughing. She told me to relax, slowly inhale the smoke, and blow it out. It worked the second time, and she and I smoked a cigarette together. I started feeling kind of dizzy, and I wanted to go home to lay down. We walked back, she got her things, and left. I laid down, and slept for a couple of hours. I felt fine when I woke up. Smoking felt like a rite of passage. AJ and I felt grown up, and started smoking in my bathroom before school, while we put on our make-up with the door closed.

Smoking caused Grant and I to have our first argument. Kate, Grant, and I went to Pizza Hut one night. While we were waiting for our pizza to come, Kate brought out her cigarettes and lit up. Grant didn't think girls should smoke, even though he smoked a pipe. When I asked Kate for a cigarette, he got up, and left the restaurant, saying he didn't want to be seen with girls who smoked. He waited for us in the car.

**

In tenth grade, I had a permit to drive, and my parents sent me to Mr. Deanovic that fall to teach me behind-the-wheel classes. Our driving route was in the middle of the city. I had to turn onto Portland, a very busy four lane, one-way street. I started in the left lane and had to cross all four lanes to make a right turn in one block. It was really tricky in rush hour traffic. I learned to turn, to back out of driveways, and the hardest trick in driving to parallel park. I was ready to take my driving test when I turned sixteen.

I had a slumber party for my sixteenth birthday. A couple of girls got into a fight, and at one point, Sara reached into Maggie's sleeveless shirt, and grabbed her bra strap, pulling it out. We were all in shock. Sara stood there with the bra dangling from her hand, while Maggie stood there braless. Suddenly, all the anger became laughter, as we realized what had happened. Later some boys came, and crashed our party.

My parents never seemed to know what was going on at the parties. My mother left sandwiches in the refrigerator for us, and went to bed. I don't think my father was even aware of the party. But I became known for my bimonthly slumber parties.

The next day, I had an appointment to take my driving test, and I passed on my first try. I ran in the house, waving my yellow piece of paper that was my temporary license. After dinner, I drove over to Logan's house. It was so freeing to be alone in the car, driving to where I wanted to go. I had accomplished another rite of passage.

Shortly after I got my license, my father brought home a brand-new, black Studebaker for my sister and I to share. My sister ended up buying herself a car. By the time I was a junior, the car was basically mine. It was black with a red and white interior, and had roll up windows. My friends and I called it the BS'er. Most nights, I picked up my friends, and we made the rounds of Porky's drive-ins. We ordered coke and fries, and waited for our other friends to show up. There were always kids from other schools, which made it a great way to meet boys.

Now that I could drive, Logan and I bought season tickets to the Guthrie. Before the matinee performance, we often ate lunch at a nearby cafeteria. I loved sitting in the theatre, the lights going down, and the stage lighting up. My world got larger. *Henry V* transported me to England, in *Glass Menagerie* I traveled to St. Louis, and in *Joan of Arc* I was in France. *The Cherry Orchard* took me to Russia, and *The Skin of Our Teeth* brought me to New Jersey. I was an empath, and I was absorbed into any play I watched. I was up there on the stage, experiencing their life and all the characters I met. I lost myself in the emotions, and didn't come to until the lights went up. I don't think any of my siblings or my parents ever went to the Guthrie. It was another way I was different.

One Saturday afternoon, I had the car, and picked up two girlfriends to go hang out at the Porky's by Lake Calhoun. We met some boys who said their parents were gone for the weekend, and we decided to go to their house and hang out. On the way there, I was driving down an unfamiliar side street with cars parked on both sides of the road.

As I passed a parked car, an eight-year-old boy riding a two-wheel bike turned into the street. He rode his bike between the parked car and me. I didn't know it, but the back wheel of his bike caught on my bumper. I heard a sound and saw the boy on the street. His bike was tipped over, and his mouth was bloody. I pulled over. Someone called the police. I waited on the curb with my head in my hands, scared and shaking.

The police called it an accident. But I saw a cute little eight-year-old boy, just learning to ride a bike, and now his mouth was bleeding. I felt so guilty because I shouldn't have been driving there in the first place, going to some strange boy's house we'd just met, whose parents were out of town. We were up to no good, and I was caught. I had to go home, and tell my parents. I had to explain why I was driving in that particular neighborhood.

Before I left, I got the little boy's phone number, and called his family the next day. His parents said that he'd gone to the emergency room to get checked out, and he was fine. I couldn't shake the feeling of shame I had inside because I lied to my parents about where I was going and why I was in that neighborhood. Deep down, I was sure it was my fault.

When I told my parents, they just seemed relieved there weren't any charges against me.

**

At sixteen, my hormones started to really kick in. But sex was confusing for me. I wasn't sure if I liked it after my previous experiences and seeing men wave their penises at me. It gave me a stomach-ache. In school, there were rumors about senior girls doing "it" at lunchtime when they left school grounds. My parents had parties, and the drunken men flirted with my siblings and me, putting their arms around us, touching our hair, kissing our cheeks, or pinching and patting our bottoms. They made comments to us that were sexually inappropriate. My father put his hands on us, and wanted us to sit on his lap. One time, he tried to French kiss my younger sister. I couldn't wait to get away from those parties.

Some nights, my father came home late from work, and announced loudly that he had just been to a "massage parlor" or he bragged about the XXX rated movie he just saw, like *I am Curious Yellow*. I could tell it turned my mother's stomach when he talked about that stuff. It felt dirty and ugly.

One night, Grant and I parked at Lake Harriet, and he did something he'd never done before: he put my hand on his private area. I didn't like it. I could feel his hardness, but I didn't know what to do. Then, he took my hand, and moved it up and down. When he put his hand on my private place, and used his fingers, the sensation felt good. I wasn't sure if I wanted to do it, and my stomach knotted up. I did it because he wanted me to, but it made me uncomfortable. This wasn't something I talked about with my friends; there was an underlying feeling that only cheap girls did things like this. I went home after, and buried my head in a book.

Books were still my best friends. When the tension between my parents got so thick, I could feel it wrap around me and make it difficult to breathe, or life's questions came at me and I wasn't equipped to answer them. I picked up my favorite book, and got lost in the characters. After the night with Grant, I got lost reading about Betsy and her new relationship with Joe. There wasn't any sexual pressure in the book, just a loving warmth.

Reading to relax wasn't working as well as it used to; I couldn't get away from the tension or a feeling of frustration and anger that started invading my inner quiet. I didn't know how to deal with it. The anger felt like my whole body was filling up with an explosive gas ready to erupt. I didn't know where to direct it or how to express it. I felt like my head was going to explode and I would disintegrate into little pieces.

I became more isolated from my family. I was always in my room reading or talking on the phone. I ran from my home whenever I could. I felt like there had to be someone, somewhere, who could love and see me without this sex stuff. There must be somewhere I could just feel loved. So, I kept searching.

The night after I'd been with Grant, I couldn't wait to get out of the house and be with my friends. I had to watch Becca and Derek until my mother got home from a meeting, and my father wasn't home. My mother said she'd be home by eight, and I could go out then. I made arrangements with my friends, saying I'd be there to pick them up at eight.

Eight o'clock passed, and then eight-thirty; people started to call and ask where I was. Soon it was nine o'clock. I hadn't heard from my mother, and my father still wasn't home. The anger that had begun to invade my inner life started to build inside my body, my heart beating faster, my hands gripped in a fist, a feeling of being trapped in my body. I didn't like the anger. I wanted to run away from it, but it followed me everywhere I went. I ended up putting my fist through a window.

When my mother got home, I ran out of the house, jumped in the car, and drove off. The anger and tension began to dissipate, and I relaxed and enjoyed the feeling of driving and getting away.

As I drove to Logan's, my mind slowed down, and I was aware of how warm the air outside felt. I realized that summer was just a few weeks away, and I started to smile.

Grant came over a couple of weeks later, and told me his family was moving to Toronto in June because his father was being transferred. At the end of May, Grant and I were riding around Lake Calhoun in his sports car, and he asked me to get something out of his jacket pocket in the back seat.

I found what he wanted, but I also found a box of condoms. We had not had sex, so I didn't know why he had the condoms. It scared me that he thought we might have sex before he moved. The next weekend, we were in my basement making out, and Grant tried to remove my shorts. I got angry, and stopped him. I told him I saw the condoms, and it wasn't going to happen. He left angry and frustrated. When Grant came to say goodbye, we kissed, wrote to each other a couple of times in the summer, and then we stopped.

A week later, Kate and I met Warren and his friend, Rick, at Porky's drive-in. Warren was short and muscular with dark eyes, black, wavy hair, and he was handsome. We flirted. Rick and Kate hit it off, and we exchanged numbers. Warren owned a boat, and the four of us water-skied every weekend. When Warren brought me home, we parked by the bushes, and made out in his van. The four of us hung out most of that summer. But a couple weeks before school started, they quit calling us.

**

In June, I started working full time for my father's construction company, doing figure work, using a ten-key adding machine and a calculator. I liked working in the office, because I got to talk to the truck drivers when they called on the CB radio needing instructions about a job they were doing. I also learned to do the payroll, writing checks for the employees, and tallying up numbers to make sure everything checked out. I was also earning a paycheck. But I soon became aware of my father's relationship to his brothers, coming to work after long lunches with them, reeking of alcohol. My father seemed to be under a lot of pressure to get the jobs done at different construction sites on time or to submit the right bid to be awarded another job at another site. There was pressure to make sure the money kept flowing through the business. I heard them often arguing in the office next door. On those days, my father came home drunk and belligerent.

In August, I noticed the whole side of our car was scratched up. When I asked my mother about it, she told me my father was drunk, and drove Derek, now six, to soccer practice. My father pulled out of the driveway, scraped the car along the stonewall scratching off the paint. When he drove down the street, he swerved, went over the curb, and hit a mailbox. I couldn't believe it. Derek was lucky he got to practice safe and sound. After that, Derek refused to get in the car alone with my father.

I worried about my father and his drinking. At times, I watched him, flashing on the one fleeting moment years ago when I saw his softness, his vulnerability, helplessness, and what I thought was love. I felt an urge to reach out to him when I saw his hands shaking and he was anxious and scared. His eyes looked wild, and he was struggling with something hidden deep inside. He looked tormented in his isolation. I felt helpless.

**

Summer was almost over, and I actually looked forward to school starting. I thought it might bring some sanity to my world. The week before school started, I went to the drive-in with a girlfriend to eat and play mini golf. Some boys parked next to us, and ordered malts. We started talking, and invited them to play mini golf with us. Afterwards, we were getting into our car, Jerry, one of the boys, asked me for my phone number. He called me later that night, and we talked for an hour.

Jerry and I started dating. We loved to go to Minnehaha Falls, walk the trails, go for Sunday drives around the lakes, and get out and walk. At night we went to drive-in movies, and we steamed up the windows, only seeing half the movie. Things felt different with Jerry than they did with Grant. Jerry was warm, gentle, and liked to just hold hands and snuggle.

Chapter 16
Nature's Prayer

One night, after we'd been dating a few months, Jerry and I parked at Lake Harriet, and started making out. Jerry stopped, looked me in the eye, and told me he loved me. I'd never had someone say that to me. What did it mean to love someone? I didn't know what to say. I just sat there with my emotions swirling around inside me. What was love? I loved Skippy, I loved Mrs. Galle, and I loved Betsy in my books. Jerry started to kiss me again, and held me close. I was grateful because I needed to think about what to say to him. I know that I liked being with him. Just having him sit near me in the car or on a couch made my heart beat faster. The warmth of his body next to me made me feel safe and connected. I wasn't invisible to him. After the next kiss, I looked at him, and told him I loved him too. We drove home holding hands, feeling the closeness of being together. But part of me felt like I was playing a part in a play, acting as if I were in love, not *really* knowing what it meant.

A couple of months later, we parked at Lake Nokomis. Jerry was a great kisser, using his tongue in such a gentle way when we French kissed. He was sensual. Something felt different that night. We had fondled each other's private parts before, but tonight, his kisses went lower and lower on my body, until he reached a very sensitive spot. I didn't know what he was doing, and then suddenly, I had an orgasm. I had never had one before, and it was amazing. I felt like my whole body was alive with pleasure soaring through my veins, building up until I felt an explosion, an energy release so powerful, it brought tears to my eyes. I wanted to live in that moment forever.

But when he came up for air, I had a mixture of feelings. It felt weird having his mouth down on my very private place. I felt dirty, and maybe guilty. But the sensation of the orgasm was so powerful. I was confused, and ended up getting mad at him, telling him to take me home. I didn't understand my feelings, and none of my girlfriends talked about sex or what was normal. Only the fast girls were sexually promiscuous. I wasn't a fast girl.

When Jerry brought me home that night, my whole house was lit up. There was nobody downstairs, but when I walked up the stairs, I heard them. I took a deep breath, and put on my strong, confident face, and walked to my parents' bedroom door. I could hear my father yelling in a drunken rage, sounding like a caged animal, and my mother, younger brother, and sister were egging him on. I opened the door and saw my father standing, every muscle in his body taught, his face bright red, and spit was foaming around his mouth. He sounded like he was possessed and talking in tongues. My mother and my two younger siblings poked at him, then, danced away, laughing. He bellowed.

I walked into the bedroom, and placed myself between them. I asked my mother to leave with my brother and sister. After they left and closed the bedroom door, I turned, and looked at my father's bloated, angry face. I saw his helplessness. I flashed on years ago when he was lying on the bed in his dirty khakis and tee shirt, looking so helpless and sad, and I felt our bond. I walked over to him, talking in a quiet, calming tone. Whatever words he was yelling, I sympathized with him, and eventually, he started to calm down. He looked at me with his clouded blue eyes, and I saw trust in them. He let me take his elbow, and walk him over to the bed. I continued to talk in a soothing, comforting tone. Eventually, he laid down, muttering to himself. A few minutes later, he was sound asleep.

At seventeen, I was the one my mother sent in to "tame the beast." I never found out on those nights why the argument started in the first place. But it was very ugly by the time I got home. It was hard to know who the parents were and who the children were. That night, I was the parent.

The next day, my father left in the morning, and came back a couple of hours later. My mother was in the kitchen baking a chocolate cake. I was licking out the mixing bowl and beaters. My father walked in the room, handed her a small box, and said he was sorry. She opened the box, and there was a ring with a very large diamond. I could see my mother's face; different emotions flitted over it. She loved the ring, but anger appeared for a second, then disgust, then resignation. She sighed, and took the ring, putting it on her finger. When she kissed and hugged him, I got a knot in my stomach. It just kept getting worse; I couldn't understand why she didn't just leave him.

That night, Jerry and I went to a different kind of party where I discovered alcohol. We went to someone's apartment where there was lots of beer, and we played drinking games. We played one called, "cowshit, horseshit." Everyone had an animal name. I was cowshit, and Jerry was horseshit. You had to say your name first, and then, another person's name as quick as possible. So, I'd say cowshit, horseshit. Then,

Jerry said horseshit, pigshit. If you messed up, you had to guzzle a beer. The next morning, I woke up with a very dim memory of what happened the night before, and I had a bad headache. It was Sunday, and I had to be at church early because I was singing in the choir.

As I sat in the choir loft singing, dressed in my choir robe, I looked up at the stained-glass window in the front of the sanctuary. Jesus was walking on water with his hands open and arms reaching out, like He wanted to gather us all close to Him. I looked around at the people in the church, sitting in their mink coats, diamonds, and pearls, everyone smelling of perfume and aftershave, looking at the minister while he was giving his sermon. I sat there, feeling my hangover after a night of playing drinking games, my hormonal body still tingling after a night of sexual exploration. It all felt so incongruent. I didn't feel virtuous. I looked at the congregation and my parents sitting in the pews, and I thought about their nights of drinking, abusive language, angry words, and a slap ringing in the air. I decided we were all hypocrites coming to church, dressed in nice clothes after taking showers or baths, smelling of aromatic scents. I remember the price my mother paid for her clothes, and I saw underneath and behind the smiles and angelic looks held for church. I saw the hidden bruises, the ugly feelings, and the guilt for past behaviors.

I began to keep a journal, writing down all my thoughts and feelings, trying to make sense of the world around me. Eventually, I wanted someone to hear what I wrote, and I asked my parents if I could read some of my writing to them. When they said yes, I shared a few things I wrote. Instead of commenting on the writing and how it made them feel, my father started talking about how I was just like his mother because she wrote poetry. Then, he went on, and talked about himself as a child. He told me about when he was a young boy, and his mother brought him to a "Holy Rollers" church, where he watched people rolling around on the ground speaking in tongues. He was so frightened, he hid in a dark corner until it was over. He talked about jumping off his front porch railing and breaking his leg while his mom was gone volunteering somewhere. I could see the hurt in his eyes as he talked about lying there all afternoon, in unbearable pain, unable to move from the spot where he fell, no one hearing him cry. His story was intense, and I knew he was sharing something from deep inside his shadows.

So, I got sidetracked in his life story, and my writings got lost in his pain and seemed to disappear into the black hole of my narcissistic father. I soon learned that with my father, it was always about him. He wasn't able to grasp other people's needs or feelings; everything got translated to his needs and his feelings. It was like talking to a brick wall. Out in the world, everyone loved my funny, charming, entertaining father. But at home, behind closed doors, he was abusive, had inappropriate boundaries, was judgmental, manipulative, and thought rules weren't meant for him. He was Dr. Jekyll and Mr. Hyde.

A week later, a new movie came out called *The Restless Ones,* written by the Billy Graham ministries. It was about teenagers, alcoholic parents, religion, angst and facing dark times. Billy Graham gave sermons in the film about God and faith. Mount Olivet church encouraged its members to see the movie, so I went with my mother. I was moved by the story because it was about my own inner pain, and it gave me hope things could be different. At the end of the movie, someone spoke, and invited anyone to come on stage if they wanted to turn their lives over to Jesus. My mother wanted to leave, and grabbed my hand. I wanted to go up on stage, so I pulled away from her. I wanted something from the people on stage; I wanted to be rescued.

But when I got up there, they brought us backstage and prayed over us, gave us a flyer, asked for a donation, and sent us on our way. I was so disappointed. I went up wanting to feel the warm embrace of people who understood and cared, but instead I felt manipulated. There was nothing "real" going on. I felt even lonelier than I did before.

At home, I took refuge in music, especially Jazz. I decided to take jazz piano, but when I went to MacPhail School of Music, they said I had to take classical piano first. I didn't want to take classical, so I took voice lessons instead. I wanted to sing like Peter, Paul and Mary, but my voice teacher had me singing opera. Songs like "Voi Che Sapete" and "Non So Pui cosa son, cosa faccio," along with some art songs. In junior high and high school choirs, I was an alto. But when I started taking voice lessons, it turned out I was a soprano, and had a strong opera type voice. I studied voice for two years and sang in recitals at a church on Lake of the Isles in a large room with windows looking out over the lake. When I performed, I stood by the grand piano at the front of the room.

At one of my recitals, I was singing Voi Che Sapete, and I blanked out on the words half way through, so I ran around the piano, looked at the music, and ran back to my spot, continuing to sing the whole time. I got a few laughs and applause at the end. My family never commented on my performance. I wanted my family to notice me, but no matter what I did, I felt invisible. So, I patted myself on the back for getting through another performance that made me so nervous I felt sick to my stomach.

My little sister Becca, now eleven, started taking piano lessons, and learned a fancy way to play Twinkle Star. My mother had her play it all the time for company because it was so pretty. I liked it too. But I wondered why my mother never sat and listened when I played piano and sang, and she never asked me to play for company. My family just howled when I sang, like coyotes howling at sirens. I was just never good enough to get their attention, no matter what I did, or how well I did it. If we trust the mirrors around us, the reflection I got from my family was I was invisible and not one of them. I never really knew if I was any good. My teachers and books were a mirror for me where I saw positive things about myself. I identified with Betsy in the Lovelace books, and I knew I was smart from my teachers.

I loved my little sister Becca, and we hung out together. Whenever she bought some new outfits, she would give me a fashion show in her bedroom. We laughed together about the silliest things, and had sleepovers once in a while in her bedroom. I was really upset one day when I came home from school and couldn't find my favorite navy-blue hip-hugger pants with bell-bottoms. I looked in my closet, in the dirty clothes, and under my bed. They were nowhere. My mother hadn't seen them. When I saw Becca, I couldn't believe it, she was wearing my pants. She had altered them to fit her. I was furious and felt so betrayed. My mother didn't do anything about it.

**

Jerry and I started hanging out at his house more, and I got to know his family. He was close to his mother, who was a full-bodied woman like my grandmother. She was Swedish, and loved to cook. It was the first time I'd heard of someone frying a steak in butter. It was the first time I had homemade Swedish Torte. They were both very good. His sister, Rose Ann, was two years younger, and he had a couple of older brothers, Wade and Harry, who were married with their own families. His brothers and dad had a roofing company Jerry worked for in the summers. His father looked like my grandfather, small and thin, and he was an alcoholic. He disappeared for days or weeks or months at a time, and eventually, they found him on skid row, drunk. They brought him home to sober up, and he was "on the wagon" until he'd once again disappear.

One Sunday, my aunt and uncle had a Carlson family reunion at their house by the river. Jerry came with me. My aunt and Jerry were surprised to see each other because she was his Swedish teacher at South High School. When Jerry went to school the next day, my aunt asked him to stay after class. After the students were gone, she told him he wasn't good enough to be dating her niece. Jerry couldn't believe it. He called me that night, and told me. I was furious. I hated judgmental people who thought they were better than other people.

Jerry made me feel special. One day, in the winter of 1966, the schools were closed because there were drifts of snow up to our chest and high winds. It was a major blizzard. School was cancelled, and around 12:00 our doorbell rang. It was Jerry, looking all snowy and cold. He tried to drive over to my house and surprise me, but his car got stuck in a snowdrift a few blocks away, so he walked the rest of the way. We gave him hot chocolate to help him warm up.

For my birthday that year, Jerry brought me to the Rosewood Room in a hotel downtown. It was fancy with a quiet waterfall in the background, white tablecloths, and candles on the tables. I felt so grown up.

I preferred hanging out with Jerry and my friends because they saw me, and I loved the things we shared. AJ and I loved to read. We lent books to each other. This year our favorite books were by James Baldwin. We read, *The Fire Next Time* and *Nobody Knows my Name*. We also read *Native Son* by Richard Wright and *Black Like Me*. I wanted to fix our world, our society, so we appreciated all cultures and skin colors. I identified with the characters and the feeling of being an underdog.

Logan and I got season tickets for the Northrup dance season. Dance performances and theatre were great releases for me. As I watched the performances, I could escape into the people on stage, feeling their energy in my body as I felt myself dancing across the stage with every move they made. My heart would beat faster; I was in their bodies, feeling the power of the dance. I fell in love with the intensity of Alvin Ailey performances. I was thrilled at the quirky Twyla Tharp company with their interesting sudden, sharply changing body movements. Pilobolus joined their bodies, and became a ball of movement, everyone moving as one around the stage, and then suddenly, they broke off into individual movements that became harmonious and synchronized. I watched Mikhail Baryshnikov with his powerful movements and passionate energy capture the stage. When I saw the American Ballet perform Swan Lake, I learned a valuable lesson. The star "prima ballerina" was doing a solo on stage, wearing her toe shoes, dancing tall and graceful when suddenly she fell, splat, on her bottom. She must have hit a sweat spot. She got up so gracefully, and continued her dance without a hiccup. It was like the fall never happened. I learned from her that we all make mistakes, even the pros, but it is how we behave after the mistake that shows our true greatness.

**

In the spring of 1966, I went out to dinner with Jerry, his mother, and his sister to the Edgewater Restaurant. It was a nice restaurant along the river by downtown Minneapolis. It was an evening with lots of dark clouds hovering in the sky. The parking lot was full, so we had to park a block or so down the street. We made it into the restaurant before it rained. I sat down, and looked around the restaurant. I noticed the front window was a wall of glass that overlooked the river. At that moment, I felt so lucky to be with Jerry and his family at this special restaurant. We ordered our meal as someone announced the performer who would be entertaining us that evening.

As the emcee was talking, I looked at the glass wall, and the view of the river was gone. All I saw was thick rain pouring down and a yellow-green color out the window. The person stepped up to the microphone to begin his performance when I saw a crack in the glass wall, and water was dribbling down the glass. I turned to Jerry and said, "Let's go downstairs. I think there's a tornado." I stood up and started walking through the restaurant. I took ten steps before the person on the microphone told everyone to head downstairs immediately. A couple of minutes later, we were all crowded in the downstairs room. There was a loud noise up over our heads, with rain and roaring winds. My ears plugged up, and then it was suddenly quiet. A man came in a few minutes later, and announced that the restaurant had been hit by a tornado. The roof of the kitchen was blown off and landed in the parking lot, crushing and trapping the cars. Luckily, our car was parked a couple of blocks down on the street.

After we got the all clear, we left the restaurant, walking carefully through the street, stepping around downed power lines that were flopping around unpredictably and throwing off sparks. Finally, we made it to Jerry's car. There was a downed power line in front of it, about one or two feet from his front tire. But there were no lines on the car, so we carefully and slowly got in. Jerry started it, backed up, and drove by the power line flopping around and sending off its shower of sparks.

We couldn't believe the devastation. All the windows in downtown Minneapolis were blown out. The news said it was unusual for a tornado to go through a downtown area. Jerry drove me home, and I made a sandwich, watching the news about what I just experienced, reliving the moments we stood in the downstairs of the restaurant hearing the winds howl and my ears plugging up. The news made it sound like a dramatic event you might see in a movie; tragic, exciting, but only seeing it from the outside. I was inside of the drama, and the newscast diminished the power, the fear, the devastation around me. The surrealistic moment of the sparking, flopping electrical wires we tiptoed through. I was still a little in shock standing there watching it all on television.

**

I was happy the last day of school because it meant summer and freedom. Everything felt lighter, freer, like there were adventures waiting at every turn. The beginning of June, I went to Pittsburgh with Jerry and his family for a wedding. I was surprised my parents said yes. It was the first trip I'd ever gone on with a boyfriend. It was fun being on a trip without my family. When I got back, I started working for my father.

Things at my father's office were getting tense; there were lots of arguments between him and his brothers. The workplace was an extension of our home: arguing laced with alcohol. My father had a bottle of whiskey hidden in the toilet tank. I was glad when my workday was over, and I could escape and be with Jerry. I saw him almost every day, and I began to realize he liked to drink beer. And now most parties had beer kegs or cases.

Patty, nineteen, and I hung out in the beginning of the summer, and brought our boat to Lake Minnetonka to waterski almost every weekend. We brought friends, packed a lunch, and spent the day at the lake. Patty was great at pulling the boat and getting it in the water. I could never have done that. We got pretty good at slalom skiing and getting our shoulder close to the water so we could get the big spray. It was fun being with Patty and our friends, feeling independent.

One weekend in the summer, my parents left town with Derek and Becca, and left Patty and I home alone. We had a party, which was big, and it spilled out into the front and back yard. Patty's friend brought beer. Everyone left around midnight. I got up the next day, and went to work, thinking I'd clean the house when I got back.

When I got home, the house was clean; all the beer bottles and cans were gone. When Patty got home, I thanked her for cleaning up. She said she didn't clean it up.

Then, we looked at each other and said, "William."

He must have come when we were at work. I knew I was in trouble now. When my parents got home, my mother opened the closet door in her bedroom, and there, stacked up, were the beer bottles and beer cans with a note from William that read: "Helen had a party." I was grounded for a month. And so, it began. It was the beginning of me becoming the black sheep in the family. The one who didn't fit in, a bad influence on my siblings.

Our family hung out on our patio, swimming in our chest-deep pool, grilling food, and eating at the picnic table fairly often. In the evening, my parents sat out there having a few drinks, and sometimes, if Patty and I were home, we sat with them and they offered us a beer.

In August, Patty's boyfriend, Parker, came to visit for three weeks. Patty was so excited because she hadn't seen him since last summer when she went to California to visit him. She was in love. A week after he left, she received a "Dear Joan" letter. When he got back to California, he found out he had gotten a girl pregnant, and was marrying her. Patty was heart-broken, angry, depressed, and started gaining weight. Muumuus were in fashion, and soon she wore them every day. She worked at an office full time, and added a part-time job. She bought her own stereo, which she put in her bedroom, and loved playing the singing nun. She played it every day.

At the end of August, I went to a weekend retreat with a girlfriend, who's name I can't reveal because she swore me to secrecy, to her church camp. We hiked, canoed, and talked. One night, we went to the girl's outdoor toilet to smoke a cigarette. We sat there for a while just smoking. Then, she turned to me, and asked if I could keep a secret she had never told anyone else. I said of course, she was my best friend. I sat there in the shadows of the outhouse, and listened while she quietly shared with me the story about her father sexually abusing her. It was so dark, I couldn't see her face as she talked about moving into their house in Minneapolis and how he brought her there, by herself, and showed her what boys did to girls when they got older. She was ten. She told me he had been doing it to her older sister for years.

After she finished telling her story, we sat, and smoked our cigarettes. We didn't talk, letting her words settle into the shadows around us. I pictured her father, who I'd never really trusted. He was a charming type, who always had some creepy joke to tell and a fake smile on his face.

Then, I quietly said, "I'm sorry."

I felt the same betrayal deep inside myself. I knew what it was like to have trusted someone, who seemed to change in an instant.

I never told anyone her story, and for years, I had blocked out my experience with my father when I was four, never telling anyone. That night, I realized my family wasn't the only one with dysfunction. I didn't have any answers, but I had a compassionate listening ear. I understood her pain. I had an abundance of unconditional love. Hers was another secret I added to the ones I kept deep inside myself.

Chapter 17
Life Is Going Very Fast Now

I lived in a house where each day held an unexpected, unwanted surprise. One morning, late summer, my father was trying to leave for work. He twitched, and made funny clicking noises in his throat, anxious. He got in his car, and then came back in because he was twitching so badly his hands were shaking. He made himself a cocktail of milk and bourbon, and downed two of them. He finally made it out the door for work where he had bottles hidden in the company's toilet tank. A couple days later, he needed my mother to visit jobsites with him because he was too anxious to go alone. When my mother wasn't available to go, I had to go, and keep him company.

Finally, in the fall, his doctor put him in the hospital because he was having another nervous breakdown. He had a series of shock treatments. When I went to visit him, I asked what shock treatments were like. He told me when they shocked his brain, it cleared his short-term memory, so he felt calmer. He said it was like cleaning the slate, and starting over. He felt peaceful after, no twitching. When my father got out of the hospital, my parents went to Portugal, and my older brother and his wife took care of us. I never quite knew what to expect from one day to the next.

**

There was something special about walking into to school my senior year, like another rite of passage, because now I was top dog. I got a parking spot in the student lot. In the morning, I picked up AJ and Kate, and we smoked on our way to school. Now, we could bask in the comfort of my car, and it was the first year the school dress code allowed girls to wear pants to school when it was below zero. My classmates and I started to go to dance clubs. I still hung out with Jerry one day on the weekend, but the other was for hanging out with my friends.

Logan and I had two favorite teen dance clubs, Bimbo's and the New City Opera House/Mr. Lucky's. The clubs had live bands, and we danced all night. We met boys from other schools. The really good dancers were black. I watched them move using their whole bodies. I loved to dance, and started dancing with Ike. We danced on the weekends at the club, and I gave him my phone number. I felt a little nervous because he had this velvety smooth voice, and I was sure my father would know he was black if he answered the phone. But the way he moved, his body really fascinated me. It was like the rhythm was stored in every part of him. There was a sensual quality to watching him; it made me want to move my body like his, to feel the music so deep inside myself. I loved his smile and his brown eyes. He seemed to enjoy the moment, and I loved his warm and inviting voice. I wrote about him in my journal. I wanted to get to know him better.

One night, Becca and I had a "sleep over" in her bedroom and I told her all about Ike and how I really liked him. As I was talking, I realized she had fallen asleep, so I rolled over and went to asleep.

A couple of hours later, my parents woke us up with their arguing. My father was in a drunken rage, yelling obscenities. He sounded like he was out of control, possessed by the devil and talking in tongues. He threatened my mother, slammed the bedroom door, went downstairs, yanked open the silverware drawer, and banged it closed. He was saying unrecognizable words the whole time. We were petrified. We heard him go back into his bedroom yelling as he slammed the door closed. Then suddenly everything was quiet.

Becca and I looked at each other.

I said, "Do you think he got a knife and stabbed her?"

We were both scared, so we got up, and tiptoed to the bedroom door. Patty was looking outside her bedroom door down the hall. She motioned for me to take a look. We were worried about what we would find on the other side of the door. I slowly opened it, afraid I'd see blood oozing out of my mother's body. When the door was fully open, I saw them both lying across the bed, passed out and snoring. I breathed a sigh of relief, and gave my sisters the all-clear sign. We all went back to bed.

I had trouble falling asleep, battling with my feelings. When I was younger, my mother seemed strong, a force to be reckoned with. She gave me a sense of safety in our house when my father was around. Now, I felt afraid my mother was no longer who she used to be. She seemed weak and frail, and was becoming a ghost of herself, like she could no longer fight against my father trying to keep her own identity. She was losing the battle, drinking as much as my father.

After that night, I watched closely when my parents started to fight. When my father was drunk, his face turned red with explosive anger, spit foamed around his mouth like a mad dog, and his fists were clenched because he was so enraged; I was afraid for my mother.

I was afraid my father would hurt her because she would egg him on, feeding the flames, while she convinced my siblings to take her side. I didn't take either side. I just wanted to diffuse the situation. I stepped in, and soothed his anger. Because of our bond, I could get him to quiet down. I didn't want the job, but someone needed to prevent any physical abuse.

I had mixed feelings about my mother, whom I never really trusted. I told her things that were important to me. Then, I heard her telling her friends about me, sounding angry or making fun of what I'd said. When I cried about Hiroshima, she seemed disgusted. When I got my period and went to her, she seemed to listen, like she understood, but then the next day I heard her on the phone telling her friend about it and laughing. That spring, we got two baby ducks at Easter. In the summer, the ducks were fully grown, and one day, they suddenly disappeared. My mother said they wandered to the creek and floated away. She was lying of course. It was hard growing up when you couldn't even trust your mother.

Years later, when I saw the movie *Ordinary People*, Mary Tyler Moore reminded me of my mother, not able to feel things, wanting everything to seem happy. She couldn't talk about sadness or hurt. When I was little, my mother stood tall, proud, and confident. As I got older, she was defeated, angry, and frustrated. In high school, there were many days I came home from school, and she was sitting in the living room staring out the window, looking at nothing at all. I asked her what was wrong, and she always said nothing. She was just taking some time out.

**

In March, we took our traditional trip to Arizona, and stayed at the Paradise Inn. This time, we flew there. It was my first time flying, and I sat next to Patty on the plane. We were laughing, and I accidentally touched her stomach. She always wore muumuus, and was quite heavy. I was surprised her stomach was hard, not flabby, but then I thought about my father's potbelly, it was hard too.

I was happy when we arrived at the Paradise Inn and checked into our small adobe house with two bedrooms and a bath. We unpacked our suitcases, and I put my suit on to go to the pool. Suddenly, I heard my father yelling and bouncing around in the shower. Derek had reached in, and turned off the cold water when my father wasn't looking. My family laughed at him. I felt sorry for him.

Patty and I hung at the pool, and visited with the bartenders who were still there from our last trip. I really got to know Derek on this trip. He was now eight, and I found he could carry on quite the conversation. He had interesting things to say, and seemed grown-up for his age. He spent a lot of time at the putting green, getting to know the men at the resort. He was a charmer.

We went horseback riding every day. Patty got side aches, so she didn't ride as long. On our mountain trail ride to the steak fry, the horse behind me didn't like my horse, so he kept biting his rear end. My horse tried to kick him, and I almost fell off. The wrangler brought the horse behind me to the front of the line. Later that week, Becca lost her balance, and fell on a cactus, coming away with a hand full of needle-sharp spines. We carefully took them out. Otherwise, it was a peaceful week with sunshine, good food, and sleep-filled nights.

We rented a car, and drove to California to visit my aunt and uncle in Las Angeles for a few days, and my aunt and uncle just outside of San Francisco for a reunion dinner. Then, we flew back home. When I got back, I found a letter addressed to me. I'd been accepted into the University of Minnesota. Jerry appeared at my doorstep that night. We ended up having an argument because he'd been drinking. He seemed to be drinking more and more. But two days later, he called, and apologized. I asked him to my prom.

**

My senior year was winding down, and the prom was in a few weeks. I wanted a special dress, and Eileen said she'd make it for me. I had picked out a pattern with a dramatic stand up collar that went down into a V-neck. It was so classy. I bought lime green material, my favorite color. The dress was floor length with a fitted waist and sleeves made of a see-through material the same color as the dress.

Eileen came over a couple of weeks before the dance to do the final hemming. The night before, I partied too hard with Jerry, and played too many drinking games. I woke up not being able to remember what happened the night before, and I couldn't find my shoes. When Eileen got there, I had eaten my breakfast, and tried to clear the cobwebs from the night before. I still felt queasy.

Eileen had a cup of coffee with my mother, and then, said, "OK, it's time to hem this dress."

I put on my dress, stood up on the chair next to her, so she could pin up the hem. I suddenly felt dizzy, and almost fell off the chair.

I sat down, and my mother looked at Eileen.

She said with a smile, "I think she had a little too much to drink last night."

They both teased me about having a hangover. They made it sound like it was a rite of passage to have your first hangover. After

Eileen had another cup of coffee, we tried it again. I stood on the chair, and got my dressed hemmed. I didn't enjoy the teasing or the headache and nausea.

A couple of weeks later, I came home from school, and my mother was waiting at the front door for me. I wondered why she had curlers in only half of her hair. She told me to sit down. My mother told me Patty called her at the Beauty Salon, and said she was in labor.

My mouth dropped, and I said, "What? Labor? Like a baby?"

My mother continued, "Yes, a baby, and she wanted me to bring her to the hospital."

I said, "But she's been living here at home; she never told us she was pregnant. How did we not know?"

My mom said, "I guess she hid it with her weight gain and baggy clothes." Then, my mother continued her story, saying, "When I got the call, I ran out of the salon with these curlers in my hair, jumped in the car, picked her up, and drove her to the hospital."

Suddenly, I flashed back to the plane ride to Arizona a couple of months earlier, when I had accidentally touched my sister's belly and wondered why it was so hard. It was hard because she was pregnant. I sat there speechless. I couldn't grasp the reality that my older sister was in the hospital having a baby. It was surreal.

Then, I realized my mother was still talking. "So, I've got to get these curlers out of my hair, and get back to the hospital ASAP. Please take care of Becca and Derek when they get home from school."

My mother pushed past me and went upstairs, and three minutes later, she came running down with no curlers and a different shirt on.

She tossed over her shoulder as she left, "I'll call you when the baby is born."

When she left, the house was a heavy quiet mixed with disbelief, a reality shattered into pieces that I kept trying to put together. I kept hearing my mother's words echo in my head *I'll call when the baby is born.* A baby was being born, my sister's baby. It was Parker's baby, I guessed. Maybe that's why she was so sad last fall when she got his letter. I felt tears burn their way down my cheeks. My sister had been abandoned just when she discovered she was pregnant. What a daunting secret to carry.

When Becca and Derek got home from school, I was still sitting on the stairs, paralyzed by my thoughts and emotions. When I heard their voices, I got up, and asked them if they wanted a snack. The three of us sat at the kitchen table eating snacks while I told them about Patty. A little while later the phone rang. It was my brother, William. He and Connie were with Patty at the hospital. My sister had a girl which she placed for adoption, never laying eyes on her baby.

When my mother walked in the door that night, she looked haunted. All the strength in her seemed to collapse in on itself. My father wasn't home, Becca and Derek were in bed, and she and I sat in the living room.

She suddenly started talking about her older sister, Maureen. I'd heard the name before, but didn't know anything about her. She said Maureen was wild, and had sex with every boy in Glendive. When she became pregnant, she was sent away to have the baby. But she never came back; she started running around the country with different men, supposedly having babies she abandoned. Then, my mother said Maureen was a pathological liar. My mother left Glendive right after she graduated from high school to get away from her older sister's reputation. She didn't want people thinking of her "like that." She wanted a clean slate, so she came to Minneapolis.

My mother looked exhausted after she finished her story, her eyes staring out the window, like she was watching her past outside in the trees. She sighed, and said it was time to get some sleep. I watched her walk up the stairs, wondering if she'd make it to her bedroom. I turned out the lamp, and went up to my bedroom. Still trying to make sense of the stories whirling around in my own life, I realized the prom was this weekend and I hadn't made an appointment to get my hair done.

I went with Jerry to my senior prom at the Calhoun Beach Club with my lime green dress. We went to a fancy dinner with twelve other couples, and then, to the dance. It was fun, but I was haunted by an underlying sadness about my sister.

**

A week after prom, Jerry called me at night. He wanted to pick me up, and talk to me about something. He had been working with his brother as a roofer after he graduated last year. When I got in the car, he was quiet. He drove to Lake Nokomis and parked. He turned, looked at me, and told me that he'd joined the Air Force. He started talking fast about how he wanted to send me money from boot camp, and have me put it into a bank account for us. With a rush of air, he said quickly, when he came home from boot camp, we could get married. Then, he stopped, taking in deep breaths; it sounded like he'd been running.

I was speechless. I stared out the window, my life flashing before me: married, tied down, children, family, more people to take care of. I always said I was going to marry a college professor, one who had patches on his elbow and smoked a pipe. Jerry was a roofer. My brain kept screaming, *NO!* Then, I started to cry. I told him I was just a senior in high school, and I was going to the U of M in the fall. There was no way I was getting married to anyone. My own life was just starting, and I wanted to find out who I was in this world. My tears turned to anger. I looked at him, said no way, and broke up with him. I told him to take me home, and never call me again. I sat there, tears in my eyes, anger in my mouth, and the feeling of being trapped. I just wanted out of his car. I had the car door open before he even stopped in my driveway. I flew out of the car, ran in the house, and never looked back. I didn't talk to him again for over a month.

Then, one Sunday night, the doorbell rang, and it was Jerry. We sat on the front doorstep, and he told me he was leaving the next day for the Air Force. He was stationed in Sweetwater, Texas, and asked if I would write to him. I said I would. He told me to take care of myself, and he took my hand, looked into my eyes, and said he wanted to protect me always. He asked me to listen to Cat Stevens' "Wild World". We hugged, he gave me a long goodbye kiss, and then, he was gone. After he left, I found my sister's Cat Stevens album, and listened to the song: *If you want to leave take good care. Hope you make a lot of nice friends out there. But just remember there's a lot of bad and beware. Oh, baby baby it's a wild world. It's hard to get by just upon a smile. Oh, baby baby it's a wild world. I'll always remember you like a child, girl.*

**

The summer became confusing and different; a new reality was emerging I didn't understand. AJ and Kate introduced me to marijuana, and I got high for the first time. Patty was back home acting like nothing had happened, playing her stereo, and keeping to herself. Until one day in July, she came out of her room, and invited me to go to Brainerd for a girls' weekend. I couldn't believe she invited me.

We drove up to Brainerd, and checked into a motel. Her friend brought beer, and we drank it in the motel the first night. The second night, we went to a club in Brainerd, and met some boys. My guy was tall, dark, and handsome. We brought them back to the motel, and we drank and partied all night long. We all passed out eventually, listening to the song "Let's Spend the Night Together" by the Rolling Stones, playing over and over on the record player my sister brought. We woke up the next day, everyone fully clothed, and we went out for breakfast. We had a great time, said goodbye, and drove back to the Twin Cities. That was the first time I'd ever slept with a boy next to me in bed. Of course, all we really did was kiss and fall asleep, but it still felt exciting. Patty closed herself off again after that weekend.

When I got back from Brainerd, I found a letter from Jerry inviting me to Sweetwater, Texas. There was a base celebration with a band, and he asked me if I'd please come. He sent me an airline ticket. It was my first time flying alone, and I felt nervous, so I brought a book and read all the way to Dallas. I had to catch another flight from Dallas to Sweetwater. It was a small propeller plane. The ride was bumpy, so I didn't read much, but it was a short flight.

After Jerry picked me up, I checked into a motel, and brought my stuff to the room. I was happy to see him. After we went out to dinner, he asked if he could stay with me in the motel. I said yes, but I didn't want to have sex because I was saving it for marriage. He slept over, and we made out, cuddled, and eventually, went to sleep. When he went to the base the next morning, I started wondering if I'd made a mistake by coming. I still couldn't think of marrying him. When he got back to the room, we went to lunch, and afterwards, he gave me a tour of his barracks and the base. I could tell he was excited I was there. When he came to get me for the dinner and the dance, he wore his white uniform, and looked very handsome. We danced all night, and went back to the motel. That night, when he slept over, I felt pressure to get back together. When he tried to be more sexual, I told him I just couldn't have sex. He got angry, turned his back, and went to sleep. When I left the next morning, I knew my feelings hadn't changed, and it was over. A year later, I got an invitation to his wedding. I went to his wedding, and wished him well.

Then, in early August, Logan and I stayed on the U of M campus, and went through sorority rush. We were both going to the university, and wanted to join a sorority. We stayed at Pioneer Hall on campus. It was like being at camp. Logan and I bunked together, and there were counselors who showed us where everything was and where we needed to go. Each day, we got up, and had breakfast in the cafeteria, where we were given a schedule of what sorority houses we'd go to at what time. We visited three houses in the morning and three in the afternoon.

After three days, Logan decided she didn't want to join a sorority, so she went home. I called my mother, and arranged for her to pick me up on Friday. I was motivated to join a sorority because my father said he'd pay for me to live in a sorority but not a dorm, and I wanted to live away from home as soon as possible. There were three sororities who asked me to join. The next day I visited the three houses, and picked Chi Omega. I signed up to live at the sorority house in the fall.

I packed up my stuff on Friday, and waited for my mother to arrive. She was supposed to be there at lunchtime. When she didn't show, I called and called, but no one was home. So, I called Logan, and she came to get me. I hung out with her till midnight, and then thought I should get home because midnight was my curfew. My parents still weren't home. I had to break in through a window because the house was locked, and I didn't have a key. I went to bed, and when I woke up, they still weren't there. I was confused, puzzled, and worried. I couldn't figure out where they could be.

Around noon, I heard someone come in the front door; it was Patty. When I asked where everyone was, she said they'd decided to go to the Ambassador Hotel with the Rowens, and let the kids swim in the pool. I asked how come no one came to get me. She said she didn't know; they must have forgotten about me. I went with her to the Ambassador, and told my mother I couldn't believe she forgot that I was sitting at the U of M, in a dorm, waiting for her to pick me up. The more I spoke, the angrier I got. When I was done, the hotel room was so quiet you could hear a pin drop.

I had tears in my eyes, my fists were clenched, and I waited for an apology, an explanation, or something.

My mother finally said, "Well, you're here now. So, go, put your suit on, and go swimming with everyone else." I walked out of their room; everyone could probably see the steam coming out of my ears. I sat, watched everyone swim, and eventually, calmed down. When Becca came over, and asked me to come swimming, I sighed, got up, and went to get my bathing suit on. My parents sat drinking with the Rowens in their hotel room.

No wonder I never felt like I could trust my mother. Time after time, she'd betray me, forget about me, ignore me, or tease me. I never heard her apologize for anything. Deep down, it always made me feel like I was defective and never good enough, no matter what I did. That day, I surrendered, and knew my mother wasn't who I wanted her to be. She was turning into my father. I didn't like who she was, and couldn't wait to move out of the house.

Logan and I continued going to Bimbo's, our favorite dance club, and watched Tony and Stella dance. They were sexual and dangerous in their sensual movements, and they were both Italian. Tony was a fighter in Golden Gloves, and a street fighter. His fights were usually over Stella because he was possessive. Tony was strong and wiry; he had black hair cut really short and intense black eyes that seemed to see through you. He had dark eyebrows that made his eyes appear even darker. His eyes drew you in, so you'd want to see inside those secrets that were hidden in them. Stella had thick, luscious, wavy, dark hair that flowed down her back. Her body was something boys lusted after and girls jealously wanted.

A week later, there were rumors that Tony and Stella broke up. They weren't in the club. Two nights later, when Logan and I were there, Tony walked in alone. When the music started, he headed towards me, and asked me to dance. My feet couldn't feel the floor beneath me. We danced all night. At the end of the night, he asked for my number. I dated Tony until I caught him in a lie. He said he joined the army and left for boot camp. He sent me letters and a necklace with a football on it. A few weeks later, I drove by the dance club in the early evening, and he was standing in front laughing with his friends. I stopped to confront him, and he said they let him out early because of an illness. I didn't believe him, went home, and threw away his letters and necklace.

Later that summer, my family got a call in the middle of the night. The cops found my older sister passed out drunk in an intersection with her head on the steering wheel of her car. My father had to go get her from the police station. After that night, she was out till all hours drinking, and met Todd at a club downtown. My father called her a slut, and they started arguing. Eventually, she took off. When my father found out she went to Todd's apartment, he asked me to come with and help get her out. We went to the windows of Todd's basement apartment, and looked inside to find her. Then, we rang the bell, but Todd wouldn't answer the door. We saw Patty, and she yelled through the door she wasn't coming home. My father threatened to call the police, but Patty was over 18. We left. Eventually, she came back home on her own.

It had been a rough summer, so many new things being thrown at me. I couldn't wait to be in the real world and away from my family chaos.

I started college with a deep loss, so deep inside it rocked my foundation. But I continued like I always did with a smile on my face, learning ways to meet my own needs, and knowing I could be what I wanted to be without them.

Chapter 18
There Are Days I Can't Hold in This Urge to Scream

I moved into the sorority house on the University campus in early September. I couldn't believe when I walked into my bedroom: it had three bunk beds and two single beds. Pam, an upperclassman, was sitting on a single bed doing her nails. She was sexy and exciting with her long black hair, dark eyes, and a body with curves in all the right places. I said hi, and as I was putting my stuff on a lower bunk, Sandy, a tall, athletic blonde, with blue eyes, came in laughing.

She said, "Wow, eight girls in one room."

Then, she threw her stuff on the top bunk above mine. Two girls wandered in: CeeCee, a cute and artsy blonde with blue eyes twinkling with mischief and Carol, a long faced blond wearing a ponytail that made her look a little like a horse. Later, I met quiet Doreen, who slept with Vaseline on her face and hands at night because of a skin condition and Amy, who was studying theatre. Suddenly I had seven "sisters" to share a room with. I learned to sleep through many alarms.

In the evenings Pam, CeeCee, Sandy, and I congregated on the fire escape in the back of the house to smoke a cigarette. Pam told us funny, amazing stories from her childhood in New York. Sandy told us about the small town she grew up in, and how it was so small, it didn't have a stop sign. Pam drove a sports car, and we loved to ride in it with the top down.

When I first moved into the sorority, I felt so free. No family issues to deal with. I was on my own to explore, experiment, and find out who I was. I had no time to read my books; any reading I did was for my classes. But I started writing more and more about the people I was meeting. I felt a heightened awareness of the life around me. It was exciting but a little scary because I didn't know who I was or where I belonged. I felt open and ready for new experiences. I was writing about what I saw and what I felt around me. I felt like I was a character in a movie or book I was writing, my only fear was that no one would ever see the movie or read the book.

Some evenings, when I needed time away from all the girls, I left the sorority house with my notebook and pencil and sat under a nearby railroad bridge. I wrote about the crisscrossing of the metal girders on the bridge or the rumbling sound I heard when the train was approaching. I felt the ground tremble under me as the train came near and went across the bridge. My senses were open, and I wrote. Writing became my new home. I felt safe, alone with my pen and paper, expressing my feelings. There was a stoplight I watched changing from green to yellow to red. I was fascinated by the repetition, and looked for some meaning.

Some evenings, I played the piano in the living room, and sang. The girls remarked about my voice, saying they were shocked to hear a full opera sound out of my small body.

A month after school started, I found a job as a banquet server at the student union; I needed money for books and expenses. I also became the house barber. My specialty was the pixie cut.

On weekends, we went to fraternity parties where there was a lot of drinking or we went dancing at clubs where I gave out my phone number using different names. Sometimes, I was Kim Jensen or Kelly Green. I told my sorority sisters if anyone called for those names, to get me. All the parties and nights at the clubs were reflected in my grades the first quarter of school; I had mostly D's with a couple of C's. I realized quickly college was different than high school.

CeeCee and I started hanging out together. One day, we walked to Dinkytown, and met two guys who invited us back to their place. They said they were artists and wanted to show us their work. When we got there, we ended up sitting on pillows on the living room floor, and one of the guys lit up a couple of joints. We passed them around. CeeCee and the guy next to her got up, and went upstairs. I was sitting with the other guy, knowing I didn't want to go upstairs. Instead I stood up to leave, and realized I was really high.

The guy took my hand to go upstairs, but I pulled back and said, "No."

I was a virgin, and I didn't know this guy. Then, CeeCee walked down the stairs, tucking in her blouse, and we left. I realized then that CeeCee liked sex.

A couple of days later, we met two guys at a party. CeeCee went home with her guy, and I stayed with Jorge, who I ended up dating for a while. A couple of weeks later, when Jorge brought me home, CeeCee was standing in the parking lot. When I got out, she jumped in his car, saying she needed to get some cigarettes. They took off, and she didn't come home that night. She hurt me profoundly, and I learned to not be quite so open and trusting. I kept my distance from her after that.

On campus, I ran into Susie, a girl from my high school. We had lunch together. She started talking to me about sex and learning how to satisfy myself, which I had never heard of before. She talked about how she loved sex, and practiced with the handle of her hairbrush. Then, she told me about the hot button, and what I needed to do to have an orgasm.

It was too much information, given so suddenly by someone I didn't know that well, but I learned things about my body I never knew before. I came away from that lunch in a daze. First, CeeCee and now, Susie: everyone seemed to love sex.

I met Jake at a fraternity party; he was from a well-to-do family. We started dating, and going to pre-parties at hotels and fraternity parties. We saw each other every weekend for a while. I liked him.

But then, things at home began encroaching on my new world. When I went home on a couple weekends, I realized my parents' drinking was worse. My mother was losing weight because she wasn't eating. One weekend, I went to a bridal shower. At the shower, my mother got drunk, and kept pulling up her dress so her slip was showing. She didn't know what she was doing. I was so embarrassed. My mother was the only little bit of safety in our house, and now, her drinking was worse than my father's. It was like she had just given up and crawled into her bottle. I heard terrible stories from my younger brother and sister, who called the police a few times in the middle of the night when my parents' drinking was bad. My parents lost their drinking buddies, the Rowens, who moved out of the neighborhood. My father was fighting with all his brothers. My parents were becoming more and more isolated with their drinking.

Alcoholism was like a cancer growing in my family. The faster it grew, the more my father had to prove to the outside world our family was fine. I had to live in a sorority, not a dorm. We had to look good on the outside to hide the disease festering inside. I went back to the sorority house after a weekend home, feeling the weight on my shoulders.

I was overwhelmed with everything coming at me, all the people and experiences. One evening, I left the sorority house, and sat under the railroad bridge and wrote about the people I'd met in the last couple of months, the new knowledge about sex, and all the drinking, trying to make sense of my new surroundings. Eventually, my thoughts turned to my family, calming my father down in his drunken rages, and how Becca, Derek, and my mother came to me when things were happening, like I had all the answers when I actually knew nothing. I looked like I had it all together, but I felt lost like them.

I knew in that moment it was up to me. Now, I was in college, and my role changed to family hero. It was up to me to look good in the world, to hide the pain deep inside my family. I suddenly felt the burdensome backpack I carried. On the outside, I was funny, energetic, and creative to everyone who met me. The darkness and shadows I kept for my journals and writings. As I sat there writing in my journal, listening to the night sounds around me, I felt like I did in my bedroom at home. I was safe here in my own little world. I picked up my notebook and pen, and walked back to the sorority house where I knew there would be lights on in every room and lots of girls talking and laughing. I knew I would walk in and get lost in the chaos of my new home

The only thing I liked about going home was seeing Becca and Derek. We were close, and I took turns sleeping one night in Becca's room, and the next in Derek's. My siblings talked the night away about everything in their lives because they wanted someone to see them. One night, Becca told me how she was playing with her hamster on her bed, and the hamster bit her finger and wouldn't let go. When she tried to shake him loose, he went flying across the room, and hit the wall. He didn't move after that. So, she ran downstairs, and turned on the TV, hoping someone else would find him because she just couldn't tell anyone. I felt important because she needed someone to listen, and not be judged. She trusted me, and it felt good.

One weekend in late fall, I didn't go home, and my older sister Patty attempted suicide using pills and alcohol. She was brought to a psych unit downtown, where she was in a locked unit for 72 hours. I went to visit her. She sat smoking her cigarette, saying it was nice there. She wasn't able to leave the hospital until she had a place to live because the counselor said she couldn't live with our parents. She moved in with my older brother and his wife in Bloomington. It hadn't even been a year since she placed her baby for adoption. I knew how much she loved the baby's father, and never really dealt with the birth. I was glad she moved into William's house because I hoped he could give her what she needed.

A week after Patty was in the psych unit, I went to a party, and got drunk. I yelled about how I hated men. I felt Patty's pain. It was the middle of winter, and I just walked out of the party without my coat and purse. I was so drunk, I didn't know what I was doing. One of my sorority sisters followed me, carrying my coat and purse, to make sure I got home safe. I didn't remember any of it. She told me about it the next morning, and I was put on social probation, meaning I couldn't drink at parties for the rest of the quarter.

When I went out with Jake the next weekend, his friend handed me a lemon because I wasn't drinking, and at the end of the evening, Jake broke up with me. I guess drinking was more important to him.

That night, I walked back to the sorority alone, and noticed a church on the corner. I was feeling down, and wanted to go in. I looked for the front door, but it was locked, and there was no other way to get in. In Sunday school, I was told churches were places of refuge. I was surprised the doors were locked. I was learning more and more life wasn't what I thought it was as a child.

For Christmas that year, I avoided going home, and decided to go on a ten-day ski trip with a college friend. We took a train to Boseman, Montana, to ski Big Sky Mountain. She had an aunt there we stayed with. When the train went through my mother's hometown, Glendive, I saw a woman with dark red hair, and I thought for a moment it was my mother walking down Main Street. I thought of her father, the railroad man, and when I saw a malt shop, I wondered if that was where he brought my mother on the days he visited his mistress upstairs. As we went by the small town, I felt my mother's ghosts. There was sadness there I didn't understand, and I brushed away a tear as the town of Glendive disappeared from view.

**

Winter quarter, I took a sociology class where we were required to do volunteer work for a social agency. I chose Stillwater prison; a group of us went out there once a week to visit with inmates and learn their stories. The first day, I hated the feeling of the two doors locking behind me as I walked in; I felt trapped. I knew, then, I could never get arrested and be in jail. It was an eye-opening, twelve-week session, learning the stories of why the inmates were arrested. It haunted me that some of their family stories were like mine.

At the end of the session, we convinced the prison to let us have a dance. I had a crush on one of the tall, dark skinned inmates, so I was excited for the dance. It was a fun night. But after the dance, I felt sad as I walked out the prison doors, and my volunteer work was over. I learned from the experience to not judge people, criminals had feelings and were people too. They could be nice, gentle, funny, and kind or manipulative, angry, and mean. Just like other people I knew. I learned not to assume things about people, knowing that each person had their own story to tell. We all had similarities and differences. Some people had more resources available to them than others. I lived with enough aberrant behavior in my own family. I became a protector of the underdog. I wanted to help those people who didn't have the resources available to them or no family or support system, people who didn't have a voice. I knew I wanted to work in social services and corrections.

When Martin Luther King was assassinated in April, I was shocked. I cried. I loved his speeches and his philosophy of peaceful demonstrations. He was such a powerful leader. My friends were all upset, Martin Luther King represented a voice of power, strength, and peace. He gave us confidence things could get better.

A couple of weeks after the assassination, the new pledges in the sorority, like me, were finally invited to the secret meetings downstairs. The meeting creeped me out. When I was eleven, my father wanted me to join Jobs Daughters, a closed club, connected to the Masons and the Shriners. I went a few times and didn't like the secret handshakes, the rituals, and memorizing worthless phrases that had to be said to enter the sacred chamber where the Queen was surrounded by her junior and senior princesses. The girls wore white silk dresses with a rope that crossed between their breasts. It was too weird, I didn't want to be in a popularity contest to become a princess or a Queen.

So, when I saw my sorority sisters wearing the same white silky dresses, I wanted to turn and run away. Instead, I learned secret words and handshakes, and went through an initiation ritual to join the sorority and receive a pin. It felt weird, cultish, phony, and not very relevant in the world I lived in. It gave me a stomachache. I was glad when the school year ended, and I could move out of the sorority house.

By the end of my freshman year, I felt disillusioned and disappointed. I realized I wasn't free of my family. In the last year, I learned more about people and relationships, being betrayed and feeling unsafe again. My family's pain weighed me down; my parents drinking, my sister's suicidal behavior and pain, the helplessness of my young siblings being stuck in our scary, abusive home. I felt guilt leaving them to deal with our parents. As the year wore on, my strength and hope started to deteriorate, and I was losing footing. I was struggling to find something I could hang onto.

My inner sanctum, my foundation, was crumbling along with my family falling apart. At the same time, the society around me was in turmoil. There was chaos, and nothing felt safe, secure, or the same. The sorority house I was once excited about represented affluence and privilege, and seemed to have no answers for how to cope with the world around me. The girls were about looking good, parties, having boyfriends, drinking, and participating in weird, secret rituals that made no sense. All these feelings were swirling inside me, waiting to break free, hoping someone would save me soon. I was still waiting for my white knight. Everything felt confusing and chaotic.

I carried all this with me as I moved out of the sorority, brought my stuff home, and got ready to work at Burke's resort as a recreation director with Sandy. I looked forward to a summer job, and working up north away from my family and the sorority.

When Sandy and I got to Bay Lake, we met Bertha, the cook, and Mrs. Burke, the owner of the resort. Mrs. Burke brought us to our cabin, and introduced us to two other girls, Judy and Donna. She told us the first weekend we would all be waitressing at the lodge, because there was a group of men coming up for a work retreat. After Mrs. Burke left, we chose the beds we wanted in the cabin, and put our stuff away.

The next day, thirty men came. We were busy serving breakfast, lunch, and dinner. There was one man, Jesse Ray, who was very handsome with dark hair and dark brown eyes. He was one of the leaders in the group. He kept flirting with me. That night, when we were done working and headed to our cabin, Jesse and his friends invited us in for a drink. The drinks were strong, and I got drunk very quickly. Then, Jesse started teasing me about meeting him for a boat ride at midnight. So, I started calling him Captain Midnight. I met him later, and we took a boat ride, parked in the middle of the lake, and made out for a while.

The next night, the men asked us to join them for drinks when we got off work. We had a few drinks, and decided to find some local clubs where there was dancing. When we got to the first club, Jesse wanted to stay in the car and make out. At the end of the night, he tried to convince me to stay in his cabin overnight, saying he'd had a vasectomy, so he was safe. I didn't know what that was, so he explained it to me. I was kind of drunk, and said I felt sorry that he had to have that procedure. When I mentioned I was a virgin, Jesse suddenly changed his tune. He told me I'd better head to my cabin, so I didn't get into trouble with my boss.

The men left the next day, and Jesse gave me his card, telling me to call him when I was in Minneapolis again. A few weeks later when we drove to the Twin Cities on our day off, I called him. Whoever answered his phone said he wasn't home, and was out for his anniversary with his wife.

They told me where he went, so I paged him at the restaurant, and when he came to the phone I said, "Happy Anniversary, I'm in town."

He was shocked, and quickly got off the phone.

Two days after the men left, resort families started arriving. Sandy and Donna cleaned the cabins, Judy waitressed, and I led the recreation activities. I oversaw the greased watermelon races, went on hikes in the woods, did arts and crafts, and taught water skiing. One day, when I was holding a boy up to ski, a huge leech swam by with a sucker the size of a suction cup on the head of a toy arrow. I kept my cool as I watched it swim away. I didn't want to scare the boy in my arms.

At night, when we were off duty, we hitchhiked into Brainerd or to Rutgers's lodge around the lake from us. In Brainerd, we went to movies or dancing, and if we went to Rutgers', it would be to see the boys who worked there.

In mid-July, Sandy and I were getting bored with the Brainerd area, and cooked up a terrible scheme. On Thursday, we visited a couple of people we knew in the Brainerd area. We asked them to call the resort, and tell Mrs. Burke that our friend Amy had been killed in a car accident, and there was a visitation in Minneapolis on Monday. We also had two people from home leave messages to make it look authentic. When we got back that evening, Mrs. Burke was waiting for us. She broke the news, and we started crying. She was so nice, and she asked if we wanted to call our friends from her house. She left us alone to make our arrangements, and Sandy and I made our eyes red with tears. When she came back later, we said we had someone picking us up in the morning to bring us to Minneapolis.

As we walked down the path from her house, we couldn't believe we had pulled it off. When we got back to the cabin, we felt guilty for our deception, but we got up the next morning, went out to the road, and hitchhiked to Minneapolis for a fun weekend.

In early August, we were hanging with the boys from Rutgers's. I was feeling invisible and bored. The anger and helplessness from deep inside me started to find its way to the surface. My inner thoughts were wrestling around, and the mask I wore with a smile was starting to crack. I felt so ugly in that moment. I opened my beer can, pulling off the tab. I took a couple of drinks from the can and studied the tab I was still holding; it had a sharp edge. I started running it across the palm of my hand; blood oozed out. It released some of my tension. It felt good.

When my friends saw me, they started freaking out, and suddenly, I had everyone's attention, so I upped the ante. I pretended to cut my wrists. Then, I ran out of the cabin, and started wading into the lake. I was playing a game of, "I scare you; you pursue me." I had someone's attention for once. I got into it. When they brought me back to my cabin, I went into the bathroom, and found a razor blade; they wrestled it away from me.

I yelled, "leave me alone!" and ran into the lake again, suddenly not caring what happened to me.

The game started to become real. All my pent up, deeply buried emotions erupted: my anger, my fear, my desperation, my sadness, and my abandonment were tossed around in the air.

My friends were so concerned they brought me to Brainerd hospital. The hospital wanted to give me a hypo, a very strong sedative, and watch me overnight. I yelled they couldn't do that because I didn't want my parents to find out. They were already having enough problems, and I didn't want to add to their worries. I started running down the halls, crying hysterically. They caught me, and gave me a hypo, which did nothing, so they gave me another one. My friends brought me back to the cabin, and took turns watching me. They respected my wish to not be put in the hospital. I slept for two days, and they were so relieved when I woke up. I saw tears in their eyes; they were worried about me.

It was the first time I let my pain show. It was the first time my façade of strength and pretending that everything was all right, slipped. It was the first time my mask cracked. It was the first time I opened my hands wanting help. It was the first time someone paid attention. I was so embarrassed I had lost control, and I never wanted anyone to see the ugliness hid inside me again.

I quit my job mid-August, and moved back home. I got a job making cold calls to sell magazines. I hated it. My parents had changed, and somehow my house didn't feel like home anymore. My mother was too skinny, she looked ill, and she was yellow all over. Life and people seemed to be constantly changing. I felt lost. All I wanted to do was party, find an escape, and get away from all the feelings and thoughts in my head.

I called CeeCee when I got to town. She lived in a one-bedroom apartment on campus with a kitchen, living room, and dining room. I spent a lot of weekends with her. She slept with a lot of guys. I thought I'd have sex when I was married, but I became fascinated by her free-loving nature. She told me how wonderful it was.

One night, two guys ran into her building, knocked on her door, and asked if we would hide them from the cops. When the police knocked on our door, we said we hadn't seen anyone. There was a squad car sitting on the street outside, so the guys stayed overnight and slept on the floor. I hit it off with one of the guys, and we sat up talking almost all night. He told me they had robbed the corner grocer with a gun. We started talking about how we could be another Bonnie and Clyde. He was really cute with blondish, brown hair that kept falling over his eyes. When I woke up the next morning, he'd left me a note, calling me Bonnie and he signed it Clyde. It was quite an adventure.

CeeCee and I started doing "street theatre." One night we met two guys at Bridgeman's, and pretended we were from South America. I spoke English with a thick Spanish accent; CeeCee couldn't do an accent, so we pretended she didn't know any English. We all went for a walk by Lake Calhoun, and stopped at our friend's apartment, all the while keeping up the charade. When the night ended, my guy gave me a ride home to my parents' house. Just before he got out to walk me to the door, he confessed he knew I wasn't from South America, I was from South Minneapolis. CeeCee had told his friend. He laughed, saying it was fun listening to me talk and continue the story. Then, he asked me out for the next weekend.

The next weekend CeeCee and I heard about a party in Mankato and drank a couple of Colt 45's as we drove. We found the party on campus. CeeCee went off with some guy she met. I didn't know anyone else until this nice-looking guy came up and asked me to dance. I ended up at his dorm, where we drank more Colt 45. We ended up in bed fully clothed, and made out. Suddenly, he started to tense up, and move up and down, up and down on top of me. He shuddered, and flopped down next to me like a wet noodle. Someone told me later it was a dry hump. Dry for me, but not for him. We both had on shorts, and I found sperm on my leg. Later, I worried about getting pregnant. Could sperm transfer through clothes and swim up? CeeCee reassured me that couldn't happen.

Later that week, I was walking down the street to the bus stop after work when a car pulled over next to me. His name was Frank, and he was handsome, with a short afro, dark brown skin, big brown eyes, and a friendly smile. I found out he worked for the airlines cleaning planes. We talked for a half hour, and he asked if I needed a ride. I thought about waiting for a bus, which could be there in ten or thirty minutes, so I said yes. I got in his car and he gave me a ride home, and asked me for my phone number.

Frank called later that night, and asked me out for Friday. I said OK, and arranged to spend the night at CeeCee's apartment where he picked me up. He wanted to stop at his apartment in St. Paul to have a drink and look in the newspaper to find a movie. When we walked into the apartment, he locked the door after us, saying it wasn't the best neighborhood. Then he fixed us rum-and-cokes, and got the newspaper to pick out a movie.

After two drinks, he suddenly looked at me and said, "Take off your dress."

I said "What?"

He said, "Take off your dress."

I looked at his face to see if this was some kind of a joke, but there was no humor in his face.

I kept eye contact, and said, "No way," my body on high alert, adrenaline soaring through my veins.

He stood up, and got undressed down to his tighty whities. He grabbed me, and tried to get my dress off, tearing it in the process. I kept telling him no, and to take me home. He tossed me on the bed, and we started wrestling. I kept fighting him and yelling. Suddenly, he stopped, got up, and went into the kitchen. I looked around frantically, got up, and sat on the floor in the corner of his apartment with furniture around me, so it was hard for him to get at me, and I wrapped my arms around myself for protection. He came back from the kitchen with a knife in his hand, and he threatened me with it. I couldn't believe this was happening; I didn't take my eyes off the knife. When he was close enough, I kicked and screamed with all my might. I kept thinking, "I'm a virgin and I'm not losing my virginity this way."

Suddenly, he stood up straight, sighed, took a step back, and laid the knife down on the coffee table. He walked over, and sat on the bed, still looking at me. Eventually, he laid down, and fell asleep. I sat there in shock not knowing what to do. There was no phone in the apartment, and cell phones didn't exist in those days. He said we were in a bad neighborhood, so I didn't feel like going out on the streets this late at night, especially with my torn dress. I sat in the corner paralyzed with fear and kept trying to weigh my options.

Eventually, I got up slowly, grabbed the knife, and hid it under the couch. Then I looked out the window to see what was out there, looking for a corner store or gas station, someplace that might have a phone. It was just houses and apartment buildings. Eventually, Frank's breathing changed, and he woke up. He got up off the bed, and got dressed without saying a word. Then, quietly, he told me it was time to take me home. He drove me back to CeeCee's apartment. I slammed the car door, and walked into the apartment building. I never thought of calling the police because I had been on a date with him and went voluntarily into the apartment. I felt like it was my fault. I didn't talk about it, but I took a long, hot shower before I went to bed that night.

The next night CeeCee had a party. Everyone was drinking. I just couldn't get into it and felt disconnected and lonely. I kept thinking about what had happened the night before. I remembered cutting myself at Rutgers that one night and how good it felt. I went into her bathroom and found a razor blade. I sat on the bathroom floor, and started to cut my palm, watching the red blood ooze out of the white cut. It felt good as my tension released. It was like I was in control of my own pain and not at the mercy of everyone else's. I started cutting, always on the palms of my hands. I went home with the palm of my right hand covered in cuts. When I went home the next morning, I sat around the breakfast table, aware of my hand. I felt more invisible than ever, because no one noticed the secret pain, hidden in my palms, buried in those cuts. I felt separate. The pain I usually wrote about in my journals and stories was now showing on the palm of my hand. It was my little secret, but I kept hoping someone would notice or see. No one ever did.

I was running from something; I'm not sure what. I knew I had to keep moving. I couldn't slow down, or I would be devoured by the pain. One night I drove by Mount Olivet Church, the church I was raised in, and I had a strong urge to go inside, sit, and look at the stained-glass window in the sanctuary. I wanted to see Jesus with His arms reaching out to gather us in close. I parked the car, got out, and tried all the doors to the church. They were all locked. Again, I felt the frustration of never being able to get something to comfort the pain I was carrying. I wanted a listening ear. I wanted the Jesus I learned about as a child, the one I wrote letters to and stuck behind His picture.

The next day, I quit my job at the magazine place, and decided not to go to back to college. I was lost. I let my parents know I was taking a quarter off and I found a job working at Fingerhut doing payroll and bookkeeping.

Chapter 19
Alcohol, You're Just Drinkin' Yourself to Death

In August of 1968, I became aware of hippies. They were chanting the slogan "Make Love Not War," at the Democratic convention in Chicago and were on the news. Hippies were a feel-good movement rebelling against our society's norms.

When I started working at Fingerhut, I met Max, short for Maxine. She was medium height with short brown hair, and had a slight resemblance to a cute little bulldog. We became friends. Then, one morning, Bobby, a full figured, busty woman with long thick, wavy black hair, started working in our department. She and her husband had just moved here from California. Bobby, Max, and I started having lunch together every day. Bobby was a "hippie," smoked dope, and believed in free love. She lived in Haight Ashbury before she came to Minnesota.

A couple weeks later, Bobby invited me over for supper to meet a friend of hers from California, Luke. The first thing I noticed was his smile. He was 6 feet tall and thin with long blonde hair, a beard, blue eyes, skin so fair I wondered if he'd ever been out in the sun, and a strong square jaw. He was very handsome. We had a great evening, and I started hanging out with Luke, Bobby and her husband, smoking dope and doing diet pills. When Luke met my parents a couple of weeks later, he and my father argued about the Vietnam War. My father wasn't happy when Luke and I started going door to door, getting signatures on a petition to stop the war. My hair was long, and I started wearing bell-bottoms and fringed tops or colorful tie-died shirts. I was becoming a hippie.

Then came the night I decided to lose my virginity. I was nineteen, and I stayed overnight with Luke. We slept on the floor of Bobby's living room on a mattress, and had sex. Because of CeeCee, I expected fireworks from the experience, but it hurt. I didn't have a climax, and I felt really sore. I went to work the next day feeling different because I'd finally taken the leap and had sex. When I told CeeCee about it, she told

135

me the first time wasn't as good as the second time. Luke and I continued to explore our new sexual relationship.

That fall, I was driving around the lakes, looking at the trees and their vibrant colors on my way to Luke's apartment when a new song came on the radio: "Abraham, Martin, and John." The words brought tears to my eyes and a sense of profound loss of innocence. I was drowning in the words: . . . *Anybody here seen my old friend Bobby? Can you tell me where he's gone? I thought I saw him walkin' up over the hill. With Abraham, Martin, and John.* Tears streamed down my cheeks, and for just a second, I felt disconnected from the world around me. Then, a car honked behind me, and I turned the corner as the song ended. The world just didn't seem to make sense. I turned off the radio, and rode in silence the rest of the way to Luke's.

After working at Fingerhut for a couple of months, we got a new boss, and work wasn't a great place to be anymore. Bobby, Max, and I started talking about quitting. I told Max she should go to college. She looked into registering at the university, and decided to try college. Bobby and her husband decided to move back to California, and I decided to go back to school. We all quit our jobs the same day.

Luke stayed in Bobby's apartment because of me. It was now mid-November, and he had the apartment until the first of December. Luke and I hung out at Max's apartment. She lived in an apartment with two other girls. I asked her about the possibility of moving in with her. I needed to get out of my house, which was driving me crazy. She said she'd talk to her roommates.

That fall Patty, twenty-two, married Todd at Mount Olivet Church, and I was her maid of honor. After the wedding, I visited Patty in her new apartment, and I got the feeling she wasn't happy. Todd was controlling. Eventually, he started hitting her. Later in the fall, Patty and Todd stayed at our house because my parents were out of town. They woke us up one night, arguing, and we heard Todd hit Patty. She divorced him a year later.

My mother's drinking was worse, and her skin and the whites of her eyes were yellow. She was way too skinny. We knew something was wrong with her, but my father wouldn't help us because he wouldn't take a look at his own drinking. My mother wasn't eating anymore, and she locked herself in the bathroom crying. Becca and Derek found liquor hidden in the washing machine downstairs. When William was over, he found alcohol hidden in a cereal box in the upstairs bathroom closet. He finally told my mother she could walk to the car or he could drag her to the car, but either way he was taking her to the hospital. When he got to the hospital, the doctor took one look at my mother's jaundiced skin and yellow eyes, and said it was from her drinking. It turned out her liver was 12 times larger than normal.

When I went to see her at the hospital, I walked in her hospital room; she turned her head, and looked at me with absolutely no recognition of who I was.

I said, "Hi, Mom, how are you feeling?"

She stared at me and asked, "Who are you?"

I told her, "I'm your daughter."

Her eyes seemed to float away from my face and focus on the ceiling. I left. I couldn't believe she didn't know me. Who was the woman lying in the hospital bed? I was totally invisible to her.

Then, the doctor told us my mother was dying, and he said he was going to give her blood transfusions to see if it would help her liver. I don't remember leaving the hospital or driving home. My mother didn't know me, and the doctor said she was dying. I couldn't take it all in; tears were sliding down my cheeks.

I drove home feeling hopeless; the darkness seemed to be devouring me. The pain inside was so great, and I felt like I had nowhere to turn. I had no friends who could understand what I was experiencing; they were having struggles of their own. I felt so lost as I left the hospital; there was nothing left. For some reason, my mother represented hope to me. On TV or in books I read, a mother always made you feel better. Mothers tickled your arm when you were sick. They made you laugh when there was nothing to laugh about. Mothers smiled no matter how beaten they felt from angry words yelled late at night. Mothers were the ones who made you feel safe after you'd fallen and scraped your knee or gave words of comfort when someone hurt you.

The trouble was my mother had no words of comfort and didn't notice when I scraped my knee; she was lost long ago to her addiction and whatever jealousies or fears she held inside. I always hoped one day she would finally be my mother, but she was just a dream I held onto: to keep going, hoping someday if I did the right thing, said the right thing, maybe she could love me. At the hospital, I realized she was gone forever, or she had never really been there. I had never felt so alone. My mother never talked about the hospital or her experience there. A year later, it was like it had never happened, and she was drinking heavily again.

At home, my father's anger filled the house. I couldn't stand being there without my mother's calming buffer. It was time to leave. The anger was back, pushing me forward, making me want to escape from the life around me. I called Max, and asked if I could move in that night. She said sure. I went upstairs, packed my suitcase, called Luke, and asked him to give me a ride to Max's. My father, Becca, and Derek were sitting in the den watching TV. I was so scared and angry. I went in, and told them I was moving out. Then, I turned before my father could say anything, grabbed my suitcase, and left the house.

I ran. I ran away from my mother's addiction. I ran away from my house and my crazy father. There was no safety in that world, so I ran away to find someplace else.

I didn't realize in that moment when I closed the front door that I was leaving my childhood behind. My Betsy-Tacy books, signed by Eileen, abandoned on my bookshelves would be given away years later to strangers who knew nothing of who Eileen was. My dog, Freckles, left behind in the shadows, was probably wandering around at night wondering when I'd be home. A couple of years later, he was hit by a car, and was gone. No one told me when it happened. Mementos and pictures of myself sitting on a bookshelf or living room table, or hanging from my bedroom wall, were eventually stuck in a drawer or thrown out.

When I closed my front door, I left a part of myself behind, not knowing whether I'd ever find it again. The looks of fear mixed with surprise on the faces of my younger sister and brother haunted me as I got into Luke's Buick Hearse and drove to Max's apartment

Max's roommates were nice at first. I had this album I loved to play called *Fire* by Arthur Brown; it spoke to how I was feeling: *I am the god of hell fire, and I bring you! Fire.* I played it over and over because I was scared, angry, and lost. I was sure no one even cared I was gone. I had no home, no sense of safety, or no place I belonged. It fit my mood; my life was a pile of smoldering ashes. Max's roommates were quiet office girls who I seemed to threaten with my intensity. One of her roommates took offense to the music, and she didn't like me. Then ,Luke had to move out of his apartment, and stayed with me a few nights. The girls didn't like a man or a long-haired hippie sleeping in their apartment. Things got really tense, and her roommates kicked us out.

We looked for a place to stay, and discovered The College Inn in Dinkytown. The seedy lobby was on the street level. When we walked in, I noticed the threadbare carpet, couches with hastily sewn patches on them, and a thin, balding, gray-haired man, badly needing a shave, standing at the registration desk. We rented a cheap hotel room we could barely afford, and carried our bags to the second floor. The hotel rooms were over the stores on the street. Our room had drab green walls with a single bed, a small table with two chairs, and a sink with a mirror on the wall. We shared a bathroom with the other guests down the hall. We kept food in a little travel bag I brought with me. It had bologna, bread, mayonnaise, and cheese in it. I put it out our window on the snowy roof, and it was our refrigerator. One morning, we found footprints across the roof leading to our refrigerator. The tenant from the room across the roof took some of our food.

When Luke and I started dating, I stopped cutting my palms because he seemed to genuinely care about me. I got a job doing figure work through a temp agency, and registered for classes at the University for winter quarter.

A couple of weeks before Christmas, Luke convinced me to try LSD. I didn't like it. Colors changed, and I watched a fire that seemed to get too big. Then, things in the room looked like they were growing. Luke suggested we head downtown. I felt really strange. Riding on elevators freaked me out, so we went back to the College Inn to lay in bed. I started hallucinating, and Luke turned into a pig. His nose was a snout. I was so relieved when I came down, and swore I'd never do that again.

I started having bad dreams about knives. The knives came at me through the air, and when I ran away, they came faster. Finally, I saw a door, went through it, and slammed it shut. All the knives hit, and stuck in the door. I breathed a sigh of relief until the knives were after my sister Becca. I couldn't protect her, and we were both running. I found a large piece of wood on the ground, and held it up. Bam! the knives lodged in the wood. Becca and I rested until the next onslaught of knives. I woke up from my dream feeling guilty I'd deserted Becca and Derek and left them alone with my father.

I called home just before Christmas, and talked to my father. My mother was still in the hospital. He said we were celebrating Christmas at William's house on Christmas day this year because my mother could only get a day pass from the hospital.

When I got to Connie and William's on Christmas, their nice, rich suburban home was a sharp contrast to my one room in the College Inn. I felt weird being there. I hadn't seen my family for a couple of months. When I saw my mother that day, it scared me. She was so skinny. Her eyes looked empty and haunted, and her smile never reached her eyes. I felt like she was acting, playing a part, but not quite all there, like she left a part of herself at the hospital. I wanted my mother back, the one who used to stand tall and strong, able to fight the battles around her, not this shrunken woman who looked like her life had been drained out of her. Everyone else at the Christmas gathering acted like everything was normal. Couldn't they see the pain my mother was in? Couldn't they acknowledge she needed help? But no one else seemed to notice. My brother's two-year-old son shrieked with joy over his presents. Everyone was laughing and unwrapping their gifts. I kept sneaking looks at my mother. One time, I thought she looked at me, and held up her open hands, wanting help. The next time I looked, it felt like she just wasn't there.

Later that week, I went home to ask my father for tuition for winter quarter. I registered for classes, and started back the winter of 1969.

My mother, who had been admitted to the hospital just before Thanksgiving, was finally discharged the middle of January. She responded to the transfusions, and went from critical to serious to well enough to go home. My older brother told me the day she left the hospital, my father brought her home, walked in the house, hung up her coat, and fixed her a drink. He didn't want to lose his lifelong drinking partner.

**

When I started back at the University, the first day I ran into Lisa, my best friend from Stevens Avenue. She was living with her boyfriend in an apartment just off campus. I told her Luke and I were staying at the College Inn, and she asked if we wanted to move in with her and Will.

The next day, Luke and I checked out of the College Inn, and moved in with Lisa. It was fun being with Lisa again. We walked to campus together, and caught up on old times. Luke and Will hit it off, almost too well. Luke was a speed freak when he lived in Haight Ashbury. Will, a nice-looking man with longish black hair, dark brown eyes, and an incredible handlebar mustache, had also been a speed freak. One day they shot up together, and Lisa and I were furious. They never did that again, and instead they drank beer and smoked dope.

Luke and I slept on a fold-out couch in the living room. One night, after we'd been there a week, I woke up because something was tickling my chest. When I opened my eyes, it was gone. The next night it happened again, only when I opened my eyes that night, I saw the end of a hanger that had been undone to be a long metal tool. I grabbed it, looked over my head, and Will was standing there, naked, trying to push down my covers with the hanger. I slept naked, so he was trying to look at my breasts while I was sleeping. He dropped the hanger, and scampered away. I went back to sleep. After Lisa and Will left the next morning, I told Luke. He said it was no big deal, and not to say anything. It was a nice apartment, and he liked staying there. After that, I wore a t-shirt to bed and slept on my side.

AJ and I had kept in contact by phone or letters since we graduated from high school. She went to Macalester College, and met Mahmood in her political science class. They quit school a year later,

140

and moved to Chicago where they found an apartment and jobs. In November, Luke and I decided to visit them in Chicago, and reserved a flight leaving Friday evening. That night, the snow was falling thickly around us and when we got to our gate at the airport, they announced flights to Chicago were cancelled. We ended up driving through the snow to the Greyhound bus depot, and rode the bus all night, getting to Chicago Saturday morning. AJ and Mahmood picked us up, and a couple of blocks later, we were stopped by the police. Because of the violent anti-war demonstrations in the summer, seeing a car with a black/Middle Eastern man driving, and a longhaired hippie in the back seat with two white girls made the cops suspicious. We showed our I.D.s, and they let us go. AJ and Mahmood showed us around Chicago, and I got to hang out with AJ while getting to know Mahmood. We took a bus back on Monday night, and I got back in time for my Tuesday classes.

Just after winter quarter started in January, there was a commotion in front of Morrill Hall. A group of students took over the president's office. They were upset about inequality on the campus. Black students could not live in university dorms on campus, and they couldn't participate in sororities and fraternities. There was no curriculum that included black culture and history. I demonstrated, and marched downtown to support the students who took over Morrill Hall. As a result of the situation, a year later, there was an African American Studies department at the U of M, offering classes like Black Family and Black Philosophy. I took every one of the classes, and graduated with a minor in Black studies.

Winter quarter, I switched my major to music, and took voice lessons, an introduction to music class, a music theory class, and I was in the University choir. The choir's big performance that quarter was a piece we performed with the Dave Brubeck trio in Northrup Auditorium. As I was singing, I felt an emptiness because there was no one in the audience to hear me. After that quarter, I went back to a social work major because music had too many little classes that were half credits or quarter credits.

Lisa and Will moved out of the apartment a couple months after Luke and I moved in, and Luke and I had our own apartment with our own bed and bedroom. I became obsessed with sex when they left because we had privacy and space. I wanted to do it all the time. I wore Luke out. It was new to me, and I wanted to explore and experiment. I had been exposed to sex and men's body parts since I was little, first not understanding, and as I got older, feeling guilty, not sure if I liked it, disgusted by men like my father or boys who put my hand on their penis. I felt like I was doing what they wanted me to, not what I wanted.

But with Luke *I* was exploring sex. I watched as he masturbated, noticing his body and face as he came. We tried different positions, and I gave my body freely to him, trying to understand what it was all about. Hidden body parts were no longer hidden behind zippers or flashing at me through raincoats and dropped pants. I loved Luke's body, and seeing all his parts. Sex took on a whole new meaning; it was enjoyable and freeing. It was my body, and I enjoyed exploring all its places.

One day, Luke convinced me to try STP; STP stood for serenity, tranquility and peace. It was a hallucinogenic drug. Luke said it wasn't as potent as LSD. It was a gentle high. He wore me down, and I tried it. It was really trippy, and the mood swings were extreme. I was glad when it had worn off. But on Monday, when I was walking to campus, I could hear the snow melting. It gave me an anxiety attack because I thought I was still high. I felt off, like I was going crazy.

Luke began to hang out with Elliot, who was the friendly neighborhood drug dealer. He was a short, white, skinny, squirrelly guy, with a moustache so thin, it made him look like he was trying too hard to be someone he wasn't. I was never sure he was telling the truth. He told outrageous stories and bragged a lot about his life. He was living with a nice girl, Mary, with long blonde hair, blue eyes, and a sweet smile. She was pregnant, and adored Elliot. It was hard sometimes. I wanted to shake her, and say open your eyes.

That winter was the first time I remember feeling totally drained of energy. Life looked gray everywhere, and I was exhausted. Years later, someone told me I had "battle fatigue" or "the fox hole syndrome." In other words, being so exhausted from having to be hyper vigilant all the time, never able to let down and feel safe. A sense of pending disaster. It lasted for a week or so, and then I bounced back.

Then, in the spring, AJ's brother died of an overdose. He was taking "downers" and drinking alcohol, and one night, he went to bed, threw up because of too much alcohol and too many "downers," and the vomit suffocated him. I had known him since I was in sixth grade. He had a dark, spooky, creative nature, and eventually lived on the West Bank, listening to Bob Dylan, Pete Seeger, and Arlo Guthrie. *Alice's Restaurant* was popular the year he died. I went to his funeral, and when they lowered his casket into the ground, I looked around at all the youthful faces just out of high school or college, all in shock that this could happen to someone so young. My knees felt weak; I wanted to sit down right there on the grass and cry. This wasn't supposed to be happening. I could hear his laughter after he scared us with his latest monster imitation. He was obsessed with art and drawing all sorts of realities that were plastered all over his room. His life was suddenly gone in the middle of his sleep when he was all alone. The knot in my stomach came back. Nothing felt safe.

Luke sold his Buick Hearse and bought a Volkswagen bus shortly after the funeral. We decided to get away. It was spring break, and we took a five-day road trip, driving through Wisconsin, Illinois, Kentucky, and Iowa. We camped or stayed at bed and breakfasts. It felt good to get away, and just drive, not having to think. When we got back, Luke started working at General Hospital cleaning cages, and taking care of animals used for research at a Rosemount facility.

I made it through spring quarter, and when the school year ended, I decided to move home for the summer. I felt unsettled, anxious, and needed grounding. I wanted to be somewhere that was familiar, and had a history, a connection to me. Luke was upset. He stayed in the apartment for another month. We didn't see each other for a while.

But moving home was worse. I thought it would feel good to be in my own bedroom, but it felt different. It didn't fit me anymore; it was too small, and there was nothing familiar on the walls anywhere. It was strange and alien. When I took a bath the first week home, the faucet seemed too high on the wall, so the stream of water was longer and fuller. I felt like I was hallucinating. I kept experiencing déjà vu that made me feel like I was high again.

Sometimes, I went to a party, and felt like all of a sudden, everything sped up, so I took a deep breath and told myself I was all right. Eventually, everything went back to normal. I learned I was having flashbacks.

One day, I sat by Lake Harriet, and had an anxiety attack because I saw floaters in my eyes. I was too aware of my own body, which I hadn't been before. Eventually, I got used to it, and life started to feel more normal. But I told my younger siblings not to mess with drugs. After I was home for a couple of weeks, Luke and I started seeing each other again.

Chapter 20
My Daddy Left Me, My Mama Did Too

In late August I saw an ad in the paper for a paperback librarian at North High School. I applied, and was hired to work the 1969-70 school year. My library hours were set around my classes at the U of M. It was kind of a sketchy school, so I wasn't too surprised when my battery was stolen out of my car the first day I worked there.

The paperback library was set up in the main hall of the school to promote reading. Students seemed to prefer a paperback book they could hide so no one knew they were reading. The students came to check out books or visit me in between their classes.

One afternoon, I was helping a student check out a book when two policemen walked in through the main door, talking on their walkie talkies and running up to the second floor. It turned out, a student got into a fight with a teacher, and gave him a black eye.

A few days later, Ronnie, the head of the North Urban League, came to the school. He walked by, winked at me, and said hello on the way to his meeting. He was tall and big, with the darkest skin I'd ever seen. He came back after his meeting, and asked if I wanted to go on break. We walked to the student cafeteria, got some coffee, and sat down at a table in the corner. Fairly quickly into the conversation, he started asking about my sex life. Did I like it hard and fast? Was I into oral sex? I looked at him stunned. I couldn't think of a thing to say. He continued, saying there was no need to be shy; sex was a wonderful, natural act. I cleared my throat, got up, and said I had to get back to work. I left quickly, confused by what just happened.

**

Fall quarter was interesting at the University. I made new friends, and became reacquainted with old ones. I ran into Marty on campus the first week; we knew each other in high school. We talked, and

144

made plans to have lunch the next day. At lunch, we started talking about dance, and she brought a flyer about an eight-week dance class at McPhail School of Music. We decided to sign up, and take the class together. We learned tap, ballet, and modern dance, and at the end of the session, we had a recital at Minneapolis Community College. Marty and I came up with our own version of Swan Lake. It was a comedy with a couple of beautiful swans coming out looking anything but graceful, chewing bubble gum. We got quite a few laughs. Then, our whole class performed a couple of dance routines.

After the show, I met Marty's mom, and I was surprised how critical she was. After Marty introduced me, her mother ignored me, and started criticizing Marty for her posture and gum chewing. She told Marty she embarrassed her. I felt so sorry for Marty, who was standing straight and tall when we approached her mother but was now shrinking and slouching. Marty and I ended up becoming best friends.

Luke and I saw each other on the weekends, and my parents learned to tolerate him. Sometimes, I told my parents I was sleeping at Marty's house, and I stayed over at Luke's downtown apartment. Marty also lived at home, so we started talking about getting an apartment together.

In my abnormal psychology class, I met Jenny, a small, petite woman with long, dark, red hair and freckles across a turned-up nose. We started talking, and after class, had lunch together. She was into astrology and the paranormal. Her father was the minister of a church on Lake of the Isles, and her family lived next door to the church. Jenny told me stories about the church being haunted and the ghosts she saw. I was fascinated because I felt a "presence" around me at times. I was aware of another dimension that lived alongside me. I met Jenny's boyfriend a week later when she invited me over to her apartment. Her boyfriend was big and tall, and they were both hippies. We started hanging out with them, and Luke and her boyfriend hit it off. We ended up spending the night in their guest room fairly often.

Luke and I also hung out at CeeCee's apartment until she quit school and moved back to St. Cloud to live with her boyfriend, Sean. One weekend, Luke and I drove to St. Cloud to visit them. It was a week after Sean had been deer hunting, and I had venison roast for the first time. While we were there, CeeCee invited us to go camping on the north shore, and said they could lend us a tent. We camped a couple of weekends later. Everyone, but me, smoked dope, and sat by the lake getting high. I sat on a large rock, and wrote, feeling the solid energy of the boulder I sat on, enjoying the lake, and watching the power of the waves, feeling okay I wasn't high.

As the weather started getting colder, Luke and I started fighting. He wanted to move back to California where there was sunshine and warmth, but I wanted to stay in Minnesota. He'd threatened to hop in his VW bus and head to California, and I'd say go ahead. But when he walked out the door, he got halfway to his car, turned around, and came back. Or sometimes he got to his car, and I ran out, telling him not to leave.

I met Ted in my sociology class. He was extremely good-looking with his short afro and his warm brown eyes, and he sat next to me every day. We started talking and hanging out after class. He was funny and gentle. One day, he invited me to his friend's apartment on campus. We ended up having sex. A couple of weeks later, I overheard him talking to his friend before class. His friend mentioned something about Ted's wife. I was stunned; I didn't know he was married. It was bye bye, Ted.

**

The beginning of December, my parents gave me an early Christmas present. For some reason, my father decided to buy me a new car. I think his motivation had to do with Luke. My father didn't like him, afraid I might move to California. My father and I went to a car dealer where he "knew a guy" who gave him a deal. I drove out that day with a brand new, white Opal Kadett. My older brother and his wife got a waffle iron for Christmas, and my older sister bought her own car after high school. There were bad feelings among my siblings.

Through the years, my father seemed to favor me; it was subtle, but his attention to me was different. He confided in me, and he seemed to trust me in his volatile dark moods. He never really saw "me;" he only saw what I gave him. My father's kind gesture caused jealousy between my siblings and me. Over the years, a lot of sideways messages were tossed my way because my father bought me that car.

On Christmas Eve, Luke was smiling when he arrived at my house. It was a smile I'd never really seen before; I wondered what was going on. When it came time to open presents, he handed me his first. As I opened it, I felt his eyes watching my every movement, and my whole family was watching me as I unwrapped my small package. My stomach started to knot up, and I hoped it wasn't what I thought it was. I opened the box, and it was a ring with a star sapphire. He got down on one knee, so traditional for my hippie boyfriend, and asked me to marry him.

I felt only panic; I didn't want to marry anyone. I felt trapped with everyone staring at me and waiting. I said yes, and put the ring on just to stop everyone from looking at me. Pretty soon, everyone was opening gifts, and colorful paper was in piles everywhere. Meanwhile,

I looked at Luke. He would never be my dream husband — a college professor or a doctor. He was a recovering speed freak with no goals. I felt sick to my stomach. The ring felt too tight on my finger; I wanted to throw it across the room. I sat there smiling like everything was O.K.

**

Marty and I signed up for classes in the Black Studies program winter quarter. We took Black Family, Black Philosophy, and Black Literature. In my Black Family class, we had an assignment to attend a black church, and compare it to our own. We went to Sabathani Church in Minneapolis. We loved it, and started attending regularly. I loved the music, but really loved the pastor's sermon that was visceral, intense, and broke into song at the end. He reminded me of James Brown. I loved his passion and energy.

One day, Marty used a word about me I'd never heard before. She told me I was sexy. She said I got a lot of male attention because I had "the look." I asked what "the look" was. She told me I was small and petite with green eyes that seemed to look right through you. I had an innocence with an underlying energy that was contagious. She told me I was pretty, but it was my sexiness that really drew men in. It was nice to hear because part of me still felt like the fourth grader my mother called fat.

I ran into Lisa on campus that quarter, and found out she and Will were living in the upstairs of a duplex on First Avenue. When I told her Marty and I were thinking of getting an apartment, she said the downstairs of her duplex would be vacant March 1st. I told Marty, and we moved into there March 1st, 1970. It was fun living by Lisa again. Our duplex had a large kitchen, a bathroom off the kitchen, a small alcove that worked as a single bedroom, a large living room, and a large bedroom big enough for twin beds. Marty's friend Leann was pregnant, and moving in with us. She and Marty took the large bedroom. I took the alcove bedroom. Eventually Luke moved in with me, and let go of his apartment. We had to flush the toilet by pouring water from the sink into the toilet. There was a dirt basement with ladder-like stairs that you crawled down through a trap door in the kitchen. But we still loved our new home.

Luke occasionally saved one of the animals from the research center where he worked. When he brought home Gulliver, a St. Bernard, Marty and I fell in love. He stayed in the basement at night, but during the day he was upstairs with us or outside in the fenced in backyard. A couple of months later, we were walking him on a leash—he loved to chase cars, so the walk was always a battle. One day, he lunged so hard he broke the leash, and headed into the street. He was hit by a car, or I should say, the car was hit by Gulliver. The damage to the car was pretty bad; the whole right fender was smashed in. But Gulliver acted like nothing had happened. He just kept trotting down the street. We caught him, and brought him to a vet who said he was fine and didn't have a scratch.

We decided a dog his size needed to be somewhere he could run free. Luke found someone who lived on a farm and wanted Gulliver. When we drove him to his new home and watched him run freely in their twenty acres, we knew it was the right choice.

Lisa and Will hung a flag upside down from their apartment on the second floor, to protest the Vietnam war. One day, there was a knock on our door. We saw two policemen standing on our doorstep. We opened the door and they asked about the flag. We got Lisa from upstairs, and the police told her that hanging the flag was OK, but she had used nails to hang it, which was defacing the flag. They told her if she removed the flag immediately or found a better way to hang it, they wouldn't fine her. We went up when they left, and helped her take down the flag.

A few days later, I was sitting on the back steps in the morning, letting the sun warm my face and thinking great thoughts, when Lisa came down without her usual cup of coffee and sat down next to me. I looked at her, and she had welts on her face and across her legs. She looked scared.

I asked, "Lisa, what happened?"

She almost whispered, "Will whipped me with a whip that had metal beads on the end."

Then, she looked at me with tears in her eyes, and asked if I heard any noises last night.

I said, "No."

I could see fear creep into her tearful eyes as she told me how Will held a gun to her head, and then, fired it just over her head to scare her. Her face lost all its color as her words came out slowly. I slid over, and put my arm around her; she put her head on my shoulder and lost all control. She sobbed, and in between her sobs, she managed a few words:

"I'm afraid to kick him out."

Before that day, when we sat on the back step in the morning, I noticed bruises she always explained away. This was the first time she told me what was happening. I told her she should call the police and get a restraining order or call the locksmith and change the locks. She didn't deserve this.

She took a deep breath, sat up straight, and said, "You're right, I don't, he's not worth it. I'm going to change the locks, and stay with a friend he doesn't know for a couple of days."

When I got home from school, Will was gone. Lisa changed the locks, and came back a week later with Will out of her life.

When I was younger, I watched life go by from my window or through books I read. I had a quiet place inside I went to for nurturing. Now that I was away from my family, living my own life, everything was speeding up, more things coming at me, quick changes that I'd quickly jot down in my journal. Life started moving very fast — no more inner quiet place to go. There was never any time, and I couldn't look back because the pain might catch up with me.

One day, I met Otis while I was hanging out on the grass in front of my class building, writing in my journal. He sat down on the grass next to me, and we started talking. He was a dark, mysterious man who had an energy like my father's: intense eyes laughing one moment and looking angry the next. I was drawn to him, even though I felt a lurking danger. Later in the week, he invited me to his dorm, and when I got there, his roommate left. We talked, and he shared stories from his past that were scary and painful. I felt his sadness as he talked. I tended to be attracted to men who shared intimate parts of themselves. Trusting them because they had shared something intimate with me. Eventually, we had sex.

Afterwards, he was different, distant and cold, and left to use the bathroom. When he came back, he told me it burned when he urinated. I reassured him that he was OK, thinking he needed comforting. I was so naïve, realizing later that was his way of telling me he had gonorrhea. He gave me gonorrhea on purpose. I realized the world was just as dangerous as my family. I went to the doctor, and got some antibiotics.

Marty and I started hanging out with three guys from school: "Jive JD," who was tall and wiry with nappy hair and very light skin; Gary, who was quiet with a beautiful smile; and Dan, who was 6' 4," big and muscular. There was no fat on his body. His big, white-toothed smile and eyes that sparkled with humor were a sharp contrast to his dark brown skin. They came over in the evenings, bringing us cases of pop and gallons of ice cream they ripped off trucks by the U of M.

I had a picture hanging on our wall I bought at a student art show at North High. It had a lime green background with purple stars bursting into an array of color. In the middle was a portrait of a black man with a strong, square jaw, penetrating eyes, and a gentle mouth. I was very attracted to the portrait's warm intensity. When Dan came over, he always teased me about the painting, saying I bought it because it looked like him. I was still living with Luke, but when Marty and I went out with these guys, he stayed home. Eventually Dan and I hooked up at his place

149

a couple of times, but it was unsuccessful because he couldn't perform, saying I was too small in stature and he was afraid of hurting me because he was so big.

Later, I found out Dan was a skilled, sought after, athlete who played baseball, basketball, and football at the university. Eventually, he became a pro athlete and played baseball for the Yankees, California Angels, and Minnesota Twins. The NFL also offered him positions, but he chose baseball. Gary became a soap opera star, and JD was just JD.

At the end of April, Marty, Leann, and I went to Madison to visit friends at the university there. Three guys from Milwaukee came over to our friend's house. One was Mack Tubbs III. He was 5' 10"and wore his hair in a medium Afro, his skin was a rich brown, and the look in his eyes was sexy and playful. He was quiet. He told me he worked for the University in Milwaukee doing upkeep and maintenance. We hung out that weekend, and went dancing at clubs. We exchanged phone numbers when he left. When I got back to Minneapolis, things were even more strained between Luke and me.

**

The spring of 1970, there were anti-war demonstrations at the U of M. We demonstrated in front of Coffman Union, and marched downtown. Then, in May, there were shootings at Kent State. Four students were dead, and others injured. Our country was in shock; shooting college students was beyond reasonable recourse to the anti-war demonstrations going on. Our country was in chaos, the University of Minnesota student body went on strike along with other colleges across the country, and all classes were cancelled.

During that quarter, I worked as an intern with Big Sisters. At the end of the internship, I planned a summer beach outing with my three "little sisters" from the program. Becca and her black boyfriend came along. When I picked up the first girl, the father opened the front door before I had a chance to knock. He asked if that was a black boy in the car.

I said, "Yes, he's my sister's boyfriend."

Then, he said his daughter couldn't come if there was a black boy going. He pronounced black boy with anger and disgust. I explained this "black boy" was nice, and came from a good family. He sneered, and said that no daughter of his was driving in a car with the likes of him. I left that house stunned. I got in the car, sat down, and started to cry. I couldn't believe someone could really feel that way.

From the back seat, Becca and Michael asked me what was wrong. I made something up because I just couldn't tell them what happened. We had a great day at the beach, but I still felt hurt by that man's attitude.

My emotions were growing more intense—new awareness, new chaos, and being too open to the world around me. I needed to get away, to experience something totally new. I needed to get away from Luke and my life I grew up in. Mack called one night and wanted me to come visit him in Milwaukee. I took a bus to Milwaukee at the end of May for a long weekend. When I stepped off the bus, I felt nervous but excited. I was about to go and look for a cab—Mack didn't have a car—when an older black gentleman, Clarence, approached me, and asked if I needed help.

He looked nice, and his face seemed open and friendly, so I told him I was here to visit a friend and might be moving here. He said he could help me get a job, and offered to drive me to Mack's apartment. I decided, why not? We stopped at a restaurant in Juneau village where he knew the manager. The guy looked like Howdy Doody with his stick out ears and pointy nose. He offered me a job as a waitress when I moved to Milwaukee, and gave me his card. As Clarence drove me to Mack's apartment, I wondered what he wanted from all this. He gave me his phone number as I got out of his car. Later, I told Mack about him, and he said to keep his information because it might come in handy. I had an interesting weekend meeting Mack's friends and becoming intimate with Mack. He showed me around the city.

In my family, I felt I couldn't express who I was growing up. When I watched Mack and his friends interacting, they were emotional and funny, playing "the dozens" and telling many stories. They seemed so free from people's expectations, and did what they needed to survive.

They felt real to me; they didn't wear masks to cover up how they were feeling like my parents did every day. William and his wife lived their perfect life in their perfect suburb, and went to the perfect church. They followed all the rules, and I always felt confined and stifled, trapped in their home. They were nice people, but so different from how I felt inside. I wanted to explore, experience, and find out who I was. I wanted to push the envelope, the boundaries, and confront the status quo. I had this creative intensity inside that needed an outlet, emotions I wanted to explore and express. I didn't want to be like anyone in my family. It was hard to leave Milwaukee, but I needed to get home, take my finals, and figure out what I wanted to do, so I took the bus back home.

When I got back to Minneapolis, I knew I didn't want to be with Luke anymore. I certainly didn't want to be engaged or married. I didn't want to be like my mother and father. I wanted no commitments. Luke was a hippie who loved getting high with no real goals or direction. I wanted to be somebody, I wanted to find myself, and I was not ready to settle down. I wanted to find love and a place I belonged. I was looking for something, feeling lost, never getting what I needed. College demonstrations resulting in the shooting of college students didn't make sense, and I wanted to get away from my family and Luke. I told my parents I was taking a year off school, packed up my car, and left for Milwaukee at the beginning of July. I didn't tell Luke, and just took off while he was at work. I told Marty I was moving to Milwaukee the day I left. She wasn't happy about it.

Chapter 21
Disconnected Lives

As I drove from Minneapolis to Milwaukee, I felt the tension leave my body, like I was breaking free. Mack's world I was driving to was connected to black street life, and the short time I'd visited there, I felt so many emotions. His life was all about the senses and the body. I grew up in a house where people lived in their heads, and feelings didn't belong. I was excited to explore a place that seemed to feel as deeply as I did, a culture where people felt and expressed themselves through stories, dance, and living in the moment. I wanted to live my life through my emotions. I wanted to find out who I was when there were no expectations from any outside sources.

It was July, and blue skies followed me on my journey. The dark clouds from my past floated away to a distant place. I drove to Mack's apartment on Capitol Drive, parked, and looked up at the windows. I felt the thrill of a new adventure behind every one. I got out of my car, walked to his front door, and pushed the buzzer. He let me in, and I walked into a world I had never experienced before.

I called the Crazy Horse restaurant the next day, and the manager said I could start work on the weekend. My shift was 3:00 till close. I settled in with Mack. His apartment was nice, but it didn't seem to be set up for cooking: no pots or pans and only a couple of plates and silverware settings. The only food was boxes of saltine crackers, bologna, and cheese in the refrigerator, so for lunch, we ate bologna and cheese sandwiches between two saltines, and washed it down with a grape soda. He didn't cook, and I wasn't much of a cook myself. One of the benefits of working at the Crazy Horse was it included a free meal when I worked. I soon found out they had great burgers and fries.

Mack worked at the University of Wisconsin during the day, gambled in the evening. I drove him to work in the morning, but when I worked, he found another way home. My shift was three to eleven three nights during the week, and one night on the weekend. Some days, we hardly saw each other except at night, and I soon found out sex was fun, playful, and adventurous with Mack.

Eventually, we started hanging out with his friends Benny and James. Benny was dark-skinned, tall, and thin with a flat nose slightly pushed in. His nappy hair was short and thin, and he walked with an air of assurance and confidence. He had mean-looking scars on his chest that came from knife wounds, and his face wore a constant sneer that seemed to mock life. When I first met his girlfriend, Arlene, who was quiet, with dark mousey hair and not very attractive, she told me she was pregnant from a rape. Benny had taken her in after the rape, and she was keeping the baby. James was short and skinny with a tight Afro and acted like a clown. He loved to play "the dozens," a verbal game to see who can make the worst insult about your mama. James was good at talking trash about Mack's mama, trying to come up with the worst insult like, "Your mama is so ugly, your papa makes her walk backwards down the street." I got the feeling Benny was the alpha male of the group, and he made me nervous.

As I sat and watched them put on their show, I felt like I was in one of those books I read years ago. I was a voyeur, watching them but not being part of them. That was how I seem to have felt most of my life, always on the outside looking in, not quite part of anything.

One night, Mack was at work, and I was visiting Arlene. When Benny got home, he asked if I'd go for a walk with him. As we walked, he said he had plans for me. He wanted me to dress up, and lure men to a hotel room where he'd wait in the closet and jump out before I had to take off any clothes. Then, we would extort money from the men. He said with my looks, we could make a lot of money. He said I didn't have to decide now, but I should think about it. He told me not to tell Mack. I avoided being alone with him again, and I didn't tell Mack.

I loved being with Mack. He was handsome and funny, and we had many passionate nights of lovemaking. But he was elusive, and I always felt like he was holding something back while I was pouring myself into him. I began having dreams that I was pregnant with his baby. When I held the baby in my arms, he looked like Mack. This baby waved his arms, and kicked his chubby legs. When I woke up, I felt a sharp loss. I had never had dreams like that before. I'd never known anyone like Mack. He teased me about always writing in my journal, but my journal was how I kept a piece of myself in this strange, new way of life.

**

One day, when I wasn't working, I went to pick up Mack from work, and James was with him. As we were driving home, Mack suddenly told me to turn right. He said he thought we were being followed. Then, he told me to turn left. After I turned left, he told me to pull over and park. When I parked, the car behind us parked, and started flashing its lights. It was an unmarked police car.

The policemen got out of their car, each approaching the car from a different side, standing slightly away and back. The first policeman asked us all to step out of the car. When we did, he grabbed my arm, and pulled me away from where Mack and James were standing. He wanted to see my license, and I showed it to him. Then, he wanted to know what I was doing in Milwaukee, and how long I'd been there with my Minnesota license. When he walked over and started going through my glove compartment, he asked who the car belonged to. I told him it belonged to the person on the registration card that he held in his hand. He told me not to get smart with him, or he'd arrest me. I told him it was my father's. When he came back over, he grabbed my purse. As he looked through it, he told me if I didn't cooperate, he would throw me in a women's prison, which I probably wouldn't enjoy. I tried to say something to Mack, but he wouldn't let me talk to him or James.

I was so confused because all I had done was pick up Mack, and now, I was standing there with these two policemen. Mack and James stood on the other side of the car, saying nothing. A squad car pulled up with its lights flashing, and the two policemen told us to stand where we were and wait. They walked over to the squad car with the flashing lights, and talked to the policemen. When they came back, they told us my car had been identified in a robbery that had occurred across town. I couldn't understand what was happening. I knew my car was totally innocent, but the squad car lights were flashing, and the policemen's shiny badges reflected the rhythm of the lights. Then a paddy wagon pulled up. I was starting to get scared. This was all bogus because I wasn't involved in any robbery. I had been home until I picked up Mack.

When the paddy wagon pulled up, the now six policemen conversed amongst themselves, looking at us periodically with suspicion and hostility. They talked on their walkie-talkies, and a couple of the cops got into their squad car and called in our driver's license numbers for outstanding warrants. The whole time, I was standing alone on one side of the car, while James and Mack were standing on the other side by the trunk. I started imagining myself sitting in a women's prison. Would I know how to protect myself? I was only twenty-one. Or worse yet, I imagined the feeling of being locked up, trapped, someone else having control over my life, no one believing what I said, that I was innocent. Suddenly, I was the star in a made-for-TV movie being harassed by cops. Who was going to come and save me? Then, a loud thud brought me back to my surroundings. It was the door of the squad car being closed.

The two cops from the squad car walked over to the other policemen just as another police car showed up. They talked to the other cops, then left. Two of the policemen came and told us that they found a white car across town that committed the robbery. But when they checked for outstanding warrants, they found that James had outstanding parking tickets that were never paid. So, they arrested him, and put him in the paddy wagon. They told Mack and I to have a nice day and left. James was released the next day, after he came up with the money for the parking tickets.

I stood there speechless; there was no apology. They just drove off. For almost an hour, I felt that to them I was guilty until I was proven innocent. It really shook me up. Mack wasn't surprised.

He just said, "Welcome to the world of being black, nigger."

He called me that often; it felt good to be part of his gang. Being called "nigger," was a sign of acceptance and trust.

**

One night, Mack was gone overnight, and he asked James to look after me. I didn't understand why I needed to be looked after. We watched some TV, and talked. James told me some interesting stories about Mack and him, how they had collected pop bottles as kids, and found discarded newspapers to sell on a street corner. It was their first hustle, he said. I was getting tired, so I called it a night, and went into the bedroom and went to bed. In the middle of the night, I woke up with James on top of me. He had pulled off my panties, and was inside me. I kept kicking and trying to push him off, but he just got this awful grin on his face. It was cruel. Up until then, I liked him. I thought we were friends, and I felt comfortable with him. So, I was shocked when I saw his mocking smile. Then he said that I better not tell Mack, because Mack would hurt us.

I never told Mack, and I was never alone with James again. It seemed I was always in situations that I couldn't tell anybody. The secrets just kept piling up inside me, tucked under a rib cage here, a kneecap there. My eyes were full of hidden stories that I couldn't share.

After I worked at the Crazy Horse for a couple of weeks, the manager kept me late to help clean up. When I brought the last of the dishes into the kitchen, he cornered me against the sink, and tried to kiss me. I put my hand on his chest to stop him. Then, he said he could help pay my rent, and he would give me the best tables for waitressing if I would be "friendly" with him. I looked around, and it was just the two of us with no one there to help me. I told him I'd think about it, and let him know the next day. I got out of there as soon as I could.

The next day, I told him, "No, *my boyfriend* didn't like the idea."

He gave me the worst tables after that.

In the middle of August, my father and Luke surprised me, and appeared on Mack's doorstep one morning. Mack left as soon as they walked in the door.

My father looked at me and said, "Do you know you are the only white person living in this area?"

They tried to talk me into going home. I said no. Then Luke asked for his ring back, which I gladly gave him. They left feeling upset. I felt relief. A couple of days later, Becca wrote me and said she and her boyfriend were having sex. She was only fourteen. I wrote to her about Planned Parenthood, and how they provided options to keep her safe.

**

I loved taking baths and playing music on Mack's stereo during the day. I listened to Quincy Jones' *Walking in Space,* and sat back to relax in the warm water. I let the soft, sensual tones of the trumpet wash over me. One day, I was playing the stereo and taking a bath when there was a knock on the door. I got out of the tub, put on a robe, and opened the door a crack. There were two cops standing there. They looked at me funny, and said they had a complaint that I was having a loud party. I opened the door, showed them the apartment was empty, and told them I was just taking a bath and listening to music before work. They apologized, and said maybe the neighbors had it in for me.

A couple of nights later, I took a bus to work because my car was in the shop. When my shift ended, the salad girl, Daneeka, said her boyfriend could give me a ride home. When he pulled up in his Cadillac, I got in the backseat with his friend Darnell. He smiled, and we made small talk. Suddenly, Daneeka told her boyfriend to make a left turn, saying she had to get something from her sister's house. When he pulled over, she told me to come with her to help carry it. We got out, and walked around the side of the house. She took my hand, and told me to run. Along the way, she told me her boyfriend had a gun, and she wanted to get away from him.

We ended up in a pool parlor on Capitol Drive where her ex-boyfriend worked. At three in the morning, I decided to walk home. It was only about a half mile down Capitol Drive. I went out the front door, and after walking two blocks, I saw a familiar car turn the corner. It was a Cadillac. I kept walking, the car pulled over, the passenger door opened, and I saw a gun pointed at me. It was Darnell. He told me to get in the car with the gun pointed right at my chest. I thought, *could I run for it?* But the gun was staring at me, and I knew I wasn't faster than a bullet. I sat in the car, leaving the door open with one foot planted on the street. He told me to close the door; he wasn't going to shoot me. He said if he wanted to shoot me, he could have done it already. I thought about that for a minute, staring at the gun now pointed at my head, and closed the door. I said if he wasn't going to shoot me, then why didn't he just give me the gun?

He sat there for thirty seconds, lowered the gun, and gave it to me. He asked me why Daneeka and I ditched them. I told him Daneeka got scared when her boyfriend showed her the gun. We talked for a few minutes, and he ended up driving me to Mack's apartment. I was so glad to get out of that car. I was shaking and felt like I was lucky to be alive. I'd never had a gun pointed at me before, and I'd never looked down the little black hole that housed the bullet. I'd never held a gun in my hand before. It was heavy. I could still feel the coldness of the metal, and I kept seeing the black hole pointed at me.

A couple of nights later, I ended up in the emergency room. Mack was gone, and I drove myself to the hospital. I had something called a Bartholomew's cyst. The young doctor was very rude and treated me like I was a prostitute. He asked a lot of questions. Was I over eighteen? What I was doing in Milwaukee? Did I have a job? Did I have any family in the area? He asked if I liked rough sex, and if I had a lot of sexual partners. I felt like he was a cop and not a doctor. I answered all his questions. I didn't like how I felt being there in that emergency room. I felt dirty and cheap by the time I left.

I was becoming disillusioned with real life. I thought policemen and doctors were here to help and keep us safe. Yet, my encounters with them caused fear and shame. I didn't know that real life had guns and men propositioning me for favors or money. I had succumbed to the reality in books I read where people's lives were glamorous or romantic, adventurous and exciting. At times, I *was* excited by the different realities I experienced, feeling invigorated by it all. I met a guy one day who just got out of prison, and we went to his mother's house. While we were sitting there, a rat ran across the living room that was the size of a large cat. No one reacted to it, like it happened all the time. When I looked at Benny, I saw a gang leader holding a knife, and he talked to me like I belonged.

I was immersed in something real, and I was free to do what I wanted. I wasn't responsible for any anyone else. I had no real friends, no ties. But I was shocked at how people treated me at times, feeling like they looked at me like I was a prostitute. Really, inside, I was a naïve girl, running away from my life, trying to find out who I was.

Mack and his friends joked sometimes that I could be an undercover cop because I didn't drink or get high. I found that an intriguing idea. I would have made a great undercover cop. I liked living on the edge, but I didn't like getting high or losing control.

Sometimes, I feared the things happening around me, but they motivated me to stay on my toes and keep myself safe. It was confusing. My home wasn't safe, college wasn't safe, and I couldn't figure out where safe was anymore. Yet, I wanted to learn, see, and do more. I still held onto the hope that there was someone out there who could love me, and I'd find a place I belonged.

Mack and I started fighting, and I realized he wasn't the place I belonged. He didn't want me hanging out with his friends. It was like he wanted me to be a prisoner in his home. He didn't care about my feelings, and got mad if I didn't do what he wanted. Around that time, Kelly started working at the Crazy Horse. Kelly and I became friends, and we started meeting for lunch or coffee. We talked. We went to her house for lunch one day, and I met her parents. I learned she was a Jehovah's Witness. She was sensitive and emotional.

Mack and I had another fight, and he gave me a black eye. I was shocked, and it brought back the memory of my father slapping me in the crib. It rocked my sense of safety. The next day, I packed up and left. I called Kelly, and we met for lunch before work. I told her I left Mack, and had no place to stay. After work that night, I met a man at the Crazy Horse bar after work. He sat with Kelly and me and heard us talking about my living situation. He said he worked nights, so I could sleep at his place if I wanted. He usually got home about the time I got up. It worked well for a few of nights, until one morning I woke up with him in bed, trying to remove my panties. I screamed, jumped out of bed, packed up, and left right away. I stayed with Kelly's parents' for a couple of nights.

Then, Kelly said, "Let's get a place together."

We found an apartment available September 1st.

Kelly and I moved into a furnished, upstairs duplex with two bedrooms, a large kitchen, a living room, and a small sitting area. Kelly and I loved to go dancing at a disco in downtown Milwaukee where Kelly met Jake. They started dating. One night when Jake was over, we talked about getting a dog. The following Saturday, Jake brought us to the pound, and we each picked out a dog. Mine was Chessie, a little black terrier mix. Kelly got Hilagus, a small collie mix.

**

Now that I was free of Mack, I started dating other men. I met a guy with the last name Bacardi. His father was one of the Bacardi brothers, who owned Bacardi rum. We dated for a while. Then, I met a man while I was waitressing, who called me over to his table one night when he was done eating. He was a blonde with a nice tan and athletic looking. He was built like an in-shape football player, and he was extremely good looking. His blue eyes looked at me with genuine interest, and he told me he watched me as I bussed the tables, noticing my frown lines. He said I looked like I was carrying the weight of the world on my shoulders, and told me I should smile more because I had a great smile.

A couple of nights later, he asked if I'd have dinner with him. The next night, we had supper at his hotel. He was in Milwaukee on business. We ended up in his hotel room, and started making out. When we got undressed, I ran my hand down his body to get him excited, and I couldn't find his penis. He had a micropenis. He got on top of me, and made the usual motions, eventually finishing. I felt nothing because there was nothing to feel. I got up, used the bathroom, got dressed, and left feeling very confused. I never saw him again.

I learned early on that men opened up to me, shared intimate stories with me which I mistook for closeness and love, mixed in with sex. I thought sex meant love, and I had been searching for love all my life. Therefore, I was open to men, encouraging them with my eyes to tell me their secrets. I went out with a social worker who was a regular at the restaurant. He had dark curly hair, brown eyes, and was very handsome. He seemed like a gentle, caring man, but after we had sex, he was cold and brought me home, no cuddling in the morning. There was also a bartender at the disco who had been flirting with me for months, and I finally went out with him. Again, on our date, he brought me right to his apartment for a quickie and a goodbye.

Eventually, I started losing respect for men who just wanted sex. When I met someone, I asked questions to find out who they were and what made them tick. I was confused and hurt when no one wanted to get to know me. They didn't want to discover the loving, passionate person I was. It left me feeling empty inside. I started writing in my journal how it wasn't safe to feel. I felt the strings of my heart snap one by one.

One night, I met Rick at the disco after work. I found out he was an FBI agent. I had never dated an FBI agent before. When he asked me to dinner, I said yes. After dinner, we went to his apartment. He got out his guitar and sang to me. I thought maybe he was a good guy, but then like the others he kept trying to get me to his bedroom. After a while, I gave in. Afterwards, I said I wanted to go out, and we went to a disco where I excused myself, ducking out the back door.

On top of the restaurant, I added a part-time, day job as a bank teller in the student bank at Marquette University. One morning, I met Edward, the son of the Bahamian ambassador, while I was working at the bank. He was six feet tall and dark skinned with a strong square jaw. He wore his hair in a medium afro, and his face lit up when he smiled. He was soft, emotional, and romantic, and his Bahamian accent warmed my heart. He asked me out, and we became involved in a very passionate relationship. We cooked meals together, went out to clubs, and spent many weekend nights in his bedroom or mine.

Kelly and I hung out during the week, taking our dogs for walks. Chessie and Hilagus got along really well. We spent the evenings talking about love and what we wanted from life.

Then one day, Mack appeared at the student bank. He waited until I took my break, we walked to the student cafeteria, and sat down. He told me he was going to jail the next week, and he asked me if I could smuggle weed into him. I'm not sure why, but I agreed to do it. Because I was working at a college, it was easy to score weed, and I brought it to Edward's. Kelly and I steamed open the bottom of a cigarette pack. I took out half the cigarettes, and replaced them with joints before sealing the bottom back up. It looked like a fresh unopened pack.

The next weekend, I went to visit Mack in jail with the cigarette pack in my purse. When I walked through the first locked door and they checked my purse for contraband, I got butterflies in my stomach.

A little voice inside said, "What if I get caught? What if I go to jail? Why am I doing this?"

I almost turned around to go back out that door. When they gave me my purse back, I walked down the long hallway. At the next door, a man buzzed me into the visiting room. He looked at me suspiciously, and I waited for him to say something. But he just watched me as I walked to Mack, and then, lost interest.

I sat down across from Mack. We made small talk as I nonchalantly opened my purse, and slid the cigarette pack out onto the table, making sure no one was looking at us. A few minutes later, Mack took the pack, opened the side where the cigarettes were, took out a cigarette, lit it, and then slipped the rest of the pack into his shirt pocket. It was slick, it worked, and when I left, I walked out the second locked door, breathing a sigh of relief, again telling myself I'd never do something like that again. But I was exhilarated I pulled it off.

After Edward's finals were over the third week of December, he went home to the Bahamas for his Christmas break. On Christmas Eve, Kelly and I went to a Catholic church. It was a beautiful service, but I was struck by all the gold I saw: chalices, candleholders, and the fine robes the clergy wore. I told Kelly it seemed so hypocritical and incongruent to the stories I believed and took comfort in as a child. My family claimed they sent Christmas presents, but I never received any. I checked with the post office, but they never found them. I had a quiet Christmas with a couple of small gifts from friends. It was lonely, but I cuddled with Chessie. We watched TV. Later that night, I heard a meowing at our front door; when I opened it, a golden-haired kitten ran in. He was cold, and seemed very hungry, so I gave him some tuna and water. Later, I bought kitty litter and cat food, and I named him Mother, short for motherfucker. I couldn't believe how well Chessie and Mother got along.

Starting the 1st of January, Cheryl, the new salad girl at the restaurant, needed a place to stay, and moved in with us. She was a beautiful girl with a medium size Afro and a dazzling smile. We sat up late at night telling each other stories and laughing. She slept on the couch in the little sitting area, and she had her own closet next to the couch. She was engaged to a guy from Evanston, Illinois. Sometimes, we all talked about selling our bodies, not having a pimp, just taking care of each other. It was always said in fun and joking around. The three of us felt close, like sisters.

In the middle of January, Edward came back from the Bahamas. A couple of days later, he came to the bank, and asked when my break was. He waited for me in the cafeteria, and told me he met someone else.

The beginning of February, I quit my job at the restaurant, and started working part-time at a jewelry store. I loved all the rings, necklaces, and bracelets. A week later, I got a call at work; it was Cheryl. She was hysterical, saying, through her tears, she'd had sex with the landlord's brother for money. He got a disease, blamed her, and was pounding on the duplex door. She wanted my help. So, I left work. When I got home, Kelly was there but Cheryl was gone. Kelly said Cheryl was too ashamed to face me. She packed up and went back to Evanston.

A week later, I made an appointment to see a doctor. He told me I was ten weeks pregnant. It was Edward's baby. I went to see Edward, and he said he wanted me to have the baby. He'd take the baby to the Bahamas in the summers, and I could have the baby during the school year. He didn't offer to be with me through the pregnancy or support me. I was on my own. I had just turned 22, and felt lost. I didn't know how I could take care of a child when I couldn't even take care of myself. I had no support system. I found a legal way to have an abortion through the University of Wisconsin.

Kelly found out she was pregnant a week after I did, and being a Jehovah's Witness, an abortion was not an answer for her. She suddenly moved out, and left her dog. I had to hunt her down, and found her at her brother's. When I knocked on her brother's door, she wouldn't answer. Instead, her brother opened the door and told me to stay away from Kelly. I said I had her dog, and he slammed the door in my face. I tied Hilagus to the door handle, and left. Her family seemed to be blaming me for Kelly's situation.

I was alone now in Milwaukee. Edward did not want me to get an abortion. Cheryl and Kelly were gone, and Mack was in jail. I sat for a few days in my dark apartment, cuddling with Chessie and Mother, trying to figure out what to do. The doctor said I needed someone to be with me for twenty-four hours after the procedure. The only person I could think of was my mother. After a couple of hours of indecision and a knot in my stomach, I called and asked her to come. I told her I had made all the arrangements, and I had found a doctor who did abortions in the hospital. Inside, I was an emotional wreck, and spent the next day crying. I just wanted someone to take me in their arms and tell me it was O.K., but I learned as a small child that there weren't any comforting arms for me.

My mother came the next morning, so I put away the tears, and appeared strong and confident. I couldn't let her see any weakness. I was admitted in the hospital that afternoon, and the abortion was scheduled for the next morning. Edward came to the hospital, and his last words to me were that I was killing his child. Then, he turned, and left. My mother didn't say a thing, except she didn't like him and his arrogance.

She didn't offer any words of comfort, and sat quietly staring at nothing. Eventually, she made small talk about my younger siblings, and was relieved when visiting hours were over. I had the abortion the next morning. When my mother came to get me, I felt empty and sad, but to my mother, I only showed that I was in control, relieved, and confident. I'd done the right thing. Inside, I was hearing Edward's last words echoing through my head. I craved a shoulder to cry on, someone I could show what I was truly feeling. My mother left early the next morning. I felt so alone. I turned to my journal and wrote, feeling numb, not being able to grasp all the emotions.

After my mother left, my landlord asked me to move to the smaller downstairs duplex. He and his recently divorced brother wanted the larger upstairs unit. I moved downstairs with Chessie and Mother, and the duplex only had a hotplate and a small refrigerator. It had a small kitchen and sitting room, a bathroom with only a shower, and a small bedroom. It was enough for Chessie, Mother, and me. After I moved in, I sat on the bed and cried.

Chessie laid her head in my lap, and Mother laid on my feet. I moved to Milwaukee, hoping to find what was missing in my life. Instead, I had many experiences, slept with many men, and only felt empty inside. I was disappointed. I thought the real world would be more loving and kinder than my family had been. But I was still invisible. Men didn't see me. I was just there for their physical gratification. I didn't belong anywhere.

A couple of weeks later, Mack showed up at the bank. He was out of jail. I saw him again, along with a couple of other men I met. I figured safety in numbers, no hurt involved, and if I stayed emotionally disconnected, I would survive.

One day, Mack left his jacket at my place. I picked it up to put on the back of the couch, and a letter dropped out. It was dated three months back, from a girl named Deborah. I was shocked when I read the letter. He had been writing her, and telling her he loved her just like he'd been saying to me. I was just another hustle to him. She wrote to him about their two-year-old child, and how she missed him when he was in jail. He had a family. I was so upset. I put up my guard so he couldn't hurt me again.

**

A couple of weeks, later my car stopped running. I towed it to my favorite gas station down the block from my apartment, and they said the engine froze because there wasn't any oil left in it. The cost to fix it was more than the car was worth. My father made arrangements to have it towed back to Minneapolis. I began having to rely on the bus. No friends, no car, which to me, meant no freedom. The only joy was bringing Chessie and Mother outside to play and do their business. At least, I had them to keep me company at night. I decided to move home and leave Milwaukee and the life I had created there. I called home, and talked to my mother. She called me a day later, and said William and Connie were driving home from Chicago in mid-March. They could swing by to pick me up in Milwaukee.

I gave a two-week notice at my jobs, and let my landlord know I was moving out. In the middle of March, William and Connie showed up at my doorstep, and helped me move from my shabby apartment. I sat in back with their children, who were two and four. It was a station wagon, and my animals rode in the back. When we got to my parents' house, William and Connie helped me unload the car. My parents now had another dog, a cat, and their wayward daughter living under their roof again. Even though I came home with my tail between my legs, I put on my defensive armor, and pretended I was fine. I couldn't show any weakness. We never talked about Milwaukee. I was back home to finish college.

Chapter 22
Devil in My Headlights, Angel on My Hood

After I moved home, I registered at the University for spring quarter, 1971, which started the last day of March. My parents agreed to pay tuition, but I bought my own books and supplies. I registered for sociology, history, psychology, and humanities. I also found a job working at The Establishment, a disco club in the Foshay Tower, in the evenings.

I had been home for two weeks when I got stomach cramps so bad I went to the doctor. He prescribed an antibiotic, and sent me home. My father went to get my prescription. When he got home, I asked him what the side effects were. After taking drugs with Luke, I was leery of any pill I took. My father said he didn't know, and I asked him if he'd call the pharmacy to find out.

He got angry and threw the pills against the wall saying, "Why can't you just trust me and your doctor?"

The reality was I didn't trust anybody or anything anymore. My life had been so separate from my parents, I felt like an alien in my own home. I experienced so many different things, and I felt like I was a different person. I felt even more alienated than I did as kid. I didn't really know where my home was.

My father, who was like Archie Bunker from *All in the Family,* and I had many heated discussions. One day, he read an article in the paper, and went off about welfare and why didn't people get off welfare when there were a lot of jobs out there and not enough people applying for them.

He said, "You'd think they'd want to *work* for a living!"

I explained that not all people had the same work ethic. I explained that a single mother with three children couldn't afford day care on minimum wage, so they turned tricks, and one trick could make as much in one hour, as working a whole day at a minimum wage job.

When you are faced with those conditions you do what you must do to survive.

My father said their lifestyle was wrong. I said no, it's just different. Another reason I wanted to be a social/corrections worker was so I could find resources and other alternatives for people in hard circumstances. He never quite knew what to do with my responses in these arguments. He wanted to judge them; I wanted to help them.

After I'd been attending classes and working for a month, I got home one night, and my parents were waiting up for me. They told me I had to leave their house that night. They were angry because they thought I was out partying with black people all night. I was shocked. I calmly told them that I didn't get off work until 1:00 a.m. and then I got something to eat at a restaurant. I was not out partying with anyone. I was working and eating. They said they wanted none of it, and told me to leave right then. I called Marty, who at that time was living with her grandmother, and asked if she could come get me.

The next day, Marty took me out to look for a place to live. I found a rooming house a mile from the University. My room was on the second floor, and it was large. One wall had beautiful natural wood built-in drawers and shelves with a floor-length mirror in the center. Built-in benches lined another wall. It had a huge walk-in closet, and a bed with a nightstand. I shared a bathroom with the rest of the boarders, and there was a community kitchen in the basement where I could cook my meals. Each tenant had their own locker to store their food and their own refrigerator shelf for the perishables. It had a large front porch, and the side yard was perfect for sunbathing. It was an amazing place.

I went home, and told my parents I found a rooming house I couldn't take my pets to. They said they would take care of them. So, I had a new home on 5th Street SE in a big beautiful rooming house that didn't allow men above the first floor. It felt safe and cozy. I moved in the next day.

I was happy with my new home because I felt safe and in control of my life for the first time. I wasn't living in the chaos of my family, and I didn't have a boyfriend. I wasn't living on the streets with life changing every few weeks. I loved the rooming house and having my own room. I bought a small turntable with speakers I put on a built-in shelf just under the floor length mirror. I sat for hours listening to music while I painted with watercolors or wrote in my journal. I became a big believer everyone should live alone. I cherished my time, and loved the stability of it. It was the first time I felt safe in a long time. I relaxed, and had time to think, write, water paint, and just be. I was alone in my own space; no men allowed. Sometimes, Marty slept over on an air mattress, and we'd lie in the sun the next day.

**

I loved working at The Establishment; I met so many different people. Until 7:00 p.m., the patrons were mostly white businessmen; after, the customers were mostly black folks who came to drink, dance, and party. The club was very popular. It had at one time been King Solomon's Mine, which had a lot of fights and police calls. The Establishment had a better reputation, and no violence or fights ever broke out the years I worked there. It had two off duty policemen working the door.

Just after I moved into the rooming house, I met Larry at The Establishment. He was in the military. He was buff and well dressed with a short Afro, and he drove a jeep. Larry spent half his time at the club sitting with me and talking while I worked. A couple of nights later, he asked if I wanted to get some food after work. We found a Perkins by downtown, and got some burgers and fries. A couple of nights later, we went out again, and he asked if I wanted to go to his place. He had a temporary apartment because he was from a military base in Texas and was here for special training. When we got back to his place, I discovered he was an amazing, thoughtful, and powerful lover. He was a great combination of gentle, loving, and rough. He showed me there were men who were kind and respectful. He was refreshing. I spent the next two nights at his place.

We started seeing each other every weekend, until one weekend, he told me his training was over. He was leaving at the end of the week. A couple of days later, I was at his apartment, and he went to get takeout for dinner. After he left, I snooped around and found a letter from his wife in Texas; it said she missed him and couldn't wait for him to come home. I sat there stunned. I had no idea he was married. I guess he wasn't as open and honest as I thought.

That weekend, I was waiting tables at work when a large man walked in the club like he owned the place. He went to Brian, the bartender, demanded a drink, and when he got it, he just walked away without paying. I asked the bartender who he was. He said Calvin, a pro football player. I asked him why he didn't make him pay for his drink.

He said, "With someone that big, you couldn't make him do anything."

When the bar closed, Marty and I walked out of the club, and a motorcycle came to a stop in front of me.

The guy on the bike said, "Calvin would like to give you a ride home on his motorcycle."

I told him I had a ride home. He left and soon there were two motorcycles heading my way. It was Calvin and his sidekick.

Calvin parked his motorcycle, leaned forward, looked at me, and said, "I would like to give you a ride home on my motorcycle."

I told him, "I already have a ride home."

On Monday, just after lunch, I was in my room when I heard a low voice calling my name. I opened the door, and there was Calvin. Men were not allowed on the 2nd floor, and he was walking along the 2nd floor hallway. I told him he couldn't be on this floor, and walked him downstairs. I didn't want to get into trouble. When I asked him how he knew where I lived, he said the bartender told him. I was seething inside because Brian gave out my personal information. Then, Calvin asked if he could give me a ride on his motorcycle. I said fine, hoping if I did, he would just go away. We rode along the river road out by the stockyards in South St. Paul. When he dropped me off, we made a date to play tennis Saturday morning. I didn't know what to do with this big lumbering man, who I didn't especially like. I went to work that night, and gave Brian a piece of my mind.

On Saturday, Calvin showed up at 10:00 a.m. We rode his motorcycle to the tennis courts on campus, and played. When we got back from the courts, he wanted to come up, and see my room. To this day, I don't know why I let him, but I did. We ended up having sex. I really didn't want to, but I learned that if I finally gave men what they wanted, they would go away. I never saw him again, so it worked.

**

I met interesting people when I started back at the university. One day, I started talking to a girl sitting next to me in class. Her name was Theresa, and somehow, the subject turned to religion and spirituality. She asked me if I'd ever heard of the Baha'i religion. She told me about the sacred Temple in Chicago, and said the Baha'i's believed in the equality of all people and rejected notions of racism and nationalism. It sounded interesting to me, and she invited me to go to their next meeting on Tuesday evening. I told her I didn't have a car, and she said she could pick me up.

Monday, the night before the meeting, I had a powerful dream. I was standing in a room with large windows. It was dark, and there was lightning flashing outside. Suddenly, a man stood before me. He was dressed in long flowing robes; he had a long gray/white beard that hung down to his chest. His gray hair was thin at the top, and the rest was long, hanging down to his shoulders. He looked at me with intense dark eyes and, motioned for me to follow him. He brought me outside, and reached out his arm to show me everything around me. We were standing on a mountaintop, and I could see everywhere. But it was dark;

169

everything was in shadows. I woke up feeling uneasy. I didn't know what it meant, but the emotions I felt were powerful and haunting.

I got up on Tuesday, and went to my classes, trying to shake the dream loose from my thoughts. After supper, Theresa picked me up. We parked in front of a small white house, and walked up to the front door. Theresa introduced me to Tom when he opened the door and led us down the hallway to a meeting room. As I walked down the hall, I noticed a photo on the wall of a man kneeling by a large rock, praying. I couldn't move, my feet were stuck to the floor, and my eyes couldn't stop looking at the man praying. It was the man in my dream: same clothes, same hair, and same beard. I got goose bumps so big I thought everyone could see them.

Finally, I found my voice and asked, "Who is that?"

Theresa said he was the esteemed prophet of the Baha'i faith, Abdu'l-Baha.

I attended the meeting, not hearing a word because my thoughts kept going back to my dream. I wanted to run out of the house; it was too weird to have a prophet be in my dream. I wanted to escape. I felt like my inner place and soul had been violated by something I knew nothing about. He had pushed his way into my dream, an intimate space. I didn't invite him in. He was an intruder in my dream. After the meeting, Theresa took me home, and after, I avoided anything Baha'i.

A couple of weeks later, I met Carla, who read palms and analyzed handwriting. She read mine, and I was amazed. She taught me about palmistry, and I went out and bought books on handwriting analysis and palmistry. I already knew about astrology. Things started to happen to me. When I waitressed, and I walked up to a customer, an astrology sign flashed in my head. I asked what they were, and I was right.

My friends would mention a new guy they met, and I'd say, "Oh he's a Virgo."

They'd check it out, and I'd be right. I studied astrology, and learned about charts and how we all had eleven signs. I bought ephemeral tables, and started working on my chart and eventually the charts of others. I used astrology to understand someone I met quickly, a filter I put someone through to see if I could trust them and let them in closer.

I also started having a unique experience called *astral projection*, which meant my soul left my body and took a journey outside while being tethered to it. One time, I woke up with my eyes open, though my physical eyes were closed. I could feel a rush as my soul started to move up and out of my body. Then, I looked down, and saw myself lying there. Sometimes, I tried to walk somewhere, and see something in the next room. I couldn't walk far before I went back to my body. At times, it felt like my soul was wrestling with something under my skin. I didn't do drugs or drink alcohol; this was something that just started happening to me when I was resting.

I ran into AJ one day after class. She and Mahmood had moved back to the Twin Cities, and lived by campus. AJ looked good. I visited them in their duplex, and found out AJ was pregnant. Eventually, Marty decided she didn't want to live at her grandmother's anymore and she moved into my rooming house. Her room was right next door to mine, and it was fun having her living in the same house.

Chapter 23
I Wonder If You're Thinking of Me Tonight

In May, I waited on a customer at work who told me he played ball.

I thought, "Oh, a softball league after work."

Then I found out played ball meant professional baseball for the Chicago White Sox. Then, one day, I met a pitcher for the Twins.

Later that week, a group of well-dressed men started coming to The Establishment for a drink later in the evening. One of them kept smiling at me. After seeing him a few nights, he came up, and spoke to me.

I think his first words were, "Do you wanna speak?"

Then, Lorenzo introduced himself, and asked if he could take me to get something to eat. When the bar closed, we went to an all-night diner, and talked. I learned he played first base for the Minnesota Twins, and was from Cuba. He asked about my family and me, and talked about the guys he played baseball with and where he played before the Twins. He told me he came from Cuba when he was 17 years old to play baseball, not knowing any English. He learned his English mostly by watching TV and movies.

The second time we went out, it was my night off, and we walked around Lake of the Isles. We held hands. The moon was full, and it reflected a path leading across the water. We each spoke about our parents and our childhoods. We went out for dinner at Embers restaurant, we just kept talking. He was so easy to talk to. He seemed to really listen and care about what I had to say, and I felt like he wanted to get to know me. He drove me home, and walked me to the door. Then, he left. On our third date, he had just returned from a string of out-of-town games. He picked me up that night, and brought me some R & B record albums. I wore out those albums when he was out of town, and every note reminded me of him. After I put the albums in my room, we went out with some of the other ballplayers and their dates for dinner and drinks downtown.

That night, when he walked me to my door, I asked him why he didn't ever try to kiss me. He said he wanted to, but he was waiting to make sure if it was OK. Then, he kissed me. It was sweet and sensual, and I felt it through my whole body. I cared about this man. On the fourth date, he brought me home to an apartment he shared on Killebrew Drive with another ball player. His roommate wasn't home. We talked a lot about our lives, and we took a shower together, making lots of suds and laughing. I felt safe with him. He was the first man I'd met in a while that wasn't just trying to get me in bed for the night. He seemed to want a real relationship. He was romantic, respectful, and interested in who I was. I ended up spending the night.

One weekend in June, my parents asked me to babysit Becca and Derek for the weekend because they were going out of town. I packed a few things, and went home. Lorenzo came over after my siblings were in bed. He was impressed with the house and area we lived in, and before he left, he handed me a gun.

I looked at him like he was crazy, and asked, "What is that for?"

He explained that anyone living in such a nice house, alone, needs protection, and insisted I take it. When I used to babysit I'd always wonder what I'd do if someone broke in. I took the gun, but was more afraid of *it* than an intruder. I slept in my parents' bedroom, and hid the gun in a dresser drawer, buried underneath my mother's nightgowns and socks. It made me so nervous, I had trouble sleeping, and laid awake with violent images playing through my mind. When I saw Lorenzo the next day, I handed him a paper sack with the gun in it and told him to put it away. When he locked it in his trunk, I breathed a sigh of relief.

When Lorenzo played home games, we spent all our free time together. If the games were close by, like Chicago, I met him there. When I finished work, we went out with his buddies to get food, and I spent nights at his apartment on Killebrew Drive. One night, we were talking, and he told me he was married. They had been separated for three years. He showed me a picture of his wife and five kids. I was glad he was honest with me. He said when he was traded to the Twins, his wife stayed in Los Angeles.

The first time I went to see Lorenzo on the road, I traveled by train to Chicago. I chose a train because I was nervous about flying. I took a cab from the train depot to the hotel where he was staying, and there was a key waiting for me at the front desk. Lorenzo said he'd call me when he was back from playing his afternoon game. It got later and later, and I couldn't figure out what happened. It was a day game, and it was almost 8:00 p.m. I was alone in Chicago, and I started feeling anxious. What if

Lorenzo didn't call? I didn't have the money to pay for the hotel room. Finally, he called. He had just gotten back to his room. We had a minor tiff. He brought me to some clubs on the southside of Chicago, and we had dinner and drinks.

The next night when I went to his game, I took a cab to Comiskey Park, and went to the will call window to get my ticket. I watched the game, and when it ended, I expected to just get a cab at a cabstand. But there were no cabs. I walked around the whole stadium looking. There were none. I started to panic—*how was I going to get back to my hotel?* I looked around, and saw a bank of pay phones a block down, and called a cab company. I kept getting a busy signal. I walked back to the stadium, and couldn't figure out what to do.

A cop, who was directing traffic around the stadium, asked if I was OK. I explained to him I needed a cab to my hotel. He said when he was done, he could give me a ride.

I looked at him, suspiciously, and said, "Maybe."

I continued to walk around the outside of the stadium hoping to hail a passing cab. I couldn't believe there were no cabs. I stood there alone. Eventually, I went back, and accepted the invitation from the police officer. He brought me to the hotel, and asked if he could come in and buy me a drink. I told him I was meeting someone in the bar in a half hour. I thanked him, and went into the hotel. I was so relieved to get to my room.

Lorenzo showed up on time, and he held me while I explained my harrowing experience. We went out for a late dinner. There was no game scheduled the next day, so we made plans to see Eddie Harris at a jazz club. I loved Eddie Harris and his saxophone. The next day, Lorenzo insisted I fly home, and bought me an airplane ticket. It had been awhile since I'd flown, and I was nervous, so I sat between two guys.

The plane taxied down the runway, and just as the wheels left the ground, I yelled at the top of my lungs, "Stop the plane! I've got to get off; stop the plane!"

A stewardess came over to calm me down, and the guys sitting next to me told me it was OK. I started to relax. I was embarrassed. It was a short flight, and when we landed, I thanked the two guys. One guy told me to fly again, right away, so I wouldn't develop a phobia. But when I was in the terminal, I breathed a sigh of relief, and knew I'd never fly on a plane again. I had lost control. Whenever I visited Lorenzo in another city, I drove or took a train. My friends and I went to several Twins games that summer with complimentary tickets from Lorenzo.

One day, Lorenzo told me his aunt from Puerto Rico called him. She astral projected, and saw me with him. She was concerned because of Lorenzo's wife in Los Angeles, and wanted to check in with him. She told him that she saw my aura, and knew I was a good person, and thought I was good for him. She told him I had the same abilities as her, meaning I was psychic and able to astral project too.

Lorenzo and I were driving around the lakes one day, and he asked about my family, whom I hadn't seen much since I moved to the rooming house. He said family was important, and he wanted to meet mine. He was so grounded and nurturing. I was twenty-two, and he was thirty-four and protective of me.

Meanwhile, my family had been limping along. My parents were still drinking too much. One night, I was talking to the bouncer, a city cop who was moonlighting at The Establishment. I mentioned I grew up on Tarrymore Avenue. He looked at me funny, and asked what my address was. He said he was called to my parents' house a few times because of excessive drinking and domestic violence. Becca and Derek called them.

In August, I heard from Becca that my parents were moving from Tarrymore and buying a house in Burnsville. I went home that weekend to check in, and my parents, Becca, and Derek, and I all piled in the car. We drove to Burnsville, and they showed me their new house, a three-bedroom, single level home. They moved in the first of September. They had a family dinner shortly after they moved in, and Lorenzo came with me. When Lorenzo walked in the house, my parents gushed over him, and Derek just stared at him. He was famous, and my father and brother were big Twins fans. After that, whenever we visited my parents, Lorenzo brought Derek a gift: a baseball mitt, a fishing rod, a signed baseball from the whole team, or something he received from a company he was promoting. Lorenzo was accepted into my family, and I became a worthy member of the household, and because of his status as a pro athlete, they accepted me going out with someone black. There were evenings at my parents' when we had rousing games of ping-pong. Lorenzo was good with my younger brother and sister and charming to my parents.

One morning, after Lorenzo and I had been at my parents, my mother called, and asked me if I knew Lorenzo was married. I said, yes, I did, but that he was separated from his wife. I *didn't* tell my mother I loved Lorenzo, and the way he treated me made me feel worthwhile and seen. Meeting him helped stabilize something inside me, keeping me from falling off the edge. He valued my going to the university, and wanted me to succeed. He believed I would be somebody. I knew he was married, but I felt like I helped keep his marriage safe because I would never take him away from his family. I only needed him in my life for a period of time to balance all the bad experiences I'd had with men. He was the prince on the white horse I dreamt about when I was a little girl. He saved me, and no matter what happened in our relationship, he was in my life when I needed him to be.

Our relationship was intense, and as summer wound down, we felt sad because he would be leaving to play winter ball in South America. We shared passionate nights of lovemaking, and many hours talking like best friends. I opened myself to him more completely than I ever had with a man. Lorenzo stayed in his apartment until the middle of October. Our last day and night were passionate because we didn't know when we'd see each other again.

The next day, I wrote in my journal, "Oh, how we loved last night, and only with him have I loved like I did last night."

Then, it was goodbye until the spring when he'd be back to play ball.

Chapter 24
Black Tears Are Falling

When I started classes at the University in the fall, I carried nineteen credits a quarter instead of the usual twelve credits because I wanted to graduate in a year. After Lorenzo left in October, I added another part-time job waiting tables Saturday and Sunday mornings at the Sherman Hotel downtown. In other words, I was keeping busy until Lorenzo returned in the spring.

I enjoyed waiting tables at the Sherman and serving breakfast. There was no alcohol or loud music playing. Just a quiet dining area with people drinking their cups of coffee, reading their newspapers, and enjoying a breakfast of eggs and toast, pancakes and bacon, or maybe just bagels with cream cheese and fresh fruit.

One morning, when I got to work, there was all this buzz about a famous conductor staying at the Sherman. When I went out to wait on tables, there was an older gentleman sitting alone. He ordered his breakfast, and when I brought him his food, he asked me a veiled question about what was there to do at night in Minneapolis and was I available to show someone around who was new to the city. I explained I was a college student, and needed time to study because I was working two jobs.

He said, "What a shame: someone as pretty as you, spending all her evenings studying or working."

Then, he winked at me, and gave me a generous tip when he left.

As he walked out of the restaurant, one of the waiters came up to me, and told me my customer was the famous conductor everyone was talking about. I told him I thought the famous conductor had propositioned me. Then, he whispered to me the Sherman Hotel was very discreetly connected to call girls. I was shocked. I had no idea.

A couple months into school, burning the candle at both ends caught up with me. On Sunday at 2:00 a.m., I set my alarm for 6:00 a.m. to get up to serve breakfast at the Sherman, and went to sleep. The phone woke me up, and I walked across the room to answer it. AJ asked me if I was OK.

I said, "Yes, why?"

She told me she called me the day before, and I sounded funny. Suddenly, feeling fully awake, I asked her what day it was. When she said Monday, I realized I had slept straight through Sunday. I decided to call the Sherman, apologize for not showing up Sunday, and tell them I needed to quit.

**

I finally got used to Lorenzo being gone, and I started to settle into a nice routine. Most nights I made supper at home in the basement kitchen. I enjoyed coming up with my own recipes as I went along. My favorite was cooking a steak cut into strips in a frying pan with a little butter, adding red and green peppers, onion, and some French dressing and letting it simmer together. Then, I made white rice. I poured the meat concoction over my rice; it was delicious. My other favorite was tomato soup with grilled cheese sandwiches. Sometimes, I put ham and sautéed onions in my grilled cheese. I felt like I was learning to take care of myself by trying to slow things down.

I started browsing in bookstores; if I had seven dollars left in my pocket for the week, I very often bought books. One day, I was in a unique bookstore, and saw a beautiful deck of Tarot cards. These fortune-telling cards, had colorful pictures: "The Hanged Man," "The Magician," "The Lovers," "The Tower," and "The Sun." I bought a book that interpreted the cards, and explained the types of readings I could do. I began reading my cards, then my friends' cards, and eventually, read friends of friends' cards. I read at gatherings. People couldn't believe how accurate my readings were. Pretty soon, when people were making a major decision in their life or facing some challenge, they came to me for a reading to clarify their path. I was finding some pieces of myself that I enjoyed inside all the chaos.

I looked forward to walking to campus every day, feeling the sun on my face. But I hated rushing when I was late, and I had to hitchhike to get there on time. One day, a guy picked me up who was driving a van; he looked OK, and so I got in. Then, something didn't feel right. I started to get a knot in my stomach. He drove off, looking me up and down.

He said, "You must be strong to be hitchhiking."

He told me that my legs looked muscular and I must be good in bed. We drove to the corner where I wanted to get out, but he kept going. I told him he missed my corner. He just looked at me, and

178

smiled. The knot in my stomach grew tighter. I said, I had to get out now; I was going to be late for class. About five blocks past my drop off place, I saw the stoplight was yellow, and would soon be red. We were in the left lane. As he slowed down for the stoplight, I grabbed the door handle, and flew out of the car, surprising the driver of the car in the right lane. I ran around his car, and took off down the block. After, I equipped myself with a five-inch long, thick metal pin used in knitting. I kept it in my book bag as a weapon if anything happened again or if I needed to hitchhike.

**

I loved working at The Establishment, especially the nights I was the disc jockey. I sat on a platform with two turntables set up by a stainless-steel dance floor. After I put on a record, I could dance if someone asked me. I knew how to pace the music, so the dance floor was always full. I started with a fast song like "The Good Foot," then "War," then I slowed it down with "Me and Mrs. Jones". I danced the night away, and got paid. I learned all the "in" dances: The Good Foot, The Penguin, The Bump, the Calypso and line dances. A man from Arthur Murray studio came in occasionally to learn the latest dances, and then went back to his studio to teach his students.

While I was working at The Establishment, guys always wanted to buy me drinks, and I told them I didn't drink.

Or they came up to me, and said, "What are you high on? I wish I had some."

I told them, "I'm high on life; I don't drink or do drugs."

They asked me what I did for fun, and I said, "The same thing as you, but I'm not getting high or drinking while I'm doing it."

I told them I liked to remember things I did. They walked away scratching their heads. The reality was I could never let go enough to drink or do drugs because I knew there was nobody who had my back if I was drunk or high. I felt like I always had to be in control.

After work, Marty and I loved to go to after-hours parties where there was dancing and good music. There was one couple always there, Lou and Sandy. Lou worked as a car salesman and a loan shark. He always asked if we needed any money. We found out, later, he charged a very high interest rate. Through my job and my partying, I got to know just about every drug dealer and pimp in the city. I knew everyone from pro athletes to the city's street hustlers. I ran into a high school friend during those years, and she told me I was really living on the edge.

Working at The Establishment was an education. I learned about undercover cops. One night, there was a new customer sitting at the bar, throwing around his money. His friend, a nice looking, clean-cut guy, came over to me. I was waitressing that night. The nice-looking guy told me his friend was looking for company and a place to stay the night. He asked if I knew of anyone who'd be interested. He said his friend had money, and was a lot of fun.

I acted like I didn't know what he was really asking, and said innocently, "If you walk out the front door of the club, and look down to the right, you'll see the YMCA. I heard the rooms are nice and clean, and it's really affordable. It's centrally located, so there are a number of places you can walk to."

The man looked at me, frustrated, and I walked away, carrying my drink orders. Later that night, Bruce told me the man who was talking to me was an undercover cop. He said there had been rumors one of the waitresses in the club was involved in prostitution.

While I was working at The Establishment, I loved to dance, I walked everywhere, and I was too busy to eat much. I never quite made being five feet tall. I dressed in style, wearing hot pants, very short shorts, and a tight-fitting top. When I walked from the bus stop to work, I always got whistles and attention. One night, there was a man I knew who worked in advertising at the bar. He started talking to me about taking my picture. He had this idea for a poster: It would be a picture of an old-fashioned bicycle with a large front wheel and two small back wheels. He wanted me pose nude next to it. He said he would photograph me from behind because I had the old-fashioned look of a woman's body with bigger hips and buttocks of the post-war days. I would be looking over my shoulder, so my profile would show, but he would brush out the features. I told him, *no*, I felt uncomfortable posing nude for anyone.

**

At Christmas that year, I felt melancholy. I worked Christmas Eve at The Establishment, and it had been three years since I'd spent Christmas Eve with my family. But I felt more at home in the darkened club, feeling the bass music thumping through the floorboards, watching people from many walks of life laughing and dancing. It felt real, and made me feel more alive than sitting around a Christmas tree singing carols with my family who kept their secrets buried, trying to be something they weren't, wearing the right clothes, and saying the right things to show the world our family was fine. There were so many lies, so much denial, and an abundance of pretending with smiles on their faces. I couldn't sit there and pretend. I preferred the dim lights and loud music, where people expressed their emotions through dancing. They weren't pretending. They knew everything wasn't all right, so they laughed and partied, and I sat there safe in my loneliness, a place I had been before.

In January, I received a letter from Lorenzo in Argentina, talking about when we would see each other again. I couldn't wait to have him back in my life. I liked how I felt inside when I was with him. Then in late winter, I heard on the radio that Lorenzo was traded to the Cleveland Indians. I was shocked. Would I ever see him again? I waited anxiously for his next letter or phone call. I was angry by the time he finally called a month later. He said he was sorry, but he didn't know he was traded until he heard it on the news. Then, he had to figure out what he was going to do before he could call me. We sat on the phone, both quiet for a moment; then he said quietly that his team would be in Minneapolis for a few games, and I could come to Chicago, and Kansas City, so we'd still see each other, just not as often. When I hung up the phone, I felt empty inside; we wouldn't really be together. We'd just have a few weekends scattered throughout the summer. I was devastated. The bubble of happiness I'd been living in burst, and I landed hard on my new reality. I was alone again.

I started dating and trying to find someone to fill in the hole Lorenzo left. But there was no one like him.

One night after work, I was feeling down. Brian and I were cleaning up after the bar was closed. We started talking; it felt good to talk to him; we had become friends over the last year. Then, he asked if I wanted to get something to eat. We went to Embers restaurant, and he invited me over to his apartment. I couldn't believe his place. It was in the first floor of a mansion by Lake of the Isles. His entrance was in the back. It was beautiful. We ended up in bed, and had friendship sex. No real passion— just let's-keep-each-other-company-for-the-night sex.

A couple of days later, Lloyd, a regular at the club, asked me to a party. He taught grade school health and physical education, and had a tight, muscular build. He was only about five-eight, and wore his afro short. When I went to his party, I ended up in his bed after everyone left. But I soon found out he was a teacher by day and a drug dealer at night. I felt so lost, and I kept looking for someone to replace Lorenzo. I dated a couple of other faceless men so I could keep ahead of my loneliness.

But at the end of April, I got real sick. I had bad stomach cramps. I thought it was a painful period, so I went to work. When I got home later, I couldn't sleep because the pain was so bad. I called a cab, and went to the County General Hospital. When I got there, they put me on a bed, and pulled a curtain around me. My fever was so high, I was delirious, and kept passing out and coming to hearing my moans and groans.

One time, I heard a nurse say, "She's lost control of her bowels and messed herself."

I felt their hands undressing me and pulling the dirty sheet from underneath me, replacing it with a clean one. Then, I passed out again until a nurse, who was taking my vitals, woke me up asking if anyone ever told me I had a heart murmur. I said no and passed out again.

When I finally woke up the next day, I was dressed in hospital scrubs, lying in a bed in a hospital ward with an IV drip of antibiotics trailing into my arm to get rid of my infection. I had Pelvic Inflammatory Disease caused from having gonorrhea. It turns out, I hadn't had any symptoms before, and it traveled up to my uterus. I wasn't contagious. I didn't know how long I had it or who gave it to me; I could have gotten it in Milwaukee, but it was probably one of the faceless men I dated after I found out Lorenzo wasn't coming back.

I felt lonely lying there because no one would even know I was missing. I started getting to know the other girls in my ward because the nurse would push our beds into the hall so we could smoke. Juanita and I became friends, and when I left the hospital, I loaned her my suitcase for a trip she and her boyfriend were taking. I never saw her or my suitcase again.

I went to the hospital early Sunday morning, and was finally released Thursday morning. When I left the hospital, the doctor told me I needed time for my body to heal and to finish my oral antibiotics before I had sex again. I worked Friday and Saturday night, but rested all day Sunday. Monday, I was back at school, trying to catch up on the work from the days I had missed.

Later that week, Lorenzo called me because his team was in town. I was so excited to see him and have him hold me. I needed to feel the comfort he provided and see the look in his eyes. I heard him say how much he missed me, and I should come as soon as possible. I called a cab. It was 1:00 in the morning, and when I got in the cab, the cab driver looked at me suspiciously, like he was trying to figure out why I was going to a hotel that time of night with my little overnight bag. I know he wanted to ask me something, but he never did. It made me feel a little like a call girl.

When I got there, I told Lorenzo my doctor told me to refrain from sex for a couple of weeks because of a female issue. Lorenzo understood, and hugged me. We cuddled and talked, kissing the night away. When the sun started to show itself, we fell asleep. I opened my eyes a few hours later, and Lorenzo had ordered room service. While we ate a very late breakfast, he gave me a necklace he bought in South America; it was gold with the word Aquario engraved on it because I was an Aquarius. It felt so good to be in his arms again, feeling how much he cared about me. I wished he didn't ever have to leave.

After he left, I decided I was sick of the male harassment at work. My hair was long — it was down past my shoulders — so I thought if I cut it all off, it would drive away the unwanted attention. I took my scissors and I cut my long hair into a Pixie style. My hair was two inches long all over my head. When I went to The Establishment the next night, Brian did a double take because he didn't recognize me. I still got unwanted attention.

**

In May 1972, there were demonstrations in front of the student union at the University. The demonstrations became violent with people throwing rocks and sticks at the police I felt like we were fighting with police officers when the real issue was the war. The police started throwing tear gas at us, and we dispersed and ran. The next day, the police were marching in formation on the University commons, and classes were cancelled.

As I was walking home across the campus, skirting around the commons area, I heard the words in my head to a Buffalo Springfield song: *What a field day for the heat. A thousand people in the street. Singing songs and carrying signs. Mostly saying, "hooray for our side." Hey, what's that sound? Everybody look what's going down.* The words echoed through my head as I became aware of the police just on the other side of the college buildings. My curiosity pulled me along, and suddenly, I was walking around the side of a building to look at the police marching. As I peeked around the building, a policeman saw me, and threw a tear gas canister at me. My eyes were watering and burning. My mouth felt like I'd been chewing on hot peppers. I ran away quickly, coughing and wiping my eyes. I thought I'd never see clearly again. I couldn't believe our world had come to this. The tears in my eyes from the gas became real tears pouring down my cheeks at the world I was living in.

At the end of the school year, I still needed five more classes to graduate. I took three classes first summer session and two classes the second summer session. In my haste to register, I ended up taking physics and chemistry, which had overlapping, mandatory labs. The people who registered me didn't catch it, and neither did I. I worked something out with the professors and alternated labs during the week, which made a very close call in both classes for getting a pass.

My physics professor was an older, pudgy, dumpy man with thinning, brownish gray hair. I went in a couple of times to get help because I was struggling with some of the concepts. A couple of times, when I was outside waiting on the steps for the class to start, he stopped to talk to me. He asked me questions, like, was I working my way through college? And what were my future plans? Then he asked me where I worked. Did I work every night? I started feeling a little uncomfortable, but then he glanced at his watch, and rushed into the building.

I was scheduled to graduate at the end of August. As my physics class was winding down, I realized I was on the edge of getting a pass for the class. I went in, and asked the professor what I could do— maybe write a paper, attend an extra lab? He said he'd think about it. He told me to call him after the final. When I called, he said he hadn't graded my final yet and he'd call me the next day.

That night I was surprised to see him walk in The Establishment and sit in my waitressing section. I waited on him, and asked if he knew anything about my grade. Again, he was evasive, and put me off. When I served him his third drink, he told me he was a Mormon and leaving the next day for Salt Lake City where his wife lived. He cleared his throat, and asked if I was busy after work that night or maybe I had some time for a lonely professor. I was shocked. I covered it by saying I had to study for a morning final. Then, I asked him if he needed another drink. He said no, and when I went by his table a few minutes later, he was gone. I knew he was avoiding telling me my grade on purpose, and by avoiding his proposition, I probably wouldn't pass. But the next day, when I called and talked to his TA, he said I had passed. In those days, I didn't realize I could lodge a complaint.

**

Just before graduation, I met Andre at work. He was from Chicago, and had a job interview at the airport. He asked me out to dinner, and after, we went back to his hotel. He told me what this job meant to him and his life. We sat up almost all night talking. He seemed so vulnerable. I just let him talk. Eventually, we ended up in bed. My girlfriends teased me about being a social worker with guys, wanting to fix and take care of them.

A couple weeks later, he came in the bar looking terrible. He was a totally different person, drunk, with a girl on each arm, acting like a jerk. He went, and sat at a table upstairs, constantly calling me to his table, demanding I buy him a drink. At one point, he got up, and grabbed my arm angrily. I told him he was acting like a jerk, and got away from him. When the bar had last call, I was at my drink station getting my last order filled when Andre came out of the bathroom. He saw me, and stood directly behind me, pinning me to the bar, asking who I thought I was. I turned, pushed him away, and walked to the other end of the bar to get my drink order.

He followed me, spitting out words like "You honky bitch, who do you think you are? You think you're better than me."

Finally, I'd had enough.

Shaking with anger, I turned, and said, "You black bastard, stay out of my face; get the hell away from me."

The bartender signaled to the bouncer, who came over, grabbed Andre by the elbow, and escorted him from the bar. I had lost control; I had never talked like that before. I was angry and scared.

My co-workers were surprised at my language, and so was I. I didn't feel negative about black people, but I wanted to hurt his feelings. I don't think I ever used that phrase again. The girls he came with told me he was kicked out of the bar down the street, and he didn't get the airport job. When the bouncer saw Andre waiting outside the bar when it closed, he escorted Marty and me to her car. It was a Friday night. I didn't see any sign of Andre on Saturday night.

But on Sunday, when I worked as a disc jockey and waitress because it was a slow night, Andre came in looking like he hadn't slept in days. He had beard stubble like he hadn't shaved, and he wore sunglasses. He came in with a coat folded over his left arm, and he turned his head towards me, following every move I made. He sat at the bar, ordered an orange juice, and kept his back to the bar to watch me. I kept serving drinks and putting on the music. I started getting the feeling he had a gun under the coat on his arm; I kept imagining something whiz by my ear. I was afraid I'd look down and see blood on my shirt. I asked the bouncer to keep an eye on Andre, and I told him what I suspected. Andre sat there all night watching me, sipping his orange juice. When he finally got up and left, the bouncer said I was lucky. He said *if* Andre had a gun, because there were so few customers, he couldn't use it without being seen.

A couple of weeks later, Andre came in on a Friday night. He looked back to normal, smiling and laughing. He was well-dressed and clean-shaven. When he saw me, he gave me a nod and a smile. That was the last time I saw him. I heard he went back to Chicago.

Chapter 25
Runnin' The Streets

On August 25, 1972, I graduated from the University of Minnesota in social work/criminal justice with a minor in psychology and black studies. My family came to the ceremony. As I stood outside on the Northrup mall, wearing my cap and gown listening to the words of the speakers, I realized I wanted to make a difference in the world. I wanted to be somebody special and help others. I wanted my life to have meaning.

When the ceremony ended, my family and I celebrated at the Decathlon Club where my father was a member. We had dinner in their dining room, and I spent the evening asking my siblings questions about their life and what they had been doing, complimenting my sister's dress and new haircut. It was fun, and there was a lot of conversation around the table. It had been a while since we had all been together.

When I was driving home, I realized that no one at the table asked about me. No one seemed interested in what I was doing or noticed my new dress or haircut. I suddenly felt drained by all the energy I put out to connect with my family. I loved hearing their stories, but it felt like a one-sided relationship. Even Becca, who I had become really close with, treated me like a stranger when it was the whole family. I felt like the black sheep.

Later that year, at family gatherings and church functions, I heard my father bragging to everyone that I was a college graduate. He'd say it with such pride, like he had something to do with me graduating. He used me to show people what a good father he was. When he did that, I just looked at him with amazement. If only the world could see I graduated despite my father.

**

A week after graduation, Marty and I left for a trip out east. We took a train to New York, and stayed with a friend of hers who lived in a rooming house for women in mid-Manhattan. We joked as we got off the train, noticing how much we looked like hayseeds from Minnesota, dressed in our red and white checked shirts, blue jeans, and tennis shoes. As we walked from the train depot to her friend's rooming house, where we reserved a guest room, we were propositioned by a couple of police officers. They made us feel really uncomfortable. After we got safely away from them, I looked at Marty, and said that New York must be a dangerous place if you can't even trust the cops.

That night, we went to see *Shaft*; it was really cool seeing it in New York instead of Minnesota. The next day, we went to a concert in Central Park and sampled New York pizza, bagels, and cream cheese. We went out to a couple of clubs for dancing and took walks in Central Park. Then, we took a greyhound bus to Connecticut where her uncle lived with his wife and three kids. We borrowed his car, and drove around Vermont looking at houses that were built in the 1800's. We took a day trip to Boston.

Marty's uncle woke me up every morning by kissing my neck, his lips traveling up to my cheek. I felt really uncomfortable with it, and Marty said her uncle always showed a lot of affection, which my family didn't. She made it sound normal, and because of my screwed-up family, she thought I was overreacting. A year later, Marty found out he sexually abused his daughters and a cousin of Marty's, and eventually, tried something with Marty.

From Connecticut, we took a train to Washington, DC, and stayed with her other uncle who was a minister who fought for social justice. We stayed in his basement for a couple of nights, and visited the tourist monuments but not the White House.

**

While I was gone, my mother invited Eileen and a couple of other women over for lunch. It was an afternoon get-together with a lot of drinking. Mid-afternoon, Eileen left to drive home. About four blocks from my mother's house, she was driving through an intersection, and a car hit her on the driver's side. An ambulance came, and brought her to the hospital.

When my mother got a call from Eileen's daughter an hour later, she said Eileen was doing okay. But the next day, there was a complication, a blood clot or something, and she died. She was my mother's "sister" and closest friend. My mother seemed lost after that.

I didn't hear about the accident or the funeral until I returned home ten days later. I was shocked, and pictured Eileen sewing my dresses and talking about the upcoming dances. I saw her family and mine at family dinners, sitting on her screened in porch telling stories of her and my mother's past. When I was younger, she "hired" me to come and wash her kitchen floors or help her in the kitchen, and I even got paid. She was the only one who gave me books over the years, and she was just suddenly gone like Skippy and Mrs. Galle. I never got to see her again, or say goodbye.

My mother didn't talk about it; maybe, she felt guilty because Eileen shouldn't have been driving after drinking so much. I went to see Eileen's oldest daughter, Cheryl, a couple of weeks later, and we exchanged stories about Eileen over the years.

**

When we got home from our trip, Marty and I decided to get an apartment and move out of the rooming house. I hated to leave my room because it felt like a safe haven to me. Even years later, when I drove by that place, I felt the same warm feelings of safety when I saw it. Marty and I eventually found a great duplex on Irving Avenue N. just off Glenwood Avenue by the projects in north Minneapolis. The little section was called "Finn Town." A lot of the homes had saunas. There was a grocery store just down the block and a great restaurant called Market Bar-B-Que with great ribs and fries.

I started working full time doing figure work for Manpower, a temp agency. During tax season, I used a ten-key adding machine and entered long columns of numbers, and then wrote down the total. I added the totals together, and that number matched another number. There was something therapeutic about working with numbers because with figure work, there was a definite right and wrong answer. I sometimes wished life was like that.

Marty got a job working at the Red Door, a walk-in clinic for people with venereal diseases and she volunteered at Planned Parenthood. Around this time, I started feeling worthless and empty. I was no longer going to school, and working temp jobs brought money in but was meaningless work. I wanted something more, and felt like I wasn't going anywhere, a feeling of being profoundly invisible with no purpose, no direction. I was just treading water, waiting.

Then, I met someone at a club; he was a great dancer and a smooth talker, and I ended up going to his place. When we got to his house, we walked down into a basement that smelled like dirty socks stuffed into worn tennis shoes. There was a couch opened into a bed, sitting in the middle of the room. It was the basement of his mother's house. I looked around, and thought I should just turn around and drive home. Instead, we started kissing, and eventually, we were lying on the bed. Things became intense and intimate, and my mind started screaming at me; I didn't have any birth control. But his hand traveled to my warm intimate place, and I stopped thinking altogether.

I went home the next morning feeling terrible about myself, and then, my period was a week late. I started to freak out. Luckily, Marty knew a doctor in the clinic who did menstrual extractions. Marty brought me, and I had the procedure performed after hours in the doctor's office. The whole situation added to my feeling of being lost, repeating old patterns, being in the same rut with my friends and jobs. I needed a change.

Luckily, I started a new temp job working for a company downtown in the warehouse district. Al was the boss of our department, and I made friends with a few of the girls. I read their palms and handwriting and did their astrology charts. It was a fun way to get to know people on a more intimate level and get away from superficial chitchat.

We went to lunch at local places as a group, and it felt good to be one of the gang. I still have a bottle that one of them gave me. Inside, is a quote from Jonathon Livingston Seagull about friendship. My friend put the quote in a painted bottle, and sealed the cork in the bottle with wax. It was a special gift, and I promised never to open the bottle and break our seal of friendship. I still have it, and I have never opened it. The woman who sat behind me in the payroll department was Jo; she had worked at the company for fifteen years. She was in her fifties, and lived with her adult son in an apartment building. We became friends, and I went to her place for dinner or Loretta's Tearoom for a special lunch. I enjoyed her friendship. I'd never gotten attention from older females like my mother I was honored she wanted to be my friend and seemed interested in me as a person. She wasn't threatened by my energy and emotions; she seemed to enjoy them.

Al invited me into his office to talk one day. He knew I graduated in social work and psychology at the U of M. He talked to me about his daughter who was having problems and asked for some advice. It felt good to have someone value what I had to say. I felt seen by Al. One time, he was planning a party, and he asked me if I would come and read palms and talk about astrology signs. I would be the entertainment. The party was fun, and everyone enjoyed having their palms read and hearing about their astrology sign. I worked for that company a long time that year.

**

In February, my parents treated me to a road trip to Arizona. It was a graduation from college and birthday present. The second night on the road we stopped at a nice hotel with individual rooms surrounded by succulent trees and vegetation.

I was at a bar with my mother and father. Becca and Derek were asleep in the room. I was telling someone about astrology and Tarot cards when a man next to me said astrology was just a bunch of bunk. I turned to him and his sarcasm, and asked him what his sign was.

He said, "Stop sign."

I said, "No, really, what is your sign?"

He said, "I don't know."

I asked him what his birthdate was and told him what I knew about Cancers. He listened with skepticism written on his face, which turned to interest as I told him about himself. When I asked to see his palm and went deeper into what I saw about him, I saw tears in his eyes. When I was finished, this sensitive Cancer, who had been hiding in a hard shell of sarcastic humor, opened up about his divorce and feeling lost. He talked about how no one knew what he was feeling inside. He was there on business, and had to keep it together. He said he was grateful for spending time with me.

My parents had left during our conversation, and when we were done, he walked me to my room. We hugged, and said goodnight. I wished him well, and he thanked me, again with tears in his eyes and a smile on his face.

Two days later, we arrived in Arizona. The Paradise Inn had closed, so my father found the Jokake Inn which was still by Saddleback Mountain in Phoenix. I had fun with Becca, who was seventeen, and Derek, who was thirteen. We swam in the pool, and ordered our lunch poolside. We went horseback riding twice a day. I spent a lot of time at the stables brushing and feeding the horses and talking to the wranglers. Derek spent time charming people at the golf course, and Becca started hanging out with Danny, our Hispanic busboy. Evenings were glamorous dinners in the plush dining room, and my parents made friends and drinking companions quickly.

When Becca flew home the day before we left because her spring break was over, she gave Danny her phone number and address. Danny suddenly quit his job, and no one knew where he went. It turned out he flew to Minneapolis, and started calling Becca when she got home. Becca went out with him a few times, and wondered who Danny really was because he lived in a fancy apartment building by Loring Park but he was only a busboy.

Suddenly, I was embroiled back in my family's chaos I had avoided for the last year, and everyone was calling me. The drinking was as bad as ever, and my father seemed to be sinking financially. One night, after we returned from Arizona, Becca called. She was freaked out because Danny had called her on her private line and told her what my father was saying on the other line. Danny said the Mafia had tapped my father's phone. Then, he confessed to her that he got a job at the Jokake Inn because the people he worked for knew my father was going to be there. They wanted him to get close to my father and his family. He said the "people" told him to quit his job, and come to Minneapolis to keep an eye on my father through his connection to her. I knew that my father's construction company was struggling because of his drinking, and I knew he owed money to the Teamster's Union. What Danny was saying was believable.

Meanwhile, Becca told Danny she didn't want to see him anymore. He got upset, went over when my parents were out, waved a gun around, and said he was going to shoot himself if she quit seeing him. Becca reassured him, saying she'd see him, and asked him to give her the gun. He did, and she hid the gun in her closet. She saw him once more, and then, tried to avoid him. One night, he came over when my parents were home, called her on her phone, said he slit his wrists, and was in the driveway. When she went out, there was blood everywhere. She got my mother, and they brought him to a crisis clinic near the house in Burnsville. Becca told me all this after Danny disappeared. She never saw, or heard from him again.

A couple weeks later, when my mother was cleaning Becca's closet she found the gun.

When Becca got home from school, my mother handed her the gun, and said, "Here, do something with this."

She didn't ask her where it came from. Becca put it in a bag, and dropped it off anonymously at the police station.

Then, I got a call from Derek. He had pushed my drunken father, and my father fell and hit his head on the corner of a TV. He was passed out and bleeding. My little brother was really scared, and my mother wasn't home. Another time, my mother locked my father out of the house because he was too drunk; he tried to break in. My mother, in her nightgown and with curlers in her hair, woke up Becca and Derek, and told them to get into the car. They drove to the Decathlon Club in the middle of the night. My mother, still in her bathrobe and curlers, got a room. Derek and Becca called me the next morning, and I went to the Decathlon for lunch. After, we watched a movie in their room. They stayed there a couple of days before they went back home to my father.

**

Before I went to Arizona, I applied to the Family Practice Clinic at the University. When I got home, they called me for an interview. I got the job as a receptionist working full time. After I had been at the clinic for a couple of weeks, I got in trouble for what I wore. Sharon, my supervisor, was cool, but her boss was a thirty-something, conservative know-it-all.

He called me into his office, and told me my attire was inappropriate for the front desk. He said it was too sexy. Sharon said I just made him nervous, and it was his issue. But after, I was careful in how I dressed.

I loved Sharon, Cindy, who transcribed the doctors' notes, and Diane, the nurse, who was funny and sarcastic. At lunch I read their palms, and told them about their astrology signs. Diane asked me to do her chart. When we took breaks together, we discussed interesting topics like the full moon and how it impacts people. A couple of doctors came in, sat down, and joined the conversation. They said during the full moon there were more calls after hours from patients in the hospital.

A couple times in the summer, Lorenzo played ball in town, so Marty and I went out with him and his teammate. Seeing Lorenzo was like coming home. He felt comfortable, and made me feel special. One time, we threw a party when he was in town. Ally came. She had been my best friend in sixth grade, and lived across the creek in a mansion, and ended up going to an all-girls junior high after boys had harassed her. I hadn't seen her in years because she went away to college. It turned out, she was moving to Chicago, and wanted to sell her car, a yellow Plymouth sedan. The front fender was dented, but it ran fine. I bought it, and finally, I had my own car. I bought car insurance, and I was free and independent. It felt great.

With my new job at the Family Practice Clinic and having my own car, I decided I wanted to live alone again. I had enough money, and I wanted my own space. I wanted to concentrate on my career. I wanted meaning and purpose. Marty liked to party, and there were always people at our house who liked to drink and get high. I wanted more from life. I started looking for my own apartment.

Chapter 26
This Lady's Not for Sale

I found a first-floor apartment by Powderhorn Park, and moved the beginning of September. I liked my new place until I started waking up with itchy bumps on my ankles and legs. I showed the doctors at work, and they referred me to a dermatologist in the University hospital complex. The doctor and interns looked at the bites, and conferred. It was decided they were fleabites. I informed the landlord that the apartment was infested with fleas. It turned out the tenant before me had a cat, and if there are fleas and the host animal leaves, then the fleas will bite humans.

I had to move out while he flea-bombed the apartment, so I stayed with AJ, Mahmood, and their son Elijah. When I got back in the apartment, I scrubbed everything clean. I washed all my clothes, towels, and sheets. I washed all the dishes, and wiped out the cupboards. I took down the ceiling light fixtures, and they were filled with dead fleas. It was a lot of work. Then, I painted the whole apartment white. I loved my new clean and white apartment.

I was happy. I had a full-time job, my very own apartment, and a car.

Next, I decided to purchase a nice stereo system with speakers that made you feel you were inside the music. The salesman I bought the stereo from asked me out. We went out the next night, and he refused to leave my apartment at the end of the night until we had sex. After a tense hour of trying to make him to leave, we had sex, and he left. I felt dirty. I heard later from someone he had done that to other girls he sold stereos to.

I loved my stereo, and played it while I danced in my living room almost every day. Then, I saw a flyer someone put up at work about dance classes at the Minnesota Dance Studio.

I went to the studio, and registered to take ballet, modern, and jazz dance because I'd always dreamed of being a dancer. I loved the feeling of my whole body working to interact with the world and the music around me. It was great exercise and release for my pent-up emotions. Towards the end of the twelve-week session, I was in my ballet class doing Tour Jetes — a turn and leap — across the floor, and I landed on the leg of a coat rack by the wall, spraining my foot. I had to quit my lessons for a while.

I still worked occasionally at The Establishment, and a couple weeks later I worked as a disc jockey. I noticed a very attractive, dark-skinned man with a compact body and a beautiful smile. On Monday, when I was working my day job, I saw the same man walking towards me, and he was smiling. When I got off the phone, he said he thought he'd recognized me at the bar Saturday night. His name was Charles, and he was a resident at the University hospital. He had just started his rotation. He was originally from California. Later, I found out he was separated from his wife because their baby died from SIDS, their relationship fell apart, and she moved back to California.

Charles and I started dating, and he eventually started spending the night. We loved going dancing, and I liked driving around in his white sports car. One night, my mother invited Charles and me to a card party they were having at their house in Burnsville. It was my mother's way of saying she was becoming OK with the men I was dating, no matter the skin color. When we got there, several tables were set up. After each game we played, we moved to the next table. Charles met my parents for the first time, and they liked him. My father said he had reconciled with the fact he might have a black son-in-law someday. It helped that Charles was a doctor.

One night, Charles and I went to a club in St. Paul. The bouncer told us it was full, and we couldn't go in. As we were leaving, a white couple came in, and he let them in right away. I stopped to question the bouncer about it, he just said that we didn't "look right" for the club. I got angry, starting to make a scene, but Charles took my arm, leading me away. He told me making a scene wasn't, worth it and we should just find another club. It really upset me.

Charles was a Scorpio, and sex was at the center of his emotional expression. He was an intense and passionate lover and had many layers to him. He always seemed a little mysterious and elusive, but when I was sick or upset, he was loving and gentle. I enjoyed being in his company, and when it was time for him to take his medical boards, he came over with his flash cards, and I quizzed him. He was someone I could get serious about. But I knew when his residency was over he had to go back to California to serve in the military for two years because they were paying for medical school.

Charles and I loved to listen to the mellow voice of Barry White singing "Love's Theme" or the sweet high voice of Minnie Riperton singing "Lovin' You" while making love. I loved listening to jazz and R & B through my primo speakers: the seductive saxophone of Eddie

Harris, the raspy voice of Les McCann, the beautiful tunes from Quincy Jones, the incredible vocals of Al Jarreau, the haunting sounds of Esther Phillips, and the sexual tones of Barry White. I could feel every word they sang. Music was my medicine, the place I went to feel whole. It was a place I could gather all my pieces, and calm them into staying in one place. Music was my home.

This year, when I went to my gynecologist for a yearly checkup, and the doctor suddenly walked out of the room during my breast exam, I was confused, and wondered what happened. A couple minutes later, another doctor came in to finish the exam. When I asked Charles, he said if an attractive woman comes in, sometimes a doctor's body has an involuntary reaction, and has to leave until it subsides. I'd never had that happen before.

**

I was still friends with Lloyd, the physical education and health teacher. In the last year, he was getting high a lot and having parties at his house. He was kind of a womanizer, and we had an off and on relationship. While I was seeing Charles, it was off, and we were just friends. He wasn't someone I could trust on a regular basis. Lloyd stopped over occasionally to catch up. He still was a grade schoolteacher by day, and dealt drugs at night.

One night, Lloyd came over, and while we hung out, he told me about the night before. He was out drinking, and when he walked to his car, he realized he'd locked his keys in the ignition. When he started to break into it, a cop saw him, and thought it was suspicious to see a black man breaking into a car at 1:00 in the morning. They arrested him. He told them it was his car, but couldn't prove it because his license and registration were in his glove compartment. They threw him in jail overnight until a friend came with a spare key to his car. Lloyd showed the police the information to prove his ownership, and drove to work. He taught his grade school students that day wearing the same clothes he had on the night before.

A week later, Lloyd called because he was trying to rent a duplex in south Minneapolis. He said he'd called the landlord, and set up a time to take a look at it. When he got there, the landlord looked at him, and said it had been rented. Lloyd asked me to see if the duplex really was rented. I called Marty, and asked her to come with, and then I called and set up a time to see the duplex. Marty and I drove over, and rang the doorbell. The landlord showed us the duplex, and said it was still available. We talked about rent and a lease. Marty and I said we'd talk about it, and get back to him. We went outside and told Lloyd, who was waiting in his car. When the three of us rang the doorbell, and the landlord opened the door and saw us, his face turned white as a sheet. He had been caught being racist. Lloyd had grounds for a lawsuit. To avoid a lawsuit, the landlord rented the duplex to Lloyd, who was a model tenant for the years he lived there.

**

While I was working at the Family Practice Clinic, I noticed foreign women coming into the clinic for hypochondriac-like symptoms resulting from culture shock. At a break, I talked to some of the doctors about it, and wondered if having a social worker working at the clinic would help these patients. They liked the idea, so I wrote a proposal for the clinic to have a social worker. I wanted to be hired as the social worker. I gave the proposal to the head of family practice, Dr. Filiatreau. He said he would consider it, and talk to the clinic's board. The idea of working there as a social worker motivated me. I worked hard, and participated in staff meetings. After a couple of months, I met with Dr. Filiatreau again. He said the board liked the idea, but I needed a master's degree to qualify for the position. I left frustrated.

I saw my family infrequently. But my sister Becca came over, and spent the night once in a while. Or she and Derek came to just hang out. My father started coming over by himself for dinner, carrying a bottle of whiskey. He ate, drinking all the while, talking about being concerned about his drinking. He thought he might have a problem. He said my mother was always telling him to quit. I told him things he could do about his drinking, but it seemed to go in one ear and out the other. Sometimes, he came and talked about work and his business not going so well. Then, he left, and the next time he came over, he brought up his drinking again. Sometimes, he came because he just needed someone to talk to. Occasionally, he took me out to lunch at a nice restaurant. I wondered if people thought I was his mistress because of the way they looked at us. He talked a lot about his drinking at those lunches, too.

One night, when he came over, he was really upset. William had quit working for him, and accused him of shady and borderline criminal business dealings. My father went on defensively explaining that buying TVs, cars, rings, and having our house painted and charging it to the Carl H. Peterson Company was OK because he was part owner of the business. After a few more drinks he complained about the Teamsters Union and the issues with his truck drivers. Sounding angry but having tears in his eyes, he told me he had hoped William would take over the business. I felt sorry for him when he left that night, watching him walk away, shoulders slumped, head hanging; he looked defeated and lost. His hopes and dreams were shattered, and he had nowhere to turn.

Later that week I called William, and he explained that he quit before someone found out the company was cooking the books. Eventually, William bought a motel in Iowa, and he and his family lived in the back. My father was so angry, he didn't talk to William and his wife for a year. Patty started working for my father part-time.

About once a month, I was invited to my parents' house for dinner. I had a reputation for being late and forgetting it altogether. My family gave me calendars and watches as a subtle pressure to have me show up. One Sunday, I went. Patty came with Paul, her second husband, who she had married a year ago. It was a short ceremony at Mt. Olivet, and it was so short that when Becca and I were a few minutes late, we missed the whole thing.

Becca and Derek were also at my parents' for dinner. My mother cooked one of her pot roasts. After dinner, things got rowdy. We tossed a football across the table. My mother got mad, but no one listened because Derek started it and my mother loved Derek. Eventually, everyone was laughing, even my mother. Then, someone brought up our cousin Cheryl, who had been left at the altar. She was older, in her thirties, and someone commented she would probably be an old maid. Then, my younger brother teased me, and said that I probably would never settle down and get married, so I could be an old maid too.

My mother piped in the conversation, and said, "Helen will never be an old maid; she'll be a bachelorette."

Everyone started laughing because that was kind of racy for my mother to say. I wasn't sure how to take that whole conversation.

Chapter 27
It Was Three O'clock in the Morning

My family's issues started to intensify, and invade my life once more. My mother started calling me because Patty and my father were constantly fighting, and Patty quit working for my father, stopping her visits home. My father's drinking was worse than ever. Becca and Derek called me because my mother's drinking was as bad as my his. They were concerned because of her liver and what happened four years ago when she almost died. Derek had physical exchanges with my drunken father where pushing was involved. My parents were out of control.

Then, my father came over one night, and tried to convince me to take over the Carl H. Peterson Company. Running a construction company with all the truckers and big machine operators wasn't my idea of a future career. I knew nothing about business. It was my father's last-ditch effort. Patty wouldn't do it, so he started pressuring me, which was absurd. There was no way I'd even consider it. But my father was drowning, his drinking was bad, his business was going under, and he was afraid of bankruptcy.

That night, when I was working at The Establishment, my father's plight weighed on me. I looked around at all the people laughing, drinking, and dancing. I suddenly felt lost, disconnected, and overwhelmed. Everything and everyone were always changing, and here was my family calling *me* to fix them.

Later that week, I was working at the clinic, and I overheard a doctor referring someone to the Johnson Institute because it helped families of alcoholics. After his patient left, I asked the doctor for information about the Johnson Institute. He gave me a brochure, and I called to make an appointment. I knew my parents had problems, and alcohol was involved, but I didn't understand what alcoholism was. In a meeting with the counselor at Johnson Institute, I learned about alcoholism, and the importance of all my siblings confronting my parents with facts about my parents' behavior while they were drinking to help break through their denial system.

We set up an intervention. I contacted my family members, and explained the intervention concept and alcoholism, letting them know about the appointment. Last, I called my mother, and told her I set up a counseling appointment for her, my father, and Patty, not mentioning anything about alcohol.

When my mother walked in for the counseling session and saw all of us there, she turned around, walked out, and sat in the car. I went, out and told her this was a family session, so everyone needed to be there. I finally talked her into coming in. When we started confronting both our parents on their drinking, she became livid. She thought the meeting was only going to be about my father, not her. She was the hardest to get through to. My father seemed grateful. He was happy that something was being done. At the end of the session, we decided, because of my mother's physical addiction and her compromised liver, she would go into inpatient at St. Mary's treatment center. My father, who had a business to run, would go to outpatient treatment.

A couple of days later, I got a call early in the morning saying a bed had opened up for my mother. I called, and told her to check in that day by 2:00. She said she couldn't because she had a hair appointment. I told her I had a couple of very strong boyfriends I could bring over to pick her up if she wasn't checked in by 2:00 pm. When I called the hospital later, she had checked in, now in the program.

My father praised me for getting him into treatment, saying I saved his life. My mother wouldn't speak to me. I didn't want his praise, I just wanted them to get better. I was tired of the many years of chaos, and hoped this would help. After my parents had been in treatment for three weeks, they had a family day where we confronted our loved ones individually, and told them how their using affected our lives. When we confronted my mother, she just stared blankly ahead, not responding to what we said, ignoring us.

When the session ended, I bawled my eyes out. Then, I looked for a staff person to talk to, but there was no one around. I hid in the bathroom, and sobbed until I couldn't cry anymore. I realized, then, that I was only seen if I was playing the family hero, taking care of or fixing people. The real deep down person inside, full of feelings and dreams, the little girl left behind in the family shadows and dysfunction covered by burdens and responsibilities would never be seen. I was glad my parents got help; I just wished I could get some help too.

After my parents went through treatment, things changed for a while. At family gatherings, I started a tradition of passing the empty cup. Whoever had the cup had to tell a family story from the past. It was fun, and no one was drinking, just talking and telling stories. It felt like some mending was going on.

One evening, I went to my parents' house in Burnsville for dinner, and because my parents were still in recovery, it was a nice quiet evening. Becca, now seventeen, asked if I'd sleep over in her room like I used to. Becca and I talked, and she told me it was hard making friends in Burnsville High School. She felt like an outsider because she was, to them, from the "inner city." We talked until she fell asleep.

I couldn't fall asleep because I'd never slept in that house before, and it didn't feel like home. The sounds and the smells were foreign. I started to feel anxious for some reason, like I'd suddenly been thrown into a new reality or a past one. I felt like a little child, lost and anxious because I didn't fit anywhere. The home I knew was gone, I didn't like my job, Lorenzo was pretty much out of my life, and I felt alone and disconnected. I lay there thinking of TV shows I'd watched when a little girl or boy crawled into their parents' beds because they were scared. I had never done that because my parents were the cause of my fear and unsafety. Their bed was never a safe refuge, and I could never have shown them my fear. But for some reason that night, I got up, feeling the adrenaline surging through my body, feeling vulnerable, and wanting comfort.

I walked into my parents' bedroom, and watched my mother sleep, feeling conflicted. I took a deep breath, and quietly, woke her up, asking if I could lay in bed with her. Half asleep, she moved over, and I crawled into her bed. She didn't say anything or touch me, she just went back to sleep. I lay there feeling like an abandoned child, needing some temporary comfort, and I pretended I was a young girl again, my mother comforting me as I heard her quiet snores. I felt my eyelids growing heavy in this illusion of a mother's love. I woke up in the morning before my parents did, and crept out of their room. I went back into Becca's bedroom, and crawled into bed. The night became a little secret no one would ever know about.

My dissatisfaction at work intensified. I wanted to be a social worker or have a job in my field. I wanted something that proved I was worthwhile and important. I wanted meaning in my life. Then, one day I got in trouble for not putting a call through to a doctor while he was in a meeting, even though I was told to take messages and not interrupt the doctors' meetings for any reason. The call was from a doctor's wife. She complained, and my boss yelled at me, even after I pointed out I was just following instructions. I turned in my two-week notice, and found another job in August of 1974.

Chapter 28
Little Child Within Sing Your Song Now

On September first, I started working for St. Joseph's home for Children in their residential treatment program. There were four "cottages." I worked in Bosco cottage with 7 to 12-year-old boys. Each cottage had a living room, an office, and an overnight room for overnight staff. There was a large bathroom with showers and bedrooms on either side of the hallway, each containing four beds. The living room area had a large circular table where we had snacks, group meetings, and breakfast. In the morning, a Sister brought in cereal, milk, caramel rolls, and sometimes, pancakes, syrup, and bacon. For lunch and supper, we lined the boys up to go to the cafeteria.

My job as a childcare worker involved making sure the boys showered and brushed their teeth, and I helped them get dressed if needed. When the kids came to the cottage, they were taken off all medications for behavior issues, meaning no Ritalin, anti-depressants, etc. Nothing to control their behavior. We ran it like a family with five fathers and two mothers taking care of twelve children. We brought them to school downstairs, and were on call for any behavior issues. We played games at night, or watched a movie before bedtime.

Hennepin County believed it was best to place the child back with their mother unless to do so endangered the child. We had family counseling for the families, and taught parenting skills to help them succeed. When the family and child were ready, the child was released to his mother's care.

At our first staff meeting I felt insecure. It was my first social worker-type job. Edin, our cottage social worker, sat there tall and confident, puffing on his pipe, looking at us like he could see right through us. I didn't want them to see the inadequacy I felt, and I didn't want to sound stupid or say the wrong thing, so I sat and watched. But by our next staff meeting, I was one of the gang. My co-workers were open and friendly, and started inviting me out after work for a drink. I didn't drink, but I ordered a Coke and talked, listening to their stories about working on the unit. I told stories of working at my old job. I began to relax, and opened up to them because I felt like I belonged.

I was assigned a couple of "little brothers." Every child had a clothing allowance when he came to the cottage. I took my little brothers clothes shopping; picking out pants, shirts, underwear, socks, pajamas and jackets and I attended their family sessions as their advocate.

At bedtime, I read stories, and tucked in the boys. After their story time, they had fifteen minutes to read their own book, and then, it was lights out. Bedtime was the scariest time for our population. It was a time they felt most vulnerable, and needed a bedtime routine that was nurturing and quiet. I sat in their bedroom making sure they quieted down and went to sleep. As I watched them, I thought about my own sleepless nights when my parents argued till the wee hours. Night times didn't feel safe, and I realized then I was in the hearts of these lost boys.

There were times at night, no matter how quiet and nurturing it was, that a boy would lose control because he couldn't handle his inner thoughts and feelings. After a family session, a boy might feel angry and abandoned when his parents left. In those incidences, they would throw an older child's version of a two-year old's temper tantrum. When that happened, the child was so full of rage, and was a physical danger to himself or others, so I held him firmly in a tight hug or sat on him to control his behavior, saying nurturing words until he was able to control himself. Eventually, the tantrum became tears, and he found words for what he was feeling. I held him as long as he needed. I felt like I was calming down my alcoholic, abusive father once again. That's where I first learned tolerance and patience for certain behaviors that others were afraid of.

Louise, the unit's schoolteacher, and I became friends, and started talking about astrology and how it could be applied to working with the children. One of my little brothers was a Taurus. A Taurus is pretty easy going until they get angry; then, they become like a stubborn bull. They dig in their heels with their bodies taught and ramrod straight. To comfort a Taurus, you need a quiet, gentle approach to calm them. Yelling or getting into a power struggle just made it worse. So, I learned to "stand next to him" like I was on his side. He started to settle down because he was feeling heard. If a child was a Pisces or a Cancer, their sign indicated sensitive insides that appear crabby and tough on the outside. So, when I saw them acting crabby or tough, I asked if someone or something had hurt their feelings. They looked up at me, surprised and with tears in their eyes. They said yes, and went on to tell me what happened.

The children's issues were all different. We had one little boy living there whose father killed his mother and then himself, leaving the five-year-old son to wander the house until someone found him. He was at our cottage until the county could find a good foster family who could deal with his issues.

We had Dannie, a seven-year old with a sweet face, big brown eyes, dimples, and a head full of dark brown curly hair. His mother was a drug dealer, and she sent him out to deliver drugs, walking down dark alleys at night to the rear door of shops.

We had six-year old Johnny, whose father called us frantically one morning, wanting to get his son in our program right away. The father was beside himself, and had tied his skinny, little, blonde-haired Johnny to a chair. At 3:00 in the morning, Johnny had gotten out of bed, and called the fire department saying there was a fire. The fire trucks came, sirens blaring, and woke up Johnny's family. There was no fire. The firefighters were angry, and told Johnny's family they'd be charged by the city for the false alarm. Johnny was scheduled to be placed in our unit at the end of the week. The social worker okayed his coming a couple of days early.

We had little Adam, whose mother was a prostitute. He was my little brother who I took out clothes shopping. At night, I braided his hair into cornrows, and applied Vaseline to his scalp. In the morning, I took out the braids, and picked it into a nice Afro.

Kenny, my other little brother, was native America. He was eight with a wiry build and very strong with dark, straight hair and intense, fiery, black eyes. He was intensely loyal to his mother, who was a prostitute; her children were products of her "johns." Kenny loved his mother, who, at family sessions, practically ignored him.

One day, I was walking a group of kids to the bowling alley, and I saw a car driving down the street that looked a lot like mine; it even had a dent in the fender. After the kids bowled, we walked back to the cottage, and I didn't see my car in the parking lot. After I dropped the children at the cottage with the staff, I walked out to the parking lot. My car was gone. I went inside, and told Branden, the lead childcare worker. It turned out a couple of boys from Daniel cottage decided to steal my car, and take it on a joy ride. The police were called, and they found the boys. I had to get the steering column repaired because they had hot-wired it.

One weekend in the summer, we took the children from Bosco cottage to a Boy Scout camp in Wisconsin. The second night, I had the overnight shift, which meant sleeping in the apartment above the room where the children slept. I was reading a book, and a bat started flying around the room, freaking me out. The bat started flying way too close to my head for comfort. I called Branden at the bar to come and capture the bat. After he got rid of the bat, we sat, and talked. Branden had been flirting with me since I started to work at St. Joe's. I wasn't used to men being so shy. At one point while we were talking, I looked at him directly, and told him if he wanted to have sex with me, he should just ask, instead of being so indirect. Boy, did he grow quiet. I had shocked him.

I saw Lorenzo in June when his team played the Twins, but after that his team wasn't scheduled to be back here. I started dating other ballplayers, trying to replace him. One ballplayer was Billie, who played for the California Angels. He and a couple of his teammates came to St. Joe's, and gave the kids pointers out on the ball field for a couple of hours. The boys were in awe of the pro baseball players. I didn't have to go through red tape with the ball club because it was just a few friends stopping over. The boys batted, and threw balls, talking with the athletes. They all had such big smiles at dinner that night, telling everyone outside our cottage about it.

My co-workers went out, and drank all the time. Someone always ended up on my couch because they were too drunk to drive. One night, when we were out, Louise looked at my palm, and told me I had a guardian angel protecting me. She told me he would always be there to guide me in my life. I hoped that was true.

**

Meanwhile, things were changing in my personal life. One night after work, I went out with Edin, and he told me he and his wife had an open marriage and were free to see other people. I had never heard of that. He said it worked well for them. Then, one night a couple of weeks later I was suffering from a really bad migraine. I was nauseated and dizzy, and it scared me. I'd never had one like that before. There was no one I could call, but I thought maybe Edin could give me some advice about what to do, so I called him. He wasn't home; I talked to his wife, Lucy. She offered to come over, and help. I said OK, and she came over, giving me a neck and shoulder massage until I fell asleep. While she massaged me, she told me she was attracted to me. I started feeling awkward because I wasn't attracted to women.

Charles, who was very supportive when I talked about my new job, had good advice, and was nice to come home to, was leaving. I was sad when he passed his boards and his residency was done. It was hard to see him go. We had a passionate last night, and said someday we'd see each other again. Then, he left, and I watched his white sports car drive away. I felt so lost and sad, like I lost a part of myself. I liked who I was when I was with him.

I thought about the words "alone" and "loneliness." I realized I liked to be alone, but I didn't like being lonely. After Charles left, I had trouble sleeping. I talked to Edin about it ,and he recommended reading. He brought me a couple of Nero Wolfe mysteries. I loved them. Reading helped relax my mind so I could sleep. Seven years later, I was reading again. Reading became my "me time." It helped me be alone again.

When AJ and Mahmood separated because he was seeing other women, their son Elijah was almost three. She and Elijah moved to a duplex three blocks from mine. Once in a while, she got a babysitter, and came with Marty and me to a club. When Mahmood found out, he threatened to take Elijah away, and he started stalking her.

Around that time, I was taking an evening class in child psychology at the U of M. I learned there were different kinds of children. There were fragile children who were devastated by a traumatic event and had trouble bouncing back and picking up the pieces, and there were children who were resilient when trauma struck them, responding like a ringing bell. They became stronger, and did what had to be done. I learned through that class I was the resilient child. I faced what came my way. I would not break.

So, when AJ came to my apartment with Elijah to get away from Mahmood's harassing calls and asked for my help, I said, yes, she could stay with me as long as she needed. An hour later, Mahmood's car pulled up in front of my apartment. I waited outside on the front steps, and told him AJ did not want to see him. He needed to leave. He started up the stairs, but I stood right in front of him. We were nose to nose. I told him he was not getting by me. He stepped to the side; I stepped to the side. I told him if he didn't leave, I'd call the police, and make him leave. This was my apartment, and he needed to go. He backed down, and left.

A few months later, when Marin had a party, AJ got wasted. I grabbed her keys, and told her I was driving. When we got in my car, she said she needed to get a bag of supplies for Elijah out of her car. When we got to her car, I gave her the keys to unlock the car door. Instead of grabbing a bag of supplies, she got in the car, and drove off. I freaked out, honking, and yelling at her to pull over, but she just kept going. I followed her, thinking I'd be close if something happened. We drove onto the freeway, heading west. She started going all over the road. She swerved, scraped along the center cement blocks, swerved back, and hit the freeway's side railing. Luckily, there were no other cars on the road at that time of night. She did that a couple more times, and then, she hit the side rail, and stopped. I pulled in behind her. She had passed out on the steering wheel. I got out of my car, pulled her out of her car, and put her in my front

205

seat. I went back to get her keys out of the ignition, and suddenly she was trying to get back in her car.

I said, "No way," and locked her car door.

She started yelling that she couldn't leave her car on the freeway to get towed because she needed her car. I flagged down the next car that came by. When he stopped, I asked him if he would be willing to drive her car, and follow us home. Then, I'd give him a ride back to his car. I thanked him for all his help when I dropped him at his car later.

AJ's drinking was getting worse. A couple of weeks later, she got so drunk, she hit the tree on her own block driving home, and ended up in the hospital with a broken arm and stitches on her face from her lower lip down to under her chin.

Chapter 29
People Come, People Go

I had weekly card games at my apartment. AJ and I were addicted to Bid Whist. We were the team to beat. One night, after a particularly fun night of cards, music, drinking, and laughter, I was exhausted. So, I left the mess and crawled into my bed after everyone left. I had trouble falling asleep, so I picked up my book *The American Tragedy.*

After reading the same page three times, I put it down. I lay on my back, stared at the ceiling, and thought about my life. I thought about the evening with my friends, playing cards, and listening to music. When they all went home with their partners, I was alone in my dark bedroom with my feelings and thoughts wrestling around in my body. I felt the loneliness start to seep from the walls. I heard a small voice urging me, a call to the streets, reminding me of the excitement of meeting new men. I never knew who I might meet. I reflected on the men in my life. I had pro athletes coloring my days; I had doctors, FBI agents, and musicians filling my nights. Being free brought new adventures to my door, but I was filling my own life with the chaos I thought I'd left behind with my family.

I looked into the dark shadows of my bedroom and felt tears on my cheeks. I wondered why crying was such a lonely event people shied away from. There were days after Skippy disappeared when I cried. I held those tears in my heart for years. There was church camp when I had the "spiritual" experience and was pulled across the water, and the tears flooded out in a church full of people. No one sat down to comfort me. There was the afternoon I was reading about Hiroshima and Nagasaki, and I was sobbing in my room. At the summer resort where I had my meltdown, the pain had reached in and tormented my soul. A feeling of abandonment took over my body, and I wanted someone to help me. So, I cried. When my parents went through treatment and we paraded our pain in a family session, tears erupted, but there was no one around who heard me. There were the nights after love making with some man I had in my bed when I felt a tear run down my cheek. I'd hurry into the bathroom and let the tears come. I had this loneliness inside no one had touched, no one witnessed, no one comforted. I filled my nights with books, and their words crowded out the confusion and pain tormenting my sleep. I played records on my stereo and let the music enter my heart and soothe it. My body relaxed, so I could sleep.

Lying there with all those thoughts, I decided I didn't want to run away anymore, I didn't want to fill empty nights with one-night stands. I wanted love and connection. As I lay there, I realized I didn't know what that meant. I was used to sudden change, people suddenly gone from my life; I didn't really know what was normal. But I knew I wanted to do things differently.

I woke up the next morning with an emotional hangover. I needed some groceries for breakfast, so I put on my game face. Looking together, strong, and confident, I grabbed my keys, got into my car, and started it. It made a horrible noise. I drove it to the nearest service station. They said the old yellow Plymouth had major mechanical problems.

After my soul searching the night before, I decided this was a sign to start a new way of doing things. So later that week, I went out and traded it in for a new car. I found the car of my dreams, my little red Mustang II.

The license plate on my new car drew attention. One day, I was teased by police officers driving by when I had my window down.

First, they said, "Hello Helen."

I couldn't figure out how they knew my name. Then, I realized they could look me up by my license plate.

Then, they pulled up as I was driving along, and said, "Did you know your license plate says Sex 184?"

When I got home, I parked my car, and looked at my license plate. It was 5EX 184. So, the police were right. I got harassed quite a few times about that license plate.

**

At work, we had a couple of new boys admitted to Bosco Cottage. One was Phillip, who hardly ever talked. No one could communicate with him. I had just gotten a rescue cat from my older brother. Cassie was white with a couple of small brown and black spots and, when she wanted attention, she kneaded me with her front paws. The first day I met Phillip, he kneaded my shoulders with his fingertips. I looked at him and asked if he needed attention because that's what my cat did when she wanted my attention.

Phillip looked at me and said, "Do you have cat?"

I said, "Yes."

He continued telling me a long story about his cats at home. When one of his cats had kittens, he asked if I wanted one. I said yes. When the kittens were old enough and Phillip had a home visit at his dad's, I stopped by and picked out a tan, long-haired kitten. I named him Maxwell. Our day always started with news about Maxwell.

The second boy came into the unit a couple of weeks later and was very belligerent. He was scared but acted like a bully to hide it. One day at lunch, we lined up to go to the cafeteria. He said something inappropriate, and I asked him to please say it again the right way. He spit a big wad in my face. I would not advise this as a healthy reaction, but it was the straw that broke the camel's back. I coughed up a big gob and sent it back at him. He was surprised. He looked at me, I looked at him, and we both started laughing. Pretty soon, all the boys were laughing. Then, I told them what he did was wrong, and what I did was not a good way to retaliate. After, though, the group had a newfound respect for me.

**

That summer, life was very busy. My sister Becca moved in with me. She had moved out of our parents' house after she graduated from high school and lived with Sean. After Sean hit her a few times, she decided to get away from him but not go back to my parents. When an efficiency apartment opened upstairs, she took it. We spent time at each other's apartments and hung out. Then, I got busy with work, and she was hardly ever home. I wondered where she was; I felt like she was avoiding me.

Finally, she told me she met a guy who turned out to be a pimp. He was priming her to take tricks. Her first night, he brought her to a downtown hotel where his girls worked. She was introduced to her first John. She felt sick to her stomach, ran to the bathroom, and threw up. She left through the back door of the hotel. She came to me that night and told me what happened. We got the guy out of her life. She stayed at my place for a few days until he stopped coming around, and we changed her phone number. A couple of weeks later, she met Curtis, who wore his Afro short, and he was a good guy with a good job. He moved in with her in the upstairs apartment, and they got a cat they named Zelda.

I was excited when Lorenzo called, and we planned to meet in Kansas City where he was playing ball in a couple of weeks. I drove to Kansas City, stopping to see William and his family on the way there. Lorenzo and I hadn't seen each other since June, and didn't know when we'd see each other again, so we spent a lot of time in his motel room. The stadium was a nice new stadium and easy to get to from my hotel. I enjoyed sitting in the stands watching him play; I felt so happy and loved when I left Kansas City.

I became friends with Rick when he moved into the apartment building next door. Marty and I hung out with him on the weekends. He was friends with Otis, a pro football player. One day, when I was at Rick's, Otis came over with his newly tricked-out van. We went out to see it; the interior walls were all carpeted, and he had put in a bar stocked with alcohol and a large stereo system. He pulled out a couple of joints and offered us some wine.

When Otis started to drive off, I said, "Stop, I have to get out. I have people coming for supper."

Otis said I had plenty of time to get back for that. Then, he drove way out to Lake Minnetonka and parked in front of a huge mansion. We all went in.

Otis and Rick went off with the man of the house, and I sat in the living room with a woman and her child. Meanwhile, I was feeling angry, like I'd been kidnapped against my will and was sitting in an awkward situation. The woman didn't want to talk to me because she wasn't happy with what her husband was doing. Finally, Otis and Rick came back, and we left. I asked Rick what they were doing. He said they snorted some PCP, an animal tranquilizer. I couldn't wait to get home. When Otis parked, I ran out of the van, wanting never to see either one of them again.

AJ, Marty, and my neighbor Tonya came for dinner and cards, and we ended up having a great evening. I told them about the afternoon escapade, and they couldn't believe it. A couple of weeks later, Otis called and asked me out.

I said, "No thanks," and hung up.

I started dating and sleeping with a Scorpio who I later found out was married, so I dumped him. I dated a couple of baseball players who turned out to be jerks. Then, I dated a man who was a Cancer. He seemed nice and polite, until one night when he was over, I walked him to the door, and he said he wouldn't leave until we had sex. I said no, but he grabbed me, and we wrestled on the floor of my apartment right next to the front door. I kept trying to push him off, but he had his way with me and left. I never told anyone.

Then, a week later, Lloyd came by and wanted to go out. I was lonely, so I went. I hadn't seen him in a while. He seemed different, hyper, and wanted me to try cocaine. I said absolutely not. During the night we argued, he got violent, hit me, and shoved me into his car. I was glad to make it home safely, and I never went go out with him again. Later, I found out he was into crack cocaine, and then, I saw him on the news. He was busted for robbing gas stations to get money for his habit. He was still a health teacher during the day.

After that, I stayed away from men for a while. The feeling of loneliness and disconnection got stronger. Money was tight with rent, a new car payment, car insurance, and food. I wanted to change jobs because I was sick of all the drinking at my co-workers get-togethers, and someone ending up on my couch. I was sick of my family's alcohol issues following me through my friends and co-workers. I couldn't seem to get away from alcohol and drug use. I wanted something more. I felt like I was always in survival mode.

Marty moved into an upstairs duplex on 26th and Pleasant not far from my place. Her duplex was nice and roomy and had two bedrooms. Felix, who lived downstairs with his three dogs, owned it. Felix was a little different. Marty had to go through his apartment to get down to the laundry room, and she said one time the dogs' butts were bleeding. Marty suspected Felix was using his dogs for sex. One day, I was talking to Marty on the phone, and asked if I could possibly move into the 2nd bedroom of her duplex for a few months to save money, while I looked for a new job.

Chapter 30
Life and Love Go on

Marty agreed to let me move in March 1976. I had to find a home for my two cats because she was allergic to them. I put an ad in the paper and found a family who wanted them. I was so sad to see Cassie and Maxwell go. When I called to check on them, the family said they were kind of unruly, so they gave them to their neighbors across the street. They said the cats were happy and gave me the new owners' phone number. In all the chaos of moving, I lost the phone number, and couldn't figure out a way to check on my cats. It haunted me for years, wondering how my cats were doing, if they were happy, and if they missed me. I know I missed them.

Everything seemed to be changing again. After my parents went to treatment, my father felt like he could finally make decisions about his company, and he sold his business. He owed money to some unsavory people, and when he sold his excavation and grading equipment, he had enough to pay them back. He also had enough left over to buy a motel like my brother did in Story City. He bought a motel in Brookings, South Dakota, and my parents moved in late spring of 1976.

Right after my parents moved, I got a call from Lorenzo. He was traded to a baseball club he didn't like, so he quit baseball, which meant I'd never see him again. I felt lost.

I sat in my room that day and wrote in my journal, realizing a weird connection. My father was married with five children; Lorenzo was married with five children. They both wore white shoes and white belts. I had an intimate connection with my father when I was very young. And in that moment, he looked like a prince lying on the bed looking at me with his soft and loving eyes while his hands traveled to intimate parts of my body. It was the only love I saw in those eyes over the years. Later, when I was a few years older, my father sat with his glass full of whiskey and talked to me about his hurts and problems. I always felt the need to protect him.

Lorenzo, I knew, could never be committed to me because he was still married even if he was separated. I thought he *was* my prince and saw love and gentleness in his eyes too, but realized it too was connected to his sexual needs. The fragile sense of security I'd gotten from them was suddenly gone, just an illusion of love that vanished into nothingness because it was never there. They had used me, and I was hungry for attention and love, so I let them. I confused sex with love. Even Charles, another man I could see myself with, was married and eventually left. Marty once told me I seemed to always need a man around. I guess I did.

The feeling of being lost was stronger than ever. I wanted a home, a connection, and a place I belonged. At four, I learned men abandoned me, and women turned their backs on me from jealousy or fear. Sex, for me, was the only connection I knew. I learned that at the tender age of four, if push comes to shove, the mistress is always left behind. I decided the next relationship I had with a man would be different; I wanted more than just sex. I wanted closeness and commitment, though I wasn't quite sure what that meant or how to get it.

I was glad my parents were in another state, and Lorenzo was gone. I needed rest, a simpler lifestyle, a new kind of relationship, and financial freedom. Marty's duplex seemed to be a temporary answer.

Just after I moved in, Becca came over in tears. She and Curtis were fighting, and she was pregnant. She spent the night, and we talked about what she should do. A week later, she asked me to come with her for moral support when she had her abortion. While I sat in the waiting room, I realized something. I had learned this year that my mother wasn't married when she had William. My father was in the service and couldn't get back to marry her in time. So, at twenty, she had a child and wasn't married. When Patty was twenty or twenty-one, she had her baby, the one she placed for adoption. I was twenty when I got pregnant and had an abortion. Now, my sister Becca, at twenty, was pregnant and having an abortion. I sat there stunned at how a family can influence your life in ways you didn't think possible. After the procedure, Becca stayed with me over night. Louise, the teacher from the boy's home, called the next day, after Becca left, and invited me over for supper because Carl, her new boyfriend, was cooking.

When I got there, I saw a man of medium height carrying an extra twenty pounds on a muscular body. Carl had a short afro, kind eyes, and looked great in his white chef's hat, which made his dark skin appear even darker. During the day he worked with violent youth. But now, he looked goofy with his drooping chef's hat, standing over the stove, cooking us fish that was fried with bananas. It was delicious. I liked him. When his friend from New York came to visit a couple weeks later, he introduced us.

Maurice was tall with a nice build and in great shape. His smile was incredible, and his face was handsome with high cheekbones and well chiseled features. His Afro was short, and he was more brown than black. But I soon realized he was one of those men no girl should ever go out with because he messed with my head. It was disastrous. He made me feel ugly while other men made me feel pretty and sexy. I was confused. Why did he go out with me if he thought I was unattractive? It started to undermine my thinking. I was always wondering what I was doing wrong. He stripped me of a sense of who I was. When he stood me up for a date and I confronted him, he had this way of convincing me it was my fault he stood me up. I drove away from his house, going over and over the conversation, trying to figure out what was the truth.

I had convinced myself I needed to be in a committed relationship instead of fleeing at the first sign of trouble. I wanted stability, so I tried to work on a relationship with him.

Maurice and I bought a family membership at the "Y," which was cheaper than two individual memberships. We listed that we were married, so he seemed to want to be with me. A couple of weeks after we got the membership, he attended a work conference downtown. On Sunday, we were supposed to work out at the "Y," but he called to cancel, saying people from the conference were going out to lunch. I went to the "Y" by myself, and after my workout, I went into the locker room and saw a tall, attractive black woman with an NYU sweatshirt on. I had a feeling she was there with Maurice. I hated being suspicious, but I never felt like he was telling the truth. When I was dressed and left the locker room, I saw Maurice talking to the girl with the NYU sweatshirt. They looked quite friendly, and they were definitely together. I left feeling furious. He had lied to me again.

I went home, sat in my room, and wrote everything down so when I talked to him, he couldn't talk me out of my feelings. When I saw him and confronted him with the facts, he twisted it around to how jealous and suspicious I was. I left, feeling frustrated and unheard. But I told myself to hang in there and make it work, because at times, Maurice was sexy and charming.

One hot summer night, I told him I had never had sex outside or in any compromising situations. The thought of getting caught was exciting. Maurice drove me home to put on a skirt with no panties. Then, we parked by Lake of the Isles and sat under a tree with me on his lap facing him and my skirt fanned out around me. We had sex while people were walking by. It was a real turn on to be out under the stars making love in the open, knowing most people didn't know what we were doing.

Also, Maurice helped me quit smoking. I started smoking when I was sixteen. I had quit once for a year in my early twenties, then, started up again to smoking a pack a day. I smoked after dinner, and I took smoking breaks when I worked at my jobs. When Maurice and I started running around Lake Harriet, we decided to quit smoking, and we threw our cigarettes away. I did a behavior modification where I bought a box of wooden toothpicks. At work, when I wanted a break, instead of going in and getting a cigarette, I reached in and got my pack of wooden toothpicks. At twenty-seven, I quit smoking for good, and never smoked again. Maurice started again a month later. Maurice and Marty didn't get along. Marty thought Maurice was manipulative and said she okayed me living there, but she didn't okay him living there. He had been staying over a lot and eating there. She felt he was invading her space.

Marty started finding fault with me. She said I used too much dish soap when I was washing dishes, and I used too much toilet paper. She thought I drank too much pop. She complained because I didn't notice things that needed to get done. So, things were tense. Marty and I had an occasional party with dancing in the living room, card games in the kitchen, and alcohol flowing freely. The parties helped relieve some of the tension. The tension motivated me to find another job, so I could move out.

AJ and Maurice got along because they both liked to smoke dope. In fact, I think AJ shared her supplier with him. AJ was divorced now, and went back to college to get her degree; she had her son to take care of, so I didn't see her as much as I used to.

I couldn't wait to quit St. Joseph's. I applied for a correctional officer position at St. Cloud prison dealing with male inmates. But given that I was a female under five feet, I didn't get the job. I applied to work at Operation de Novo, an organization that helped troubled youth, and didn't get that job. I applied at a group home; they offered me a job, but I turned it down. I looked into taking the LSATs, so I could go to law school and become a lawyer. I applied to be a police officer in Bloomington. I passed all the tests and was put on a list. But veteran's preference put me further down the list. I put my application in to Anoka County to be a probation officer, which I really wanted. I was so excited when I got called for an interview a couple of weeks later and could quit my job at St. Joe's.

Chapter 31
Guitar Man

In June,1976, after three interviews, I was hired as a probation officer in Anoka County.

I drove home that day, looked in my rearview mirror, and said out loud, "I am a probation officer."

I loved how that sounded; I felt like I had an identity and a meaningful purpose. I was a juvenile court probation officer, so my caseload was twelve to eighteen-year-old females. In the juvenile division, female probation officers only had female cases. Which meant I had a large geographical area that covered all of Anoka County.

I started work July 1st, and soon, met Sherrie, a fellow probation officer. I asked her about places to live near Anoka. She told me about her apartment building in Brooklyn Center. After work, I went and looked at the apartments and rented one that day with a move in date of August 1st.

I was excited for a new life in Anoka County away from my old friends. But I was still involved with Maurice, and he moved some of his stuff to my new place. For some reason, I couldn't break up with him. Then, Maurice got a call. His father owned a bar in Florida and was arrested for murder. Maurice said he needed to help his dad. When we went to the airport and I watched him take off, I realized I never wanted to see him again. He was bad for me and this latest development put me over the edge.

I went home, packed up his stuff, and brought it to Carl's. I was freaked out and called Patty, who lived nearby, and asked if I could sleep on her couch for a couple of nights. I was feeling anxious and needed something familiar. I packed some clothes and headed to her place. I slept in their den and got to know my nephews. Patty and Paul drank a lot in the evenings, reminding me of my parents' drinking. I felt uncomfortable; I went back to my apartment after a couple of nights.

When Maurice called, I told him I never wanted to see him again and that his stuff was at Carl's. Then, I hung up. I couldn't sleep because I felt so alone; my old friends felt like they were part of another lifetime and miles away from where I was. I didn't really know anyone at my new job. So, after three nights of no sleep, I worked up the courage to call Sherrie's apartment at 3:00 in the morning.

When I explained I couldn't sleep, she said, "Come on over."

The door was open when I got there.

She called out, "I'm in the bedroom." She was lying in her king size bed, threw open the covers, and said, "Hop in, we'll have a slumber party."

We talked, and I told her about Maurice, his father in Florida, and how I broke up with him. I talked forever, releasing my pent-up energy. It felt so safe being in her bed, talking late at night with the lights off, hearing words of encouragement, and feeling the safety of her non-judgmental world where everything would be OK. I finally fell asleep in the warmth of her friendship. Until that night I had hardly spoken to her. The next morning, she sent me off to work with a hug. It felt great.

I had never had a friend like her; she was warm, sensitive, nurturing, emotional, and caring. My other friends had been running buddies who shied away from intimacy. Their caring came out as teasing and joking around. They were survivors in their own lives, and warmth, gentleness, and emotions were too threatening. It was safer to keep a distance and be tough. We were there for each other as fellow survivors walking the same path. Now, I was on a different path, and I felt their hostility because I was a probation officer, carrying a badge, and was not supposed to be associated with illegal activity, like drugs, which eliminated the parties I used to go to.

When I heard Maurice was back, I had my locks changed because he had a key. I felt safe knowing visitors had to be buzzed in. When Maurice came over, buzzed me, and tried to talk his way in, I told him I never wanted to see him again. He left, and a huge weight was lifted. I was free and excited to start my new life.

I wanted to be someone and make a difference. I wanted my world to slow down, but I didn't know how. My focus was always about taking care of others. I kept feeling one word inside of me: HELP. But there was no one to help me.

The first thing I decided to do was make my apartment into a "home" for myself, a place I wanted to be. I reupholstered an old love seat with material I found with a white background and big splashes of orange and brown. I bought a new glass and silver coffee table with a matching étagère. I invented something I called the "Passion Pit," which was a double mattress with a faux fur cover. By hand, I sewed huge body pillows that matched the couch. I had a swing lamp hung over the passion pit and a floor lamp next to the love seat. I bought plants: a big schefflera, dieffenbachia, and a split leaf philodendron. My new apartment felt airy and artistic. I had framed posters of Alvin Ailey dancing, a ballerina on toe shoes, a modern art piece containing the same colors as the couch, but I still had my same bed with its lime green headboard I painted. Now, I had a home.

I loved my new job. Sherrie was becoming a good friend. She had a friend Leila, a volunteer probation officer, who was a high school teacher. I started doing things with them both. We went out to dinner or got takeout, which we brought to my new home, and the three of us talked and ate for hours in my living room. I found out Sherrie was in school getting a marriage and family therapy degree, and Leila was bisexual. I shared some of my own past. Sherrie sometimes fell asleep in my passion pit while Leila and I talked. Eventually, we woke Sherrie up, and they went home. It was nice having a real home to hang out with friends.

One day, when Sherrie and Leila came over for lunch, AJ called out of the blue, and I invited her, too. It was nice to see her again, but I realized we had grown apart. She still was into drugs and alcohol and had sampled cocaine. I was steering clear of that past. My childhood friend I had felt so close to, my confidante, was gone. So, I hardly ever saw AJ after that.

Dave and I were hired the same day. We had lunch occasionally to swap information on cases; he lived at home temporarily, and we'd have lunch with his mom if our home visits were close to his house. Our boss had a get-to-know-each-other party for the juvenile and adult POs. I read palms and talked about astrology signs. A few people asked me to do their charts, and someone asked me to do a horoscope feature in the Anoka newsletter. It was fun getting to know my co-workers.

Every once in a while, I was drawn to my old life. Living in Brooklyn Center took me away from the city and my old haunts, but sometimes an old hook up called and wanted to hang out. He'd end up spending the night, and I always felt guilty afterwards.

One night, I went out with Marty, and I met Tyrel, who needed a place to stay for a couple of nights. I let him stay with me, but I told him absolutely no drugs. He said he could live with that. We ended up sleeping together, and when I woke up in the middle of the night, he wasn't in bed. I went out into the living room, and he was listening to Stevie Wonder and had lines of cocaine spread over the album cover. He was snorting a line as I walked out into the living room. I was livid. I told him to pack up his stuff and I drove him to Minneapolis and dropped him off. Then I drove back home, took the Stevie Wonder album, and threw it away. I didn't want anything to do with cocaine or people like Tyrel.

Every morning, I went to Sherrie's apartment to visit while she got ready for work. When I had a morning after a bad night and I felt anxious and angry with myself, I told her what happened. She hugged and reassured me. There was nothing I could tell her that could shock her; she had no judgment, just a listening ear and a hug. I looked forward to those hugs. My family and old girlfriends didn't hug. Sherrie loved hugs and to talk in the wee hours about everything. A few months later, when I started writing songs, she came over, got comfy on my passion pit, and asked me to sing her my songs. She helped me get comfortable with my creativity because she liked what I created.

She was different than any of my other friends. She went to potlucks, was in a book club, had little girly knick-knacks around her house and decorative candles, and was the first person I ever cried with. She taught me a lot about friendship. Before, I always had plenty of friends and if I decided not to do something at the last minute, I just didn't show up. But Sherrie showed me a whole new way to be a friend.

A month later, Sam and Jon were hired. Pretty soon, all the juvenile probation officers were hanging out together. We went to a movie called *The Centurions*. After, we started calling ourselves The Tomah Centurions because Harry Tomah was our boss. Harry had a lunch meeting one day, and Sam sat next to me. He was tall with blonde hair, and when he sat down, I noticed his striking blue eyes. We started talking, and I found out he played guitar and sang. I asked him if he'd play for me and maybe even teach me.

A week later. he asked what I was doing after work.

When I said, "Nothing," he asked if he could come over and bring some takeout.

I said, "Sure."

He brought Chinese food, two guitars, and a songbook. We ate and talked, and afterwards, he sang for me. I loved watching him play and sing; then, he taught me four chords and left one of his guitars for me to practice on. I was so excited because I felt like a whole new world had opened up to me. Every day after work, I went home and played the four chords and sang. The first song I learned was "The Wreck of the Edmund Fitzgerald." I had written some lyrics a year before, and the next time he came over, Sam helped me find chords for my song.

I liked being with my new co-workers. When I worked at St. Joe's, everyone drank too much, and by the end of two years, I felt like I was working with a bunch of alcoholics. My friends for years liked to drink, smoke dope, and do cocaine. So, it was refreshing to be with my co-workers in Anoka who weren't big drinkers. They were involved in other things. Dave loved to fish and boat. He took me waterskiing a few times. Sam was into music and singing at gigs. Sherrie was into potluck suppers, book clubs, and playing racquetball. So, when we got together to play cards, maybe someone brought a six-pack.

We started having 500 parties, and meeting for lunch during the day. Sometimes, we went out to get a meal after work. Occasionally, spouses joined us. But most of the time, it was just us. It was great having time to talk to others who experienced the same kind of day we just had.

**

It was my job to go on home visits, interview the offender and their family, and come up with a recommendation for the judge when the case went to court for sentencing. Home visits were the hardest because I didn't know what I was walking into. I went to homes in Anoka, Coon Rapids, Circle Pines, Blaine, and Ramsey. Some homes were way out in the country, very isolated, where the closest neighbor was anywhere from one mile to five miles away. Most of the time, the visits went like clockwork, but some visits, I felt something in the air. It stayed there through the interview, and I knew when I left, there was abuse going on. It wasn't in their words. It was just a feeling. Later, I got a phone call, and heard a girl whispering on the phone, telling me that her father did things to her sexually. Other times, the call was about physical family violence. I followed up with another interview that took place in my office, and I talked to child protection.

Along with home visits, I did school visits. I talked to the school counselor, vice principal, and maybe a teacher or a coach, someone who knew the juvenile offender, to determine what resources were available to her. I had students in junior and senior high schools, and because I looked so young, the teachers kept mistaking me for a student. I visited several cases I'd inherited from the previous P.O. that were in various group homes, foster homes, and the Lino Lakes Correctional Facility. Then, I recorded a full report for the judge and progress report for my other cases.

My cases involved robberies, incest, rape, attempted murder, assaults, drug use, intoxication, burglaries, and runaways. I had a girl who stabbed each of her parents 30 times while they were sleeping. The father woke up in the middle of being stabbed, looked at his daughter, and told her to call 911. She stopped and made the call. Because she missed all their major organs, both parents lived. I had a girl who took a pair of scissors and shredded the clothes in her mother's closet before she ran away. I had a father who was an over-the-road trucker who sexually molested both his daughters, and the mother caught him in bed with one daughter. When I talked to the mother about it, she just said she had married him for better or for worse. I had a boy in 6th grade who burglarized a couple of homes and told me in his interview that he did it to get help for his sister, who was pregnant and in ninth grade. He thought if he got in trouble, someone would come in and fix his family, like he saw on TV. So, my co-workers and I had stories to tell, and our shared reality created real camaraderie between us.

I was assigned a volunteer probation officer on a case where one of the children in the family was kept in the closet and had cigarette burns all over his body. That's when I met Karen for the first time. She was a volunteer probation officer and helped me investigate the case. After the case was over, Karen was assigned to another probation officer, and I lost track of her for a while because she was working in the adult unit.

**

That winter, there was a corrections conference in downtown Minneapolis. After the sessions were over, we went out to a club.

It had only been three years since I worked at The Establishment, and when I walked into a club, guys came up to me and said, "How's it going? Helen, haven't seen you in a while."

Some of the guys were pimps I knew from waiting tables, and some were drug dealers and hustlers. My co-workers looked at me like I had three heads. I explained I used to work part-time at a club downtown. They were impressed. My co-workers were suburban white people who didn't hang out with black people, so they had awe in their faces when I talked about my days as a disc jockey and the people I met. I felt so accepted by my co-workers.

Sam and I were getting together regularly to play music. He was comfortable to be around and became someone I trusted, which was hard for me. I found living and working in the suburbs felt alien, a sense of not belonging or connecting anywhere. I grew up in a city, continued to live in cities, which felt different with all the energy and people everywhere. There was always someplace to go: a club, a walk around the lakes, a good restaurant, or a music concert close by. Living in a suburb, I had to drive everywhere; it felt open, sterile, and lonely. I felt a little like a fish out of water. I think I was suffering from culture shock. There wasn't any passion, no throbbing sexuality pulsing in the air, just freeways, highways, and flat land with no lakes and not many trees. The city had lots of trees. My old friends seem distant and far away.

There were days I felt so anxious, I wanted to jump out of my skin. On those days, I'd call Sam and ask if he would come over and keep me company. He felt the most like the people I used to hang out with because of his love of music and his passion about the world around him. I could talk to him. I called him when I was down. I could show my vulnerability and trust knowing he wouldn't expect sex because he was married. He was my white knight protecting me and keeping my loneliness at bay. I loved playing guitar. Sam wrote music, and I listened as he sang, falling in love with his lyrics and the emotions they showed. Our connection really grounded me.

One day, I surprised him and did his astrology chart. He was an interesting man. His chart said he was the master of illusion and good at sleight of hand. It was true; he created a persona around him that kept people wondering. He was also creative, romantic, and sensitive. He was touched by the astrology chart I gave him and began opening up more about his own life. He became one of my best friends.

In the spring Jon, another juvenile PO, and Sherrie hung out sometimes. When Jon came over to my apartment and asked if I'd go out with him, I was confused. I asked about him and Sherrie because I never dated any of my friends' boyfriends. He said they were just friends, and I confirmed it with Sherrie. She was having an affair with married Matt, who was also a PO.

So, Jon and I started dating. Jon was handsome with his blues eyes, dimples, and a sexy moustache. He was medium height and very fit, and I found out he was traditional about relationships. When we started sleeping together, I began feeling pressure to be the girl cooking for the boy who held open doors and protected me. I felt stifled. After a month, we decided to just be friends.

That summer, Sam and I took walks during our lunch break at work. He started telling me he was attracted to me but couldn't act on it because he was married. I said I felt the same way, and it was hard for me, too. But I wanted his friendship more than anything, so we needed to respect the boundaries. He told me when I was dating Jon, he was jealous, even though he had no right to be. We continued to play guitar weekly over the summer with a walk thrown in here and there.

One week, our whole unit attended a workshop on the MMPI. When we broke for lunch, I saw Karen, the volunteer PO, at the fast food place. We started talking and ate lunch together. In our MMPI test, we both scored a high four and a high nine, which meant we were rebellious and independent. Criminals and policemen were usually high four-nines. Karen told me she had been trying to talk to me for months, but I was always so busy or I was hiding behind my hair, so I never saw her. She was glad we were finally talking. She lived in an old farmhouse in the country, played guitar, and sang. She invited me to get together and do music at her farmhouse. She lived with an older guy, who worked construction, by the name of Del. I never knew what I'd find at Karen's farm, one day she had a litter of puppies that I wanted to take home. Karen was quirky and fun, and we shared a love of music. She wasn't into drugs or drinking and seemed just high on the life around her.

Karen and I started hanging out. We had lunch, played guitar, and went to movies. We saw *Prince of the City*, a movie about a police officer agreeing to investigate police corruption. He had to make a choice of bringing his friends down or he'd end up going down.

After the movie, Karen turned to me and said, "I'd never sell you out. I will always have your back."

I was so touched by her loyalty, a loyalty in my life I hadn't felt by many people. She was a friend I could trust. When I started writing songs, Karen created great harmonies for them. She was the first woman I let mother me, and she gave me neck rubs and nurturing hugs. She gave me motherly advice I listened to.

When Sam taught me guitar, it opened a whole new world for me. I loved singing, playing guitar, and writing songs. I started by singing and playing Gordon Lightfoot songs, then I learned "House of the Rising Sun," random songs like "Kumbaya," and "Michael Rowed the Boat Ashore." I put Barbra Streisand on my stereo and sang along to her greatest hits: "People," "Secondhand Rose," "Sam You Made My Pants Too Long," "My Man," and "He Touched Me." I sang at the top of my lungs, transported to a stage, standing in front of hundreds of people listening to me with their faces filled with emotion. I went to see *A Star is Born* twice, and my heart overflowed with the emotions of the songs. They just pulsed through my veins until I got home, and I could stand in my living room and sing those words and feelings, releasing the energy into the world around me. I was the star. I was also in love with my Porgy and Bess album. I sang "Summertime" feeling myself in the hot steamy sun, and I sang "It Ain't Necessarily So," or "I Got Plenty of Nothin'," and the medley "Here Come da Honey Man." I was in that world walking down a dirt road, fields and land surrounding me, and I was wearing a faded sundress torn in places, searching for love. I was the hungry singer, singing her songs while walking through life. I loved my alone time in my apartment with my guitar and my stereo.

**

A couple of months after the MMPI training, there was a two-day workshop by the Johnson Institute about alcoholism that changed my life. It was very detailed, and it was the first time I'd been part of something like this. The very first lecture about alcoholism and how it affected the family started releasing my own hidden memories from a young age. Hearing about the alcoholic's behaviors, I felt like they were talking about my parents and my childhood: my parents deflecting their pain onto us, never admitting their drinking problem. It always became about something bad that we had said or done.

The words of the lectures felt like knives stabbing into my heart. I felt my childhood innocence go up in smoke with every word they spoke.

I ran to the bathroom, hid in the stall, tried to swallow the tears that were in my throat, only to have them pour even harder down my cheeks. Memories and flashbacks of my childhood—the many lies, the physical abuse, the violent temper, the inappropriate touch, the smell of alcohol on their breath, the bloodshot eyes looking at me unfocused, the knot in my stomach from sleepless nights filled with anger and crying, and the chaos, never knowing what to expect when I walked through the door. I sat there and cried my eyes out. My whole life was passing before me in their words. I felt the pain they were describing. I couldn't pretend anymore everything was all right. My parents were sick with a terrible disease that had been slowly killing them over the years.

The workshop broke through a lot of denial. I felt by the end of the workshop my soul had been laid bare for all to see. I'd never felt so vulnerable. Something broke open in me and flooded out. I couldn't stop crying. Karen and Sherrie came in the bathroom and took turns comforting me. I suddenly understood my feelings over the years of not ever really trusting people and how my parents' drinking made me doubt my own reality because they twisted the truth or minimized actions to cover up their drinking. I was always hypervigilant and on guard. I saw what alcoholism had done to my parents, but until that workshop, I didn't realize how much their alcoholism had done to me.

After that workshop, I was different. I felt like I didn't know who I was, like the rock I was standing on was falling away. I started having trouble sleeping. I realized I didn't know what "normal" was. As a young child, my normal came from the books I read because my family was so chaotic. I couldn't wait to leave home and get into the real world to find out what normal was, but once I was out there, I couldn't find what was normal for me. Then, working in the jobs I worked and the families I worked with, I was just continuing the job

I'd been doing all my life: taking care of a dysfunctional family. Over and over I was trying to fix my family. I had lost myself somewhere in all the chaos. I didn't know if there was a normal.

I had a friend who was involved in contest debate, and the issue that year was, "What is happening to the American family?" He asked me to speak. I stood in front of 200 adolescents who listened with rapt attention and took notes about everything I said. I was shocked because the only adolescents I saw were in trouble with the law. So, what was normal? When I visited a group home or treatment center for potential placements for my juvenile offenders, I sometimes felt jealous. The structure and care the treatment homes provided, felt safe, comfortable, and predictable. I wished I could stay there and have the attention focused on me. I was always caring for everyone else. I didn't know what I needed, and maybe I never knew.

**

When Jon moved into a new place, he wanted me to see it, and invited me over for supper after work. We talked while he was cooking, and I told him what happened with me at the workshop and my family stuff. Until then, I was a master at keeping secrets and hiding the truth about what went on at home. When he heard I had trouble sleeping, he invited me to sleep on his couch. I ended up staying there for a couple of nights. The second night I couldn't sleep, and he heard me walking around and invited me to crawl in bed with him. We messed around a little but didn't have sex. When he held me, I slept.

The next day, I went back home and over to Sherrie's. When I walked in her apartment door, she handed me a piece of paper with the name Keith Flanders, a psychologist, and a phone number written on it. She told me she and other POs had been to see him over the years.

Later that week, I saw Sam at work, and he asked me how I was doing. He said his wife was gone for the weekend, and they had a guest bedroom where I could spend the night. So, I went over after work and Sam made us dinner. After dinner, we talked and played guitar until I got sleepy. He settled me into the guest room, and I crawled into bed. I couldn't sleep and felt anxious. I felt so vulnerable and disconnected. I wanted hugs; I wanted friends who knew me. I wanted someone to take care of me. But I didn't really have anyone. I woke Sam up and asked if he'd come lay with me. He came and held me. We started to get sexual, and I stopped him. So, we just laid there, and I fell asleep. I was so happy in the morning because I slept well. I thanked Sam, and the messing around was left unmentioned.

When I arrived at work that day, my boss asked me to come to his office. He told me the adult court needed a person to perform alcohol assessments on DWIs coming through court. He thought it would be a great little side job for me. The next week, I found myself sitting across from adult men and women interviewing them on their drug and alcohol use. I had been trained for this job all my life, and I recommended treatment interventions for a number of people, anything from AA to an in-patient facility.

A couple of nights later Sam, came over and we played music for a while. I was feeling vulnerable and Sam hugged me. The hug turned into a kiss, which turned into oral sex, something I'd never done. My only experience with something like it was when I was in high school with Jerry. But I'd never participated in doing anything myself. Now, I understood why people used the term 69 to refer to oral sex. It was mind blowing. I had never felt so lost or swept up in my physical wanting. It scared me; I didn't want to want him like that; he was my friend; I respected his marriage. I trusted him to set the limit because he was married. I looked at him after and said that could never happen again. I wanted him in my life, so we had to stay just friends.

Chapter 32
So Many Lies, Where's the Truth

I made an appointment to see Keith, the therapist Sherrie recommended. I'd never been in counseling before, so I was nervous. At my first session, I walked in, and Keith was sitting at his desk, writing. At first glance, he looked like a young Santa Claus. His hair had gray in it, and his short-trimmed beard was almost all gray. His belly was just starting to form over his belt. When he looked up at me, his blue eyes were intense with shades of warmth and gentleness. He resembled my father slightly, but only the good parts my father hid away.

I felt anxious and afraid. What truths would come out, and could I really trust him? I was aware of all men's sexuality, and it made me nervous. I didn't want to see him as a sexual being. I wanted to trust him. I sat down on the chair opposite him. He was smiling and started telling me a little about himself, trying to put me at ease. When he turned the conversation over to me, I took a deep breath, started to say something, and instead burst into tears.

He invited me to sit on his lap, which I did, and he held me. I became uncomfortable and went back to my chair. I couldn't believe I sat on his lap and cried in front of him. Sitting on his lap felt kind of good but also inappropriate. Because Sherrie and others recommended him highly, I worked up the courage and told him I didn't feel right sitting on his lap. He apologized, told me I looked so vulnerable, and he felt a need to protect me. I had never had a man nurture me without there being sex involved, so I was suspicious and wasn't sure if I trusted him. I told him a few stories about the men in my past, and eventually talked about what happened at the Johnson Institute workshop. I told him how it had broken through my delusions and defenses, and how I saw my family with more clarity.

As our talking continued, I began to relax a little and told him I felt anxious and out of control because my reality had suddenly changed. I wasn't feeling grounded.

He listened intently, expressing words of encouragement. I talked until I felt drained and empty. His kind eyes looked at me, and he said he understood what it must have felt like to grow up in my family. He talked about alcoholism. I told him my father was diagnosed as bipolar, but I always thought it was the use of alcohol that created his mood swings. He explained how bipolar people often self medicated with alcohol. When I shared some of my past, he didn't criticize me, he just told me he understood my behavior and my need to break free from the dysfunction in my family. Trying to find my own identity by dating hippies, people of color, and different cultures were my way to live outside the lines my family created. He said it was a sign of strength and resilience. I left that night feeling stronger inside, like I was OK because someone finally listened to me and understood.

At our next counseling session, I tried to control the sessions with my talking and analysis of things I was angry about. Then, quietly, Keith interrupted and threw in an insight that hit deep. I was suddenly crying, not in control anymore. It was uncomfortable for me and confusing. It took my breath away, and my life seemed uncertain. I didn't have all the answers; I really wasn't in control. I began to relax in those healing moments. Keith helped me understand that when I was younger, I didn't know I could be angry. I had learned if I was hurt and angry, I could distance from the feelings if I analyzed what happened. If I could understand the reason it happened, then I'd feel better. If my mother yelled at me, and I later found out she wasn't feeling well, I could forgive her. It helped me forgive my father for things because of his mental illness and drinking. As I got older and in touch with my anger, it motivated me to make changes. I started to stick up for myself and not accept certain behaviors.

Keith added that under my anger was fear. I could have become a victim and let my fear win, but instead, I got angry, which motivated me. I became a survivor. That's where I got my strength. He commended me for trying to find my own truth, one that made sense to me, since my parents' attitudes didn't. My resilience kept me looking for who or what I could trust and hold onto. Because of my parents' drinking, there were so many lies, secrets, and shame buried inside our home, and my parents created barriers to keep out the truth. When I tried to break through the barriers, it threatened their existence.

At the end of the session, I was exhausted. I started to walk to my car and lost my vision. I had squiggly lines of lights flashing through my eyes, which I'd never had before. I walked back to Keith's office, and he asked me if there was someone I could stay with. The only person I could think of was my sister Becca, who now lived near downtown. I got my car, and he followed me to Becca's to make sure I made it OK. I slept on her couch, told to her about counseling and what I had learned at the Johnson Institute workshop, and we cried together.

That night, lying on her couch, I had trouble sleeping. There with so many thoughts and memories running through my head after the counseling session. I felt like that little four- year-old girl again with leeches covering my legs at the resort where I was trying to catch minnows with my net. When I caught one, I didn't know what to do, so I threw it back in the water. My thoughts were like the minnows swimming around aimlessly. I kept trying to catch hold of one to make sense of my sleeplessness, or understand the words running around my head, about family, alcohol, and my life. Just when I thought I caught one, and it started to show me something important, it got away. I lay there staring at the white ceiling, hoping all my thoughts would come together and finally give me the answer. Eventually, I drifted off into a restless sleep, waking up exhausted. Becca was gone when I got up, and I went to work.

Sam came over a week later. He brought his guitar and played a song he wrote about me: *how does it feel to be alone, lost in your ideals, how could you have known just how lonely life could feel.*

After my counseling sessions in the last two weeks, those words hit a place deep inside me. I cried, Sam held me, and told me he loved me. He said he wanted to leave his wife and move in with me.

I pulled away from him, looking into his eyes, and he was serious. It freaked me out. I started talking fast, saying we couldn't do that because we worked together, and he was married. I was attracted to him, but I told him that we had to be just friends or I couldn't hang out with him. I liked his wife. When I stopped to take a breath, he got up, looking hurt, grabbed his guitar, and left. I felt so sad because I cherished our time together playing guitar and I didn't want to lose our friendship.

**

I saw Sam at work on Friday morning, and he asked about getting together to play music. We hadn't gotten together since the night he talked about leaving his wife a week ago.

I said, "Sure."

He brought food and his guitar, and we played and sang for hours. It felt so good. I loved having him in my life and sharing music.

But after we finished playing our last song, he turned and kissed me; we ended up in a wrestling match on the floor. He wanted to have sex, and I said no vehemently. We argued, and I asked him to stay away. He picked up his guitar angrily and walked out the door.

Sam started making weird comments at work about how he saw me doing different things, like swimming in my apartment building's indoor pool or watching me when I used jumper cables to start my car outside my apartment building. It felt like he was stalking me. I missed getting together with Sam, but I knew I had to keep my distance. I saw him only at work.

Meanwhile, at work, things were changing for Sherrie. Matt and his wife separated. Sherrie was happy because now she and Matt could date openly. But once Matt was divorced, he wanted to see other women. Sherrie had waited for him to leave his wife for months, so she broke it off.

Sherrie and I started having many late nights of girl talk with food and my guitar, commiserating about men.

Playing guitar was very important to me. A lot of people went home after work and had a cocktail, a beer, or class of wine to relax. I got home, took out my guitar, and practiced for hours. I started writing my own songs. Music started to open me up, and I heard melodies in my head. I'd hum and find chords to match what I was humming. A couple of days later, words started to come to me and suddenly I had written a song. Sometimes, they were sad with minor chords; other times they were happy with major chords.

It was really nice to have a built-in groupie section with Sherrie and sometimes Leila, who came over and asked me to play my songs when they were having a bad day. Music was also my way to free myself of all the built-up emotions from working every day with chaotic families. I worked so closely with such intense situations in other people's lives, I needed a release, so I wrote words and melodies to free the energy I had collected that day. It felt good to sing loud with anger or joy or sing soft with love or sadness. It was my escape; it was my refuge. I finally started finding some equilibrium. I was finding a new sense of myself and I was doing better.

**

Meanwhile, my caseload at work was as intense as usual. One of my juvenile offenders, Mandy, ran away from her group home. I was walking out the door to see a concert one night when the phone rang. It was the sheriff's department in southern Illinois. Mandy was picked up for shoplifting, and he noticed she was wanted for running away from her group home in Minnesota. I made arrangements to fly her home and found someone to pick her up and bring her to the group home. I missed the concert and a good night's sleep.

Elena was a girl on my caseload who was the daughter of a government official who had passed away a couple of months earlier. She was caught joy riding in a stolen car with stolen merchandise in the back seat. When I did an investigation, I found out that after her father passed away, she changed her friends, started smoking and drinking, and eventually, went joyriding and skipping school. She was just a couple of months from graduating and had good grades prior to losing her father. She was put on house arrest, ordered to get back into school, and to stop drinking. She and her mother went to grief counseling, and her mother took a parenting class for single mothers. Her father had been a stern limit setter, and, as her probation officer, I became the limit setter. She started attending school regularly; no more joyrides and shoplifting adventures. And, she got back with her old friends. Elena did great and was soon off house arrest. I was invited to her high school graduation party.

Another girl I worked with was Tracy. She was in high school and was stunningly beautiful with long graceful fingers, well-manicured nails, a full head of luscious brown wavy hair, and stunning green eyes. She was the granddaughter of a retired judge. When she was little, her father shot her mother and then killed himself, so her grandparents raised her. At fifteen, she was caught smuggling drugs into the jail to her twenty-four-year-old boyfriend. She got probation.

I also had two sisters, Denise and Brandy, who were burglarizing homes for their father, who was a fence, and shoplifting at Target for their mother, who returned the items they shoplifted for the money. The girls got caught. Again, these were some very attractive girls who could often charm the judge, faking sweet innocence. The older girl, Brandy, made a real mistake. Her judge was a softy, and started giving her fatherly advice.

She turned, looked him straight in the eye, and said, "Judge, why don't you just shut the fuck up?"

He pounded his gavel, face red, and sent her to Lino Lakes.

I had, Laura, who was in the ninth grade and on probation for shoplifting. When I interviewed her, I learned that one day her mother left for work, and her father, who was unemployed and depressed, said he was going to take a nap. He went in his bedroom and a few minutes later, he suddenly yelled out with pain, so she ran in. He had stabbed himself in the stomach, trying to commit suicide. She called 911, the ambulance came, but he passed away en route to the hospital. Laura told me she took his bloody sheets, washed them, and put them in the dryer. When she saw a piece of her father's skin stuck on the side of the washing machine, she lost it, and started crying. All the time she was telling me the story, she had no expression on her face. She was one of my hardest cases because she was so quiet and withdrawn and it was hard to get a read on her.

The female juvenile probation officers started grumbling because of the large geographic area we had to cover. If we had boys and girls on our caseload, it would be smaller. So, we got together and wrote a proposal to the court to change the rule. Our proposal was heard, and we were granted the request to have boys and girls on our caseloads. Our driving area was cut in half, and the system became a lot more efficient.

**

Craig, an adult PO, and I moved into an office in the Coon Rapids police department. Craig was strait-laced and serious. But I enjoyed sharing an office with him. One day, I was filling out an application to the U of M to get my master's in social work and scheduling a time to take the GRE test to get in. Craig asked me what I was doing. After I told him, he said he'd always wanted to be an FBI agent. I said, so did I, so we looked up the credentials we'd need. At that time the FBI was looking for people with a master's in accounting or economics because there were a lot of crimes involving financial institutions.

We looked at each other and said, "No way. Accounting degree, boring."

The next day, I was driving home from the Anoka office, driving down Coon Rapids Blvd and noticed a car following close behind me. I sped up, and so did he. I slowed down, and he did too. I changed lanes, and he went along with me. When I stopped at the next stoplight, he nosed his car against my rear bumper and started to gun his car and push my car into the intersection against the red light. I slammed down on my breaks, and just as I reached to put on the emergency brake, the light turned green. I gunned it through the intersection and turned into the Coon Rapids police department. He took off then. I waited a couple of minutes to make sure he didn't come back, and then I drove home. I wondered if it was someone on my caseload or was it just a random act. No one followed me home. I sighed with relief.

The police officers in Coon Rapids stopped in occasionally to visit. They invited us on a ride-a-long to experience what happened on their watch. The following Friday night, I rode with them. Our first call was a domestic disturbance at an apartment building. On the way there, they told me these calls were always the most unpredictable because of the intensity of the emotions mixed with alcohol or drugs. When we entered the building, they told me to stay back and wait down the hall. I could hear two people yelling, and someone was crying. The officers knocked on the door and stepped back. A man answered the door, and the police went in. I walked up and watched through the open door. I could hear them talking quietly to the man, whose face was red with rage. One officer put his hand on the man's shoulder to comfort him. The woman was crying, cowering on the couch. One officer sat with her while the other one steered the man down the hall of the apartment. Eventually, everyone was talking in quiet tones. The woman decided not to press charges, the two hugged each other, said they were sorry, and we left.

When we got back in the squad car, there was a call to a wooded area by the river where an armed robber was seen fleeing. We got down to this very isolated, deserted area, thick with trees. The officers drove in as far as they could, and then, they took off on foot, leaving me alone in the squad car. It was at night, very dark, and no one was around. I waited nervously for the officers to come back, and the longer they were gone, the more nervous I got. I was alone down there. No means to contact anyone, I didn't know how to operate the comms in the squad car, and the officer took the car keys with him. My mind started imagining all sorts of scary scenarios; an angry man charging the car, or a wild animal. Finally, I saw the bobbing of a flashlight and I could make out police uniforms. I breathed a huge sigh of relief.

**

When my GRE test score finally came, I found out I was two points too low to be accepted into graduate school. I was disappointed. I liked being a probation officer, but it was long, intense hours, filled with cases of families and individuals suffering from major life events.

I used to say I could take my caseload and divide it in thirds. The first third were juvenile offenders with a first offense; the court experience and probation were all the person needed to change. The second third were juvenile offenders who needed more intervention, like chemical dependency treatment or group and family counseling, and they probably wouldn't be back in the system again. The third group were juvenile offenders who appeared in court several times, been sent to Lino Lakes, participated in chemical dependency programs, and had a family history of court involvement. They would probably never really change, and they were the part of my caseload I spent the most time and energy.

The first two-thirds of my cases kept me going, inspiring me to work harder, and the last one-third created burnout. So, I started to want something different.

**

In my sessions with Keith, I talked about wanting to fix myself so I could fit into my family. I always felt I was defective and wanted to belong. When I went into my next session, I was upset because of something my family did; I asked what I could do to fix them. But Keith's response was I wasn't responsible for fixing them, and the only person I could fix was me. Eventually, I realized I wasn't defective, and I deserved hugs and honesty. Once I realized there was nothing I could do to change my family, I felt defeated. I didn't know how to belong and lost hope of things being better. Keith told me I had to mourn the loss of my family, even though they were still alive. I had to mourn the loss of the family I wanted.

When Derek graduated from high school in Brookings, I drove to his graduation. I saw my family, who I hadn't seen for a while, and I met Derek's friends and saw the golf shop he was going to work at for the summer. My brother took me aside and whispered that he was concerned because our parents were drinking again. My hopes were shattered once again. When I talked to the rest of the family, we decided to have a family intervention when they were in town for Thanksgiving. The intervention didn't go so well. My parents said their drinking was under control, and they didn't feel the need to change their ways.

In the next session with Keith, I brought up my mother and how I couldn't understand why she never liked me and seemed to avoid me when I was little. Now I was an adult, and she would call my sisters periodically, but she never called me. I always had to call her. The tears started trickling down my cheeks as I once again felt like the ugly duckling in our family.

I started talking about how scary it was when William had polio, and then I heard myself telling Keith about the day a piece of me went missing. I talked about seeing my father lying on the bed, looking at me with sadness in his eyes and a smile on his face. I was suddenly that little girl again climbing on the bed to comfort my father, not understanding what my father's hands were doing. I felt his sadness, and then I felt my mother's hands suddenly yank me off the bed, screaming and telling me to go to my room. I felt the confusion I had back then with tears pouring down my cheeks. Keith and I sat there quietly for a couple of minutes until I got myself under control.

When I looked up at Keith, his eyes were soft and warm.

He said quietly, "I'm sorry that happened to you."

I took a big breath and slowly released it as I relaxed in my chair. Keith understood.

He said what my father was doing that day was not my fault. My parents couldn't face what happened, so they couldn't face me. He said I felt abandoned because I was. It was emotional abandonment. I had to become invisible so they could stay together. No matter how loud I screamed or how far I jumped, they couldn't see me. He said they took my innocence, a sense of belonging, and feeling safe and protected from me that day. He explained that at some deep level, my mother was jealous and threatened by me because of the affection my father showed me. It was something he hadn't been giving her. She did leave me that day, like a sudden death, and that incident changed my life completely. He talked about emotional incest, and how from what I had told him, I seemed to be my father's confidante, and my mother pushed me to take care of him. That's why he came to me to talk about his problems even when I was a young girl.

Keith looked at me with fondness and said, "What a resilient child you were, so smart and resourceful."

In our next session, he started helping me give voice to my special, lost, invisible child. He knew so much about me now, so many things I never shared with anyone, and he saw my beauty and who I really was. In his eyes, I wasn't defective. In my sessions with Keith, I started to unleash my creativity and the need to express myself through music, writing, dance, and creative outlets. I learned to not bury my vulnerability and my emotions anymore. I learned to take risks. He helped me express myself and learn to love and see myself. He helped me reclaim parts of my childhood I left behind. I bought self-hardening clay and sculpted figures like the "thinker" or representational busts of people I'd met. I went out, bought the Betsy-Tacy series, and read it again.

As a result of our sessions, I signed up for a performance class at MacPhail School of Music. I performed an "audition" piece to get in the class. I wore my leather jacket and jeans and brought my guitar. I sang a song I wrote. I felt shy, and I hid behind my long hair so I couldn't see the audience. The teacher called me that night and said she looked forward to working with me. She liked my song and my voice. In class, I worked on two performance songs, "Sam You Made My Pants Too Long," and "Secondhand Rose," by Barbra Streisand.

Our first performance was at a mansion in Kenwood. It was a huge house with a grand piano in the middle of their living room and a grand staircase at the entrance when we walked in. It was an intimate setting with a small audience of maybe twenty people. The accompanist sat at the grand piano, and we all performed our two songs. It felt so special. It went very well, and I started to build a little confidence.

Then, we performed at a restaurant, Howard Wongs on the 494 strip. It was a piano bar and restaurant. When I got there, I thought I was going to throw up. The dining room was packed, and every table was full. I told the teacher I didn't think I could do it; I'd just sit and listen.

When everyone had performed and I was the only one left, the teacher went to the microphone and said, "OK, Helen, this is your time. Do you want to sing or not?"

I slowly stood up and walked to the microphone, feeling put on the spot. The music started, I swallowed a couple of times, saw a painting of a lake with two swans on the wall. I sang my two songs looking at the painting. Towards the end, I ventured a look at the audience. They were listening, and when I was done, I got a lot of applause.

After that experience, I saw an ad in the paper for performers to sing telegrams. It was the "The Original Singing Telegram Company," and it operated out of an office that was over a photography shop. I was hired and worked evenings and weekends. I could sing covers, or I could sing songs that I wrote. Weekly, I checked in with the office and got names and phone numbers to contact. I called the client and asked personal questions about the person I was singing to. Then, I wrote a song with all the personal, poignant, funny details about them. I did birthdays and weddings.

One day, I went to a hospital and sang to the woman's father whose head had been hit by a closing garage door before the current safety features. He was in bad shape with stitches across his shaved head. I'm not sure how much he heard because he kept nodding off. One time, I dressed as a gorilla; another time, I wore a black leotard with a top hat and tails, walking in with a rose in my teeth and standing on a table to sing a personalized happy birthday to someone's co-worker. I must admit, the first few times I went out to perform, I felt nauseated with nerves. But eventually, the jitters turned into excitement. I loved doing them and getting the applause and positive comments. It helped balance out the harsh reality and angry words I heard from my juvenile offenders and their families.

My counseling with Keith was a monumental change in how I saw myself. He was the first person who mirrored back to me what he saw. He wasn't the men I was seeing who mostly just wanted sex, and he wasn't my alcoholic parents who were self-absorbed. He was someone who helped me understand who I was and validated my inner dreams. He told me once our counseling sessions felt to him like he was giving me the parental advice I never got growing up.

The sessions awakened me to my love for music and creativity. I had felt for years like I had this powerful energy trapped inside an armor of protection. I didn't know how to express all the emotional energy that was trapped inside. Sam helped with the guitar lessons and bringing out my songs, and Keith helped by reflecting back to me who I was. I found something I needed so badly.

**

I had my astrology chart done by a well-known astrologer. When it was finished, they told me I had so much creative energy, I would always need a lot of creative outlets or I would have trouble sleeping. I needed outlets for all my intense energy. It was a good thing I was singing, playing guitar, and writing songs and stories while I was a probation officer.

One day, I was visiting a girl at Lino Lakes, and I started thinking about incest victims. I learned from my own experience that incest victims are not connected to their bodies and emotions, and they lived in their heads for survival. Also, people who were raised in institutional settings learned to talk a good game and sound sincere because they knew how to play the system. So, I came up with the idea of teaching classes that worked the body and emotions, using creativity. I got special funding on a trial basis for a two-month period to work a couple of evenings at Lino Lakes. One class was Disco Dance, which was big at that time. The juvenile inmates loved it, and it was a healthy physical way to release pent up negative emotions. I also taught a sculpting class, bringing in self-drying clay. The juveniles loved making things that came from deep inside they didn't have to talk about. I also taught creative writing. The stories they had were many, some sad, some hilarious, but all an expression of things hidden inside coming out in safe ways to show the world.

I enjoyed teaching the classes so much, I decided to look into creating my own degree at the U of M. I met with an advisor on campus and showed him my proposal for using a few disciplines in the degree. It was a degree in counseling that included massage, music, movement, and art therapy. As a counselor, I could use a variety of skills to help the client access emotions. Our body holds emotions in our muscles, and I could access them using movement or music to help release the emotions. I could use creative, artistic expression to go in and find buried emotions and traumas or massage using therapeutic touch for those who had suffered physical abuse or trauma. He was interested in my proposal and said he would get back to me. When we met again, he told me the people he talked with said it was too ambitious and had too many components, so they turned it down. I really thought I had an answer. I saw what I did at Lino and how it changed the girls. I wanted the skills to help people in what I called a holistic therapeutic environment.

After seeing Keith for a year, we decided I should come in only when I needed a session. He was a psychologist, and he wasn't covered by my insurance, so I had quite a hefty bill. When we changed my counseling status, he explained that he knew he was encouraging me to change my job and pursue who I was. So, he slashed my bill in half.

**

A month later, The Bailey Institute hosted a conference, and the Anoka county probation officers were required to attend. I went to a women's workshop where I heard Cynthia, a therapist from the Bailey Institute speak. As I listened to her, I thought about my close friends in the past, who were never vulnerable with me but we helped each other to survive, each of us coming out of our own family dysfunction. My friends weren't looking to get married, have children, and take care of their husbands. We were forging our own paths. My old friends, in some ways, were a lot like my mother; they didn't talk about feelings, they avoided intimacy, and they thought I was too emotional and sensitive. I was the one who took care of them, being a designated driver, or just a listening ear to their frustrations. None of us really trusted men. I had temp jobs where I worked with women who talked about shopping, redecorating their house, what clothes labels were the best to buy, getting married, and gossiping about other women, and I thought they were boring. Sherrie and Karen showed me a whole new way to be friends and that women with goals could be vulnerable, sensitive, and not afraid of intimacy. As I listened to Cynthia at the conference, I wanted to understand more about my own feminine side, and I signed up for an individual session.

I saw her for a couple of private sessions, and then invited my mother to a session, which didn't go so well because my mother became defensive and couldn't accept my feelings. Cynthia talked about how much I wanted to have an honest relationship with her, one of support and love. But my mother seemed threatened by the session. After the session, she was even more distant.

Cynthia started a women's group and invited me to participate, instead of doing individual session. It was a good place to work on my issues about men and their role in my life.

It was an interesting group of women. Sandy, a tall, beautiful, athletic woman lived in an exclusive, wealthy neighborhood. She loved horses and outdoor activities. She was married to a very rich, important man who had a weird fetish. He liked to wear women's pantyhose to bed and rub up against her. Julie was a little chubby with black curly hair and was newly divorced with three children. She had MS. Sue was medium height, very slim and blonde, and was a lesbian. Her family rejected her when they found out. She was very involved in the NOW movement. Donna was petite with long dark hair, very timid, and shy. And Carla was uptight, strait-laced, and married to a man who was a youth minister. I liked the women and felt safe in the group. It was an atmosphere where I got some mirroring about myself. One day, I talked to them about a girl on my caseload. I told them she was like a little animal living on the streets, following her instincts, not connecting or trusting, just reacting to people around her.

The group said, almost at the same time, "Yes, like you."

I was surprised, but the more I thought about it, it was true.

Sandy and I became friends, and I slept at her house a couple of times when her husband was out of town. She started seeing another man and fixed me up with his friend. I found the men to be very unattractive and boring. They were small, skinny, rich white guys who talked about their country club and playing tennis. Then, the three of them talked about horses and whether they should race a certain breed. I couldn't relate to anything they were saying because my background didn't include country clubs or horses. I was about parties and living on the edge. So, I barely said three words. I am not a shy person, but my attempts at conversation fell flat. So, we never double dated again, but we remained friends.

My counseling experiences gave me insight. I had felt most my life like a rudderless boat, caught in the middle of conflicting currents tossing me to and fro. Sometimes, I caught a current and went in that direction; then, a wave came and changed my course. I didn't know the rules. The rules my family had changed with the alcohol flow in the house. I grew up with a sense of how far I could comfortably go in any situation, but a code of conduct escaped me. Reasons for rules eluded me. I lived what felt right at the time and reacted to events around me by surviving the situation. When I heard people talking in black and white language, right and wrong rules, I always thought *according to whom?* There are so many ways to live, to look at things, to experience things; it all depends on your own life experience. I wanted to feel the comfort of absolute truth or absolute reality, but it escaped me.

My parents' prejudice was wrong. I had friends I cared deeply about in grade school, and I read books with characters that suffered from prejudice in their lives: Anne Frank and her sad, poignant story about being a child in the world of Hitler; the young girl, Francie, in *A Tree Grows in Brooklyn* and how reading helped her escape growing up in a world of poverty and her father's alcoholism; and Asher Lev in *My Name is Asher Lev,* about a Hasidic Jew whose inclination to artistic endeavors threatened his family and traditions. I loved the people I met in my life and the stories I read. It was like my parents were afraid, and they lived in a walled off city that was their life. Their blinders kept out anything that might upset the apple cart of their daily existence. Their alcoholism colored everything in my childhood, and I felt like a prisoner. With counseling, I started to understand how different I was from them. I liked who I was and felt sadness that they would never know me. I was the honesty they wanted to avoid.

The rudderless boat that was being tossed by the river's current was changing into a free spirit. I was excited to create and experience the life around me. I became the fingers playing the strings of my own life.

When Sherrie talked about renting a townhouse together, I was excited. We found one on the outskirts of Brooklyn Park, which felt far from the cities. I liked the idea of living with a close friend, but as it came closer to signing a lease, I got a knot in my stomach because the townhouse seemed too isolated. In my sessions with Keith, he helped me look at probation work and how it perpetuated my family script. He encouraged me to find another job. I realized I wanted to study creative outlets, like music and writing. I wanted to go back to school at the U.

Just before Sherrie and I were to sign the lease, I backed out. We had already given our notice and she was upset but understood. She found another roommate. I found an apartment in South Minneapolis close to the University where I wanted to go back to school, and it was close to my beloved lakes. It was time to quit my probation job, so I handed in my two-week notice.

Chapter 33
Music Man, Fill My Heart with the Notes of Your Love Song.

I moved into an upstairs duplex in Minneapolis with the help of my friends. Peggy, who was my age, owned the house and lived in the downstairs apartment. Her roommate, Jenny, was also our age. We became friends. The "front" door to my apartment was on the side of the house. I had a kitchen and a small living room with my "passion pit," love seat and chair. I had a small area to set up my stereo and guitar. There was one bedroom and a bathroom with a tub. And best of all, off the kitchen was a little balcony that could seat maybe two or three people comfortably. I sat out there, writing songs and playing guitar. I loved it. For the first time, I moved into an apartment when I wasn't running away from something because now I was finding myself.

I started my own singing telegram company called "Sing O Gram." I still worked for "The Original Singing Telegram Company." If I went out and performed for the Original Singing Telegram, I promoted them and passed out their cards.

Performing telegrams was an adventure. I wrote a "get-back telegram" to a man who did actuarial work at an insurance company. He and a female co-worker were friends and found themselves in bed together one night. After, he backed off. She wanted me to embarrass him at lunch at his insurance company downtown. I asked her if he had a sense of humor because I didn't want to get hit. She said he was a Leo and would love the attention. So, I wrote a song about a man who loved his figures, so long as they were 36-24-36, then I went to his work and walked through the crowded lunchroom in my top hat and tails, yelling his name. When I found him, I said, "This singing telegram is for you," and sang it.

He loved it, and everyone around him laughed. When the song was finished, I handed him the lyrics and a cassette tape of the song.

One day, I got a call from a woman who wanted to send a birthday telegram to her friend Dorothy, who worked on the eighth floor of the Soo Line railroad building. I wrote the song, drove downtown, and went in with my top hat and tails carrying my guitar. I went to the eighth-floor receptionist, asked where I could find Dorothy, and she pointed her out. I got my guitar out and told Dorothy who the telegram was from.

I got a third of the way through the song, when a very angry man came charging out of his office, yelling "Stop that, stop that!" Then, he looked at me and said, "Get the hell out of here."

He didn't want "my kind" in his workplace and told me to leave immediately.

I gave the woman her song and tape and left. In the elevator, a man got on with me and apologized for Fred, who was the man who yelled at me. He said Fred was unbalanced and often yelled at his employees. For instance, if he saw two people standing and talking, he would run out of his office and tell them to get back to work or he'd put a stick up their butt. He was very irrational.

When I got home, the client, who hired me, called and said her friend got fired because I sang to her at the office. I couldn't believe it. I got the name of the president of the Soo Line railroad and called him. I told him the experience I had and how I had been treated. I explained Fred's unstable and irrational behavior and how he fired the person I sang to, who had no idea I was coming. I said that if Fred didn't want me in the office, he could have calmly asked me to leave, instead of being abusive and swearing at me. The president listened, took notes, apologized for what happened, and said he would investigate. The next day, I got a call from an employee on the eighth floor of the Soo Line railroad. She told me the whole eighth floor took up a collection and wanted to take me out for dinner and drinks at the Black Angus to thank me because when Dorothy came to work that morning to get her things, Fred called her into his office, and apologized for his irrational behavior and gave her job back. They said Fred had never apologized to anyone before. They thanked me for talking to the president and making things right. The next night, I had dinner with some wonderful people from the eighth floor of Soo Line railroad.

**

A couple weeks after I moved into my duplex, Karen and I went to a piano bar downtown. We met an extremely good-looking man from California who was here on business. He had striking blue eyes, a nice tan, and wavy blonde hair and was tall and trim. We hit it off, and he had a great sense of humor. He invited us back to his hotel room when the piano bar closed. We went up there and visited for a while. Then, he asked me what I was doing the next day. I said I had nothing planned, and he asked if I would show him around Minneapolis. We made arrangements for the next day, and I picked him up around 10:00 a.m.

We drove around the lakes, and eventually, parked and walked. He told me that he lived in the L.A. area and was in advertising. He was the person who came up with jingles and ideas for the ads; he was their "creative thinker." He said he had never been to Minneapolis. I told him he was lucky it was summer. We had a great time together, and he said he'd like to extend his trip a day, if he could spend the night at my place.

I said, "Sure," so we got his luggage, and he checked out of the hotel.

He took me out to dinner, and we went to a club to listen to music.

When we got home, we made love with a soft summer breeze drifting through my bedroom window. It was magical. He was drop dead gorgeous and in my bed. He was a gentle lover, and the next morning, he made love to me again.

After, we were lying there, and he said, "Thank you."

I could hear tears in his voice. I propped myself up on my elbow and looked at him. Then, with a couple of tears running down his cheeks, he told me I was the first woman he'd been with in a long time. He said that after a horrific divorce, he'd turned to men for comfort. He said I had helped him by being warm, caring, and free of game playing. Because I was so genuine and open, he was able to have such a special night and morning.

Later, we went out to lunch, and I brought him to Anoka to get my last paycheck. When we got there, he asked if he could use the phone. I went to get the check.

Sherrie, Lori, Carla, and a couple of other people came up and asked almost drooling, "Who is that guy?"

When he came over, I introduced him. Later, we went out for dinner, and I drove him to the airport. I dropped him off, and he thanked me for our time together. I received a letter from him a couple of weeks later; he thanked me again for my hospitality and loving, warm personality. He said he returned to California feeling like a new man.

That weekend, my cousin Mary, who was older and one of the cousins who lived up the block from me when I lived on Queen Avenue, called. She was taking a watercolor class and met a man there she thought I might like. He was a priest who left the clergy and was starting to date women. I told her to give him my number. Michael called a couple of days later; we talked for a while, and then, he asked me to brunch. When he picked me up Sunday morning, we drove downtown to a trendy place. Michael was handsome with chiseled and sharp looking features. We went to a cafe that had a garden area with flowers and a small waterfall. The food was nice, the atmosphere was peaceful, and Michael was a good conversationalist. His hair was silvery white. He told me it turned gray at an early age. He was a retired Jesuit priest and worked in Chicago for years at a seminary as the principal of the school. Now, he was exploring life after priesthood.

When he brought me home, I invited him in. We sat on my loveseat and talked for a long time about books. Suddenly, he lunged at me, held me down against the cushions, kissed me hard, sat up, and said he'd better go. I sat there, stunned.

He called the next day to set up a date to play racquetball at the Decathlon Club; we had both discovered we liked to play. The following Saturday, we played in the afternoon and went back to his place where he made dinner. Afterward, we sat on the couch and talked. He told me about the seminary and becoming a priest. He shared how he was brainwashed about women. First, he was shown pictures of women in disturbing ways and told over and over women were dirty and evil. His desires shriveled up and died. When he had an awakening serving in the priesthood, he didn't agree with the teachings about women and wanted to live like a regular man.

I talked to him a little bit about our first encounter and how uncomfortable I felt with the sudden change in behavior. We talked for quite a while and again, he suddenly made a very abrupt move on me. After a few minutes I said I had to get going. I was glad to get out of there. I felt attacked and uncomfortable. I didn't go out with him again. I heard later, from Mary, he became a male model and a soap opera star in New York.

I suddenly started getting phone calls from Sam again. We had stayed distant friends at work and said goodbye when I left my probation job. I was surprised when he called, but he said now that I wasn't working at the same place as him, maybe we could see each other again. He came over one night, but things felt different and he started pressuring me for sex again. I still cared about him; he had given me support through a hard time. But it wasn't the same, and I didn't like the pressure. When he left, I knew I'd never see him again, but periodically through my life, I would get a random phone call from him.

I continued to play my guitar every day and wrote songs. One day, I bought the Twin Cities Reader and saw ads for band auditions. I went to a couple of them, and the first band offered me drugs and alcohol before the audition, which I declined. The audition didn't go well. The second audition was even worse, and I got too nervous. Then, Karen found an ad in the paper, and we went to audition together. We drove out to a bar on a small two-lane road. It felt like we were way out in the country. I realized later, it was the outskirts of

Eden Prairie. We pulled up to a deserted bar, parked, knocked on the front door, and wondered if we had the right address. When the door opened, there was a six-foot, dark-haired man towering over us with biceps my hands wouldn't have fit around. He had a full beard and looked like he just hopped off his Harley after a night out with his motorcycle gang.

Then, he smiled and said, "My name is Mike."

He asked if we were there for the audition. He had a beautiful smile, and a soft voice.

We stepped into the barroom where there was a drum set and microphones set up in the middle of the room, instead of tables and chairs. There was a guy on the drums and a guy with a guitar. Mike played lead guitar. Karen and I took turns auditioning, and at the end of the audition, we hung out a while.

Mike kept flirting with me, and we started talking just the two of us. Karen was talking to the rhythm guitar player and drummer. Mike hesitated and then said that he wanted to ask me to be in the band, but he never dated anyone in the band. Then, he paused and said he really wanted to ask me out. He said it was my choice; I could either be in the band or date him. I chose to date him, and Karen became the singer in the band.

Later that week, I saw a flyer for the Zoe Sealey Dance studio at the corner store. The dance studio was close to my apartment, and I started studying dance again. I took ballet, modern, and jazz. It was a great form of exercise, and I loved dancing to the rhythm of the music, learning ways to move and use my body in a healthy, strengthening way. I still held on to a secret dream of being a dancer with a lean muscular body, moving with grace and passion on the stage. I wanted to float on the musical notes, interpreting them into visceral movements that grounded me.

The women's group I was going to was ending. Cynthia was getting married. In an individual session, she told me she was attracted to me. I said I was flattered but I only liked men that way. She talked about her upcoming marriage. She had just completed Hebrew school and felt ready for the Jewish wedding her parents were planning for her. At the next group session, Sue told me she was attracted to me, and knew she wasn't my sexual preference. Then, Julie spoke up and said she was attracted to me, too. I was confused. I had been raised to feel invisible and not very attractive. When I worked at The Establishment, I became overwhelmed with the attention I was getting from men, so I cut my hair short to get some relief, and now, here I was with women saying they were attracted to me. It was overwhelming. I started wondering what I was doing to get this kind of attention. Cynthia helped me sort out it was nothing I'd done, and there was nothing I had to do about it.

Carla from the women's group heard me talk about taking dance classes. Her husband was a youth minister who needed a dancer to perform at his church up north, someone to interpret the music in a dance moving down the aisle of the church. I said I would do it. I rehearsed and came up with movements that flowed with the music and interpreted the message of the song. I enjoyed the rehearsing. The weekend we were supposed to leave to drive up north, I got the stomach flu. I had to cancel; there was nothing I could do.

The women's group had one more session before Cynthia left on her honeymoon. We had a potluck and said goodbyes with hugs and tears.

Chapter 34
Art's Song: You Were So Warm and Gentle Last Night

Mike and I started dating. He was not like anyone I'd known before. His parents lived in the back of the bar where we auditioned. They ran the bar in the evenings, which was a popular dive bar in the country. His mother must have weighed at least three hundred pounds, and his father was small and thin. Mike had a private entrance to the basement where he lived. Mike and I ate with his parents and his sister Jody once a week. He built his own guitars, wrote his own songs, and was the lead guitar player and singer in his band. He was a country boy and very introverted. He worked out with weights every day and had wide shoulders and narrow hips.

At first glance, he looked like a tough biker traveling with a bike gang, but when I got to know him, he was gentle, soft-spoken, and sensitive. His family was religious, and Mike believed in what the Bible said, especially the part where the man should have the last word. I loved to watch him sing and play guitar. We became lovers fairly quickly, and he was passionate and intense. He made me feel fragile and treated me like a precious flower. I went to his gigs, watching him and Karen perform.

Mike's sister, Jody, lived in a big ramshackle house with sloping floors and long windows. She was a country mouse who was quiet, dressed plainly with short brown hair and no makeup or frills. I attended my first Tupperware party at her house. When I was with Mike, I felt like I'd been transported to another time and another life that was in the country. What a contrast from my past ten years.

**

When I moved back to Minneapolis, Marty and I started hanging out again. She had the summer off and asked if I wanted to travel with her. We started planning a three-week road trip, driving across the United States to Seattle and then to Vancouver and across Canada to Winnipeg where we'd head back down to Minnesota. When I told Mike about our trip, he got upset. He was worried I'd find someone on the road. I reassured him that I'd only be gone three weeks, and I'd write and call him.

Marty and I took off the second week of August, and the first night, we stayed at my parents' hotel in Brookings. My mother and I sat by the pool the next morning, and she told me that I was nothing like anyone in the family because I took risks and did things no one else would ever do, like this road trip. What I really wanted to hear were words like, you have hair like your older sister, you are athletic like William, or Becca is musical like you. I wanted to hear I was part of the family puzzle; I fit somewhere, instead of being a puzzle piece lost from another box that didn't quite fit. I wanted to feel like I belonged. But eventually, I realized my role in the family was not to belong, and I would always be the outsider. That role seemed to follow me most of my life.

When we left Brookings, we drove to the Black Hills and set up camp. We pitched our tent and heated up some canned stew for dinner. After dinner, I was playing guitar, and the guy in the tent next to us came over. His name was Ken, and we hung out by the campfire. He invited us to the rodeo he was riding in the next day. We stayed another night so we could go to the rodeo. We watched Ken ride in a barrel race, roping calves, and ride a bucking bronco. After we had dinner with Ken, we headed to Yellowstone, where we camped for two nights and stopped and saw Old Faithful on the way out of the park.

The next day, we drove all day and found a campground just before suppertime. When we checked in, they warned us about bear sightings in the campground and stressed the importance of no food in our tent. We found a campsite up on a hill that looked down over a sea of RVs. That night, we had to work long and hard to get our canvas tent set up. It was getting harder to find that tension spot for the poles. After a hot shower, we crawled into our sleeping bags to play backgammon. During the second game, the tent collapsed. We flew out of the tent to catch who did it.

I looked at Marty and said, "You know, we could have run out of the tent and into a bear."

We looked around and saw our tent poles thrown to the side but didn't see anyone. We set the tent back up, laid in our sleeping bags, and wondered if it was a bear or unstable tent poles.

Our next destination was Seattle. We stayed with my step-grandmother, Amy, who I hadn't seen since I was in grade school. Amy was a receptionist for a Psychiatrist, and after I'd been there for a day, she pulled me aside and told me she felt guilty for how my mother was brought up. Working for the psychiatrist, she learned the importance of hugs and nurturing. She said my mother didn't get that, and after my mother's father married her, Amy, and she became pregnant, he brought my mother back home to Montana to help with the baby, which she thought wasn't fair to my mother. Some of my cousins came over the day before we left and had dinner.

The next day, we left, and our destination was Vancouver, BC. We found a nice hotel downtown that was clean and inexpensive. The next day, we visited her friend Valerie, who took us to a nude beach. It was strange walking on the beach and seeing everyone around us naked. I didn't think I'd take off my suit, but I did. It felt good to be totally open to the elements. But being sunburned on places that weren't usually exposed to the sun wasn't so great. The next day, it made sitting quite uncomfortable. The last day, we packed up, and as we were heading out of town, a guy in a postal truck flirted with us. Then, he motioned us to pull over and asked us to go have coffee. Gary told us we couldn't leave Vancouver because the next day was the Bicentennial with fireworks and the tall ships coming in. He invited us to stay overnight at his house, and the next day, he'd take us to watch the tall ships sail into port with fireworks overhead. It was a dramatic conclusion to our adventures in Vancouver.

The road trip across Canada was beautiful. The Canadian Rockies were more dramatic than anything in the U.S., and the state parks were very well maintained. Canadians were so friendly and down-to-earth. When we camped near Banff, we were greeted by a black bear waddling down the road between tents. There were very stern warnings about keeping food in our tent. One little potato chip or a corner of a cookie could mean you'd come back to a tent torn to shreds.

We visited Lake Louise and drove up to see the glaciers. On the way, we saw a sign indicating a hiking trail. We stopped and took the 45-minute hike. When we reached the end of the trail, we were standing on a platform on the side of a rocky area. I stood and looked out; I was speechless.

I saw a huge valley with the most rugged and dramatic Rockies towering over me. The mountains were stone giants surrounding me with their strength and power. To the left was a glacier, glistening with white and turquoise colors and water running off creating the most beautiful bright blue-green lake. The scene was tremendous, and I felt like I was an ant, standing, surrounded by the gigantic landscape.

It brought tears to my eyes as I felt the insignificance of my life in the scheme of all things. I was but a minute speck in the universe. I felt free.

I was seeing the beauty and greatness of the Creator. It brought me to my knees with tears on my cheeks. I will never forget that moment.

The next day, we camped in the Banff area for a couple of nights. We hiked and visited Banff, which was one of the most beautiful towns I'd ever seen. Its backdrop was the dramatic, snow topped Canadian Rockies. There were cute shops and timeless architecture that made me feel like I was in the Swiss Alps. There were hikers walking into town after a month in the mountains, backpacks on their backs, hair in reggae knots from lack of combing, grime covered faces, smiling, their stomachs rumbling from hunger, well defined calf muscles, looking strong and sturdy, and hiking boots laced up tight. I saw the hikers everywhere, stocking up with food and water, repacking their packs for the rest of the journey. I wondered what it was like hiking alone in those powerful mountains.

Marty and I were sad to leave the area, and the next night, we camped in Calgary where it rained all night. The next morning, our air mattresses were floating in four inches of water. We had to pack our heavy canvas tent, soaking wet.

We started driving early, and in the evening, we found a motel. After we checked in, we unpacked our stuff and laid our wet tent out to dry. We curled up in our nice warm beds and got a good night's sleep. Our tent was dry when we got up the next morning; we packed it and were on our way. We camped the next night at a little campground and got to Winnipeg late in the afternoon the following day. We found a hotel for the night, unpacked, showered, and headed out for dinner. After dinner, we went to a club downtown and met Jim, a Native-American, from the Dakota Ojibwa tribe who brought us to the Assiniboia Downs racetrack the next day. Winnipeg was our last stop before heading back to Minnesota. We got up the next morning, and with Canadian flag stickers on my car and guitar case, we headed home. When Mike appeared at my doorstep, I realized how much I missed him. We caught up, and he spent the night.

I loved camping, and a week later, I bought a tent, a nylon Timberline tent with tent poles that had bungee cords so they snapped together when you set them straight. The tent was lightweight and took maybe fifteen minutes to set up. It was nothing like the canvas tent, which at times took forty minutes. I camped a lot that summer and brought my guitar to play by the campfire.

**

I wasn't a person who waited around for things to happen. Because I wanted to sing my songs in coffee shops and there was no one to accompany me, I learned to play the guitar and piano. I became what I needed to be to get what I wanted. When I heard a record company was auditioning artists and their original music at the Sheraton Inn in Brooklyn Park, I had to audition. Mike told me to call him when I was getting ready to go in for the audition. When I drove to the hotel that evening, my whole body shook with excitement. I couldn't believe I was doing it. I got there, signed up for a 10:00 p.m. audition time, and waited, my guitar by my side. I decided to call Mike around 9:00 p.m. and went to a wall of phone booths. I picked the phone booth in the middle, and dialed Mike's number.

Just as Mike and I started talking, a man who'd had too much to drink came and knocked on the door of my phone booth, saying he needed to use the phone. I told him to use one of the other booths. He wouldn't leave, knocking louder and getting obnoxious. Mike was getting concerned at his end because he could hear what was happening. Finally, the man left.

Ten minutes later, he came back and yelled, "Tell him you love him. Have you told him you loved him yet?"

Then, he opened the door of the phone booth, and told me to hang up the phone or he would hang it up for me. I told him he needed to get out of the phone booth as I pushed the door closed. He slurred his words as he yelled and walked away. When I got back on the phone, Mike told me to hang up and come home because he was concerned for my safety. Three minutes later, the man came back, forced open the door to the booth, grabbed the phone, and hung it up. Then he grabbed my right arm and yanked me out of the booth. I pushed him away and looked around at all the empty phone booths, wondering why he kept bothering me. I said I was going to get the manager of the hotel, so he took off.

I found the manager, and he contacted the police. He and I went into the bar, and I found the man who had accosted me. The manager asked the man's name, which was Terrence, and told him to come with him until the police arrived. After yelling a few obscenities, Terrence went with the manager. The police came and talked to Terrence, his party, and me. I lodged a complaint, and the policeman said I'd have to go to the police station to make a formal complaint later that week. The policeman left. I got my guitar and sat on a chair in the lobby.

I played through my songs quietly because my audition was in fifteen minutes. At 10:00 pm, I walked in for my audition. My fingers were shaking, and I took a deep breath to sing.

I said to myself, "You can do this, Helen, come on. Go for it."

I opened my mouth to sing. I sang "Young Boy" and "Alcohol," Two of my favorite original songs. I felt like I did well, but I was still shaking after what had happened in the phone booth. I didn't hear back for a second audition. I was glad I did it anyway.

A couple of days later, I went to the police station to file my complaint. The policeman tried to talk me out of it, saying that it was my word against Terrance's, and cases like this rarely went to court. I said I wanted to file, so he brought me the forms, and an hour later, I left the police department feeling disappointed by the lack of support by the policeman.

Terrance, the drunken man, was brought to court, charged with assault, and found guilty. He paid a fine and served some weekends in jail. I had grown. In the past, I wouldn't have complained or stood up for myself, thinking it was my fault.

Chapter 35
This Lady's Not for Sale

Earlier in my life, I was always looking outside of myself to find something or someone that made me feel loved or like I belonged. I explored the world outside my body. I was so open and let too many people in. I got hurt, felt betrayed, and couldn't believe all the dishonesty when all I wanted was to have someone love me and to be seen. When I started therapy, I explored the places inside my body. I discovered my creative passions and started looking inside myself for answers, instead of giving my body away to get love. I couldn't create if I didn't feel, and I couldn't feel if I wasn't aware of myself. What I created came from deep in my heart, and it loosened old knots in my stomach. I shared my energy with the world through writing, music, songs, sculptures, and photography. My feelings went on the paper. I heard them flying through the air when I sang my songs, and I felt them in the words of my stories. What I experienced in my life could be seen in the street people I photographed.

Growing up invisible was lonely, so I found a place inside me where I could see myself in the books I read. As I grew older, I lost that place, and was always taking care of someone else. I became invisible to me. Now, I began to see myself, feel who I was, and know what was important to me. I took weekends and hibernated away from the world, writing songs and stories or creating a sculpture. I came away feeling refreshed, strengthened, and rejuvenated.

I decided to study photography at the U of M in the fall of 1978. I signed up for a photography class, and I fell in love. I needed a camera, so Mike bought a Nikon and loaned it to me. I shot pictures downtown at night, capturing shapes and colors. I shot photos on campus, studying lines and textures. I worked in the dark room bringing my pictures to life.

I continued to work temp jobs and perform singing telegrams. Karen and I started singing at the Malt Shop where they served malts and trendy sandwiches with lots of alfalfa sprouts and veggies. Karen played piano, I played guitar, and we took turns singing lead and harmony. I performed my original songs, but we also performed songs by Linda Ronstadt,

Barbra Streisand, Gordon Lightfoot, Smokey Robinson, and some Joni Mitchell. We performed at cafes and coffee shops at least once or twice a month.

I joined a racquetball club in St. Louis Park, and I went there to work out. I found women there who played racquetball. I began playing tournaments and won trophies. At one tournament, I won a turkey. I was addicted, and every Saturday, I played for three hours. That year, my family had Thanksgiving at my brother's motel in Story City, IA, and I challenged William to a game of racquetball. My older brother was very competitive, so we had some hard-fought games. I did win one of the three games, and in the other two the scores were close. When we got back to his motel, my brother told the rest of the family that he couldn't believe he got beat by a girl. That was quite a moment to have my brother share my victory with everyone else.

Later that fall, my relationship with Mike started to change. We had our first fight when Sherrie had a party, and I asked him to come. He came, but just sat in a chair and never said a word. If someone talked to him, he acted like he didn't hear them. It was weird. I was upset that he didn't join in with my friends. After the party, he told me he was shy and wasn't comfortable with people he didn't know. He was fine on stage, but not out in public.

A month later, we went to his friend's party. It was in a garage, instruments were set up for performing, and there was food and liquor. There were people of all ages: kids, teens, and adults. More than one teenager approached me, asking if they had seen me on TV, saying I looked familiar. There were men who came up and talked to me about music and singing. When we left, Mike was quiet, and I couldn't understand what I had done. I asked him what was wrong, and he, finally, said I was too pretty, and it was hard for him to watch me talking to other men. I told him I was only interested in him. When he dropped me off at home, he broke up with me. I was angry because I didn't do anything wrong. After a few minutes, I got in my car, drove to his house, pounded on his door, and told him he couldn't break up with me. I did nothing wrong. We ended up making love in his van, and I spent the night.

At Christmas, my parents gave me a Nikon camera. When I saw Mike later, we unwrapped our presents from each other. He gave me the camera he bought for me to use in my photography class. When Mike heard what my family gave me for Christmas, he got quiet and said that he couldn't seem to ever do anything special for me. He talked about breaking up because he just wasn't good enough for me. I explained having two cameras was a bonus for my classes. We ended up having make-up sex, and he spent the night.

A couple of weeks later, he asked me to marry him, and inside I freaked out. He sat there looking at me; I had to say something, so I said yes, thinking I could just get engaged. Some people were engaged for years. A week later, when he talked about living together, I got a knot in my stomach. We started looking at homes outside of the Twin Cities, like Jordan and Lonsdale. The concept of getting engaged and living with him was kind of exciting. I loved the musician in him, his creative, passionate soul. But with his jealous, possessive quirks, I felt stifled. I loved being with people, eating at restaurants, and dancing. I always had a lot of friends, male and female. I started having trouble sleeping at night, thinking about being with Mike isolated in the country. I knew I couldn't do it. I broke up with Mike in March.

**

A month later, Peg knocked on my door at 2:00 a.m. and asked if I was OK.

I said, "Yes, why?"

She told me that Jenny had just been raped, and the police were on the way. Peg wanted to make sure the rapist hadn't come upstairs. Then, she explained what happened. Both Jenny and Peg were from small towns where no one locked their doors. Peg was teasing Jenny that night about not locking the front door, and Jenny just blew her off. Around 12:30, they both went to bed. Someone came in the front door and went into Jenny's bedroom. He grabbed a pillow while she was sleeping, and as he placed the pillow over her face, she woke up. Then, she felt a knife at her throat. He told her if she made a sound, he would kill her and her roommate. He climbed on top of her, tore off her panties, and raped her. When he was done, he whispered in her ear to count to 100 before she opened her eyes. If she opened them before that, he would slit her throat. She counted to 100 and slowly opened her eyes. Then, she screamed and woke Peg up.

The police never found the guy, and Jenny wasn't the same after that. She couldn't sleep at night, so she quit her day job and got a night job. She was anxious and jumped at sudden noises. She locked the doors to her house obsessively. Eventually, she started answering phones at a crisis center and met other victims of violence. She became more relaxed but always kept the sense of being on guard. I made sure my upstairs and downstairs doors were locked every night.

**

Karen and I discovered the Uptown Bar, and sometimes, Peg came with us. It had a live band and a dance floor. The first night I went, I was carded; I couldn't believe it because I was thirty years old. Karen and I danced and left a couple of hours later. We started going regularly.

One night at the bar, I met a good-looking guy and we started dancing. We hit it off, and he asked if I wanted to do something the next night. I said sure, and the next night, we went out for dinner and talked. It turned out he was only twenty-five, and I'd just turned thirty. After dinner, we went to a movie, and he came to my apartment and spent the night. When we got up the next morning, he wanted to hang out. We went to a buddy's place of his who offered him a beer. I thought to myself, *drinking beer in the morning is not a good sign.* Then, we stopped at his parents, and he had a beer with his dad. We had talked about playing racquetball earlier, so I challenged him to a game. We went to the racquetball club and played three games. I won two out of three, and he didn't like that. After we got a bite to eat, we went back to my place, and spent another night exploring each other's bodies. When he left the next morning, he said he would call me later, but I never heard from him again.

In some ways, I was glad he didn't call because I didn't like his drinking habits. But I wrote a song about him. It was a get back song with sexual overtones. A couple of weeks later, Karen and I saw him at the bar, and I told him about the song. He wanted to hear it. I had a guitar in my car and invited him to the parking lot. I got my guitar, and Karen and I sang the song. He laughed and clapped at the end. Then, I asked him why he didn't call me. He said he didn't like being beat at racquetball and decided I was too much for him. I never ran into him again, but I got a lot of attention for the song, *Young Boy.*

**

I continued studying at the U of M. I took a studio art class and an art history class winter quarter, and in the spring, I took a sculpture and another photography class. I loved taking pictures and developing them in the darkroom. I was still taking dance at Zoe Sealy Dance Studio and Clarence Teeters, a well-known dancer, was coming to teach a class. I loved watching him move and got permission to photograph him during a class. I shot the photos and wanted to represent movement, so I made them into photograms. The photos were about movement of the dance and not the dancer. I loved those pictures, and eventually, sold them.

One Sunday, I went to the art institute and saw photography by Jerry Uelsman. I fell in love with his work and the way he blended photos into one picture. One was a bedspread that looked like a woman's face was growing out of it. His work reminded me of Salvador Dali and his melting clocks. When I was at the art institute, I heard a woman talking about him, like she knew him. So, I approached her and asked where I might be able to contact him about taking a workshop. I found out he taught at a university in Florida. I sent him a letter asking if he was doing a workshop anywhere in the United States that summer.

For my photography class I photographed nudes; my sister and Marty both posed for me. I did a series on my sister's breast. I took a pierced earring and taped it with beige masking tape to give the illusion of a pierced nipple, which people actually do nowadays, but not back then. The photo worked; it really looked pierced. I posed Marty with hats and certain lighting. I photographed her doing absurd positions and created blended images. I also did street photography and tried blending negatives for photos and photograms showing motion. I took photos of people on the street: homeless people, bag ladies, and street musicians. I captured on camera passengers waiting at the airport to leave as well as some just arriving. I loved taking photos and seeing people through the lens of the camera. They were all black and white stories just ready for me to write.

In my sculpting class, for my project, I built a life-size man. The assignment was to use plaster, but other materials were welcome. I wanted a cuddly, soft sculpture so I used wire and wood to create the bones and joints, newspaper for muscle, and a layer of soft cotton substance for just under the "skin." The skin was made from beige cotton sheets. He had a beard and hair that were made out of yarn, and his features were embroidered on his face. He was dressed in jeans and a jean shirt. He looked a lot like Mike. I called him, Jeremiah. He was displayed at the end of class on the front porch of an abandoned house, sitting on a porch railing, playing a guitar. After my work was graded, I brought it home, and Jeremiah sat on my living room couch or my living room chair and footstool. I liked having him there to keep me company. One day, when I had a weekend to myself, I decided to build a female sculpture, so I started building Sara.

I had heard back from Jerry Uelsmann in April that he would be teaching a photography class in Victor, Colorado which was near Colorado Springs. I also noticed a flyer on the bulletin board, advertising a writer's workshop at Copper Mountain, Colorado. The dates coincided so I could go for a weeklong workshop in June for photography at Victor. Then, I drive to Copper Mountain where I would start a weeklong writing workshop. I signed up for both workshops.

**

My brother Derek, who graduated from high school in Brookings and tried a year of college, suddenly showed up on my doorstep. He was upset at my mother and father's behavior and wanted to come see me for some counseling and nurturing. He needed my sisterly love. While he was there, he told me he and his buddies were drunk one night, and they burglarized a cabin. They brought the furniture home for their apartment. He felt guilty but was too scared to return the stuff. Derek brought and introduced me to new music: punk. My music collection expanded to include: the B 52's "Rock Lobster," the Buggles who sang "Video Killed the Radio Star," Devo's "Whip it," and albums by Blondie. A couple times, he appeared with a girlfriend; their trip started when they were drunk and decided to get away from Brookings. I heard stories about my parents and their drinking that concerned me. I no longer felt responsible for getting them help. I did what I could and let the rest go.

Patty hosted a family dinner and asked me to bring pie for dessert. I didn't know the etiquette of bringing dessert. I brought a couple of frozen pies, still frozen.

My sister got angry and said, "Don't you have a brain in your head? You're supposed to cook them before you bring them."

I said, "I thought pie was better fresh out of the oven, so I thought I'd just cook them while we were eating dinner."

She took the pies, mumbling under her breath about how I went to college, but I had no common sense. She wasn't angry about the pies—she was envious because I graduated from college.

In early August, I visited Derek and my parents in Brookings. When my mother and I were alone, she asked me if it was rape if she didn't want sex and my father forced her to. I told her it was if she didn't want to do it. She went on to tell me my father liked to do it in the morning and she did not want to do it.

Later that same year, Patty called and asked me if she had to have sex with her husband just because he wanted it. Her husband seemed to believe it was his nightly privilege and her responsibility to please him. I told her the same thing I told my mother. I couldn't believe she shared such intimate information with me, especially after the frozen pie fiasco.

Chapter 36
What Did I Do?

Sherrie hosted a couple of slumber parties at her mother's house. We all brought sleeping bags, food, and snacks. We ate and talked the night away. At one of the slumber parties, Sherrie told us she applied at graduate schools in marriage and family therapy and got accepted into Purdue's master's program in Indiana. She asked me to go with her when she looked for an apartment, and we talked about camping there.

Middle of May, we drove to Indiana. I brought my tent, and we set it up in a campground close to town. The first night we went out for supper, checked out the Purdue campus, headed back to the campgrounds, and went to bed. We left the outside door flap and back window open to let the air blow through. In the middle of the night, something woke me up; I thought I saw a face looking at me. I went back to sleep. In the morning, we had breakfast, and headed to the campus. Sherrie found a nice one bedroom, filled out the paperwork, and gave a deposit for rent. Later, we went out for dinner and a to club to listen to music.

We got back to the campground around midnight. When we pulled up to our site, there was no tent. We thought we made a mistake, so we checked the number, butit was the right site. We went to the campground office to report it, and they called the police. When the police came, I told them about the night before when I thought I saw someone peeking in the door. The policeman said there probably was someone peeking because behind the campground were homes and a residential neighborhood, and my tent was a nylon Timberline and lightweight. All someone would have to do is take out the stakes and pick it up with a friend, hauling it away still assembled with everything in it. The police didn't find my tent. Luckily, we had our purses and some of our clothes with us. But most of our clothes, our sleeping bags, and our pillows were taken with the tent. Sherrie and I checked into a motel for the night. We drove home tentless the next day. Luckily, I had renter's insurance, so my tent was covered. When my insurance money arrived a couple of weeks later, I went out the next day and bought another nylon Timberline. Sherrie moved to Purdue in the fall and started her master's program.

**

The third week of June, Karen rode with me to Victor, Colorado for Jerry Uelsmann's photography workshop. When we got in town, we were directed to a high school at the end of Main Street. There was a large gymnasium with cots lined up on both sides for us to sleep in. The first day we got there, we walked to a café in town, and I suddenly felt lightheaded, nauseated, and dizzy. I had to sit down. Someone in the group said it was altitude sickness; we were at 9700 feet, and I'd feel fine in a while.

Every morning, we attended a class where Jerry Uelsman lectured on photographic techniques, and then, we went out in the afternoon to shoot pictures. The first day, we went to an old mine shaft, and he let us loose with our cameras. In the evening was darkroom time to process our photos. Each day was a new topic and a new place to explore. At the end of the workshop, we went to Jerry's house for dinner and a session with his wife, who was a Jungian therapist. We showed her our photos, and she told us what she saw in our body of work. She told me that I had a lot of varying styles, and I was very good at everything I did. But to reach excellence in a project was hard for me because I got bored easily and started exploring other avenues that challenged me.

When the workshop ended, Karen rode with me to Copper Mountain, where I dropped her off at the airport, and she flew home.

I checked in at the Copper Mountain resort for the writer's workshop, and there was a get together to meet other students and the teachers. I met Ricardo there. He was a well-known author who wrote a number of books and screenplays that became movies. He and I stood on the balcony and talked for a long time. He told me about New York City, and I talked about Minnesota. It turned out he was the instructor for one of my courses. Later, he asked me if I did mushrooms, and I said no. I thought he was talking about mushrooms you eat, but he was talking about hallucinogenic 'shrooms. After the get together, I checked in at the campground.

When I got there, it was full. I panicked and asked where else I could camp.

There was an older couple standing by me looking at a map, and the woman turned and said, "Why don't you pitch your tent behind our RV?"

So, I did.

Their names were Jackie and Leo, and they were from Montana and attending the workshop also. I set up my tent, got some dinner, and crawled into my sleeping bag. In the morning, Jackie invited me in for breakfast. We talked, and I found out she was a retired teacher. Jackie and Leo made me feel safe because I was camping by myself. After breakfast, I drove to the workshop, excited to immerse myself in writing.

Ricardo taught my fiction class in the morning. The first day, he talked about using descriptive language, and the second day, he talked about using dialogue. Our homework in the evening was to write a chapter using the tools he described. In my afternoon poetry class, we wrote haikus and poems. We hiked, sat on rocky mountaintops, and wrote about what we saw. When we broke up for the day, we were given an assignment to write a poem. In my classes the next day, we read what we wrote, and our work was critiqued.

On my lunch break, I sat, played guitar, and sang. The second day, Nick from my fiction class sat with me at lunch. He was a principal in Illinois and was recently divorced. The third night, he asked me out for dinner, and he sat with his arm around me in the booth. After dinner, he came back to my tent, and we messed around for a while, kissing and exploring each other's bodies, but we didn't have sex. The next morning, Leo and Jackie invited us in for breakfast.

Ricardo and I started talking after class. He asked me how I thought the class was going and seemed to be flirting with me.

In my poetry class, we were assigned to find a famous poem and change the words to fit our experience on Copper Mountain. I picked the poem "Chicago" by Carl Sandburg. My teacher asked me if I would write a song about the workshop for the last night's celebration.

That night at a poetry reading, Ricardo stood next to me the whole night, trying to get a conversation going. He was shy when he wasn't the teacher. He seemed kind of lost, and I wanted to comfort him. I sneaked a look at Ricardo and wondered what it would be like living with him in New York, a famous author with famous movies under his belt. Would it be exciting?

The last day of classes Nick and I hung out, and we sat on the mountaintop talking, writing, taking pictures, and exchanging phone numbers. That night, all the participants shared our poems and stories, and I sang the song I wrote about Copper Mountain.

After the celebration, Ricardo asked me if I wanted to hang out. He said it was so quiet in the mountains, and he couldn't sleep. New York, he said, was so noisy every hour of the day that the quiet there felt deafening. We went to his room and talked, started making out, and eventually, went to bed. He didn't have a condom, and I had left my diaphragm in the tent at the campground. He pulled out early the first time, but not the second time. I thought, what are the chances of getting pregnant after just one time? We didn't get any sleep that night, and he asked if I'd take him to the airport. After I packed up my tent and said goodbye to Jackie and Leo, I swung by to pick him up.

We drove down the mountain together. It was a beautiful hour and a half ride. Ricardo shared stories about New York and compared them to life here in the mountains. I loved talking to this accomplished author who had been part of writing movies everyone saw on the big screen. He was an interesting person. When I dropped him off at the airport, we exchanged phone numbers. I drove home thinking about him and the mountains.

**

When I got back from the workshop, I needed to find a job to make some money while I was in school. I applied for a part- time, clerical job at Integral. I interviewed with Barb, who hired me on the spot. I started work the next day and met Joan, my office mate, who was engaged to a chiropractor. I heard a lot about her wedding plans and asked her if she'd like to have her astrology and compatibility chart done for an early wedding gift. She said yes, and I worked one up that night. When I brought it to her, she couldn't believe how accurate it was, even the issues she had with her fiancé. She told other people at work, and I did a couple more charts.

I did filing and scored exams for Integral, which was a business that provided workshops on personality traits and who you work best with. They had a psychologist on staff and business trainers. To work there, you were required to take classes. I signed up for a training class Ron was offering: "Building Self-Esteem." We did trust and truth exercises. On the third day, we all had to stand up and tell one thing about ourselves that no one else knew. One guy got up and said that he was a hit man.. The man was from Pittsburgh and looked young and strong. He freaked us out. We were speechless afterwards, and Ron didn't ask him any questions. He said he wanted to see him after the class. The next day, the man wasn't there. Ron said we had signed a confidentiality agreement, so it was a delicate issue. Then, he said we didn't know if the man was delusional or using attention-getting behaviors to shock us. Someone asked if it was true, and were we in danger because he told us what he did? Ron explained the man didn't give any names, so we weren't in any danger. Ron was looking into how to handle the information, and we didn't need to worry about it.

One day, Barb from work invited me to her house. Her son was into astrology too.

I was sitting on the couch talking to her son when Barb suddenly blurted out, "You need to use your psychic ability or you'll get sick."

I looked at her, shocked. She said she was sorry, but sometimes she was "used" as a vehicle to give messages to people, and the messages just suddenly blurted out. I didn't know what to do with her message to me, but I tried to keep myself open.

The next day at work, I mentioned my singing telegram company to Joan. She thought that was so cool and said she wished she could sing. A couple days later, she asked me if I would sing in her wedding. I said sure.

**

Marty decided to move to New York City where Planned Parenthood had an opening. Before she left, she threw a party at her duplex. When I got to the party, she introduced me to Bill, a guy she had dated. Bill was a tall, good-looking man with a kind face and beautiful smile. He had a short Afro and finely chiseled features. I said hi and started mingling. At the end of the evening, I found myself standing next to him. We started talking, and he told me he played guitar, sang, and wrote music. We kept talking until he asked about getting together to play sometime. I hesitated because he was dating Marty. He looked at me and said he and Marty were just friends. We set up a time to get together and play music at my place the next afternoon.

When Bill arrived, he was surprised to see someone sitting on my small couch. Then he looked again and saw Jeremiah, my soft sculpture. I told him I sat Jeremiah in my apartment so I never felt alone. We talked, played guitar, and sang, working on harmonies. When he was getting ready to leave, I asked him to sing with me at Joan's wedding. With a little coaxing, he said he'd do it. I told Joan the next day. She was excited and brought in a list of songs. Bill and I started rehearsing them every few days.

Bill and I could talk about everything, and, soon shared intimate stories of our lives. I loved singing with him, and we worked hard on the songs for Joan's wedding. The day of the wedding, we sang in the big church. Our harmony in "The Lord's Prayer" brought tears to our eyes as we sang it. The other songs went well, too, but there was something about our harmony in "The Lord's Prayer" that stayed with me for days. Bill and I started singing together at places like the Malt Shop where Karen and I sang. We did songs by Stevie Nicks, like "The Chain and Songbird." We performed "Summertime" and Billy Holiday songs like "Lover Man" and "Good Morning Heartache." He brought an interesting, complex rhythm to songs and had his own unique style. We performed "Dream Weaver" reggae style. I loved performing with him.

My family drama started up again. Becca and her boyfriend Curtis broke up, and when Marty moved to New York, Becca moved into her duplex. Then, Becca started attending the Aveda school to learn to cut hair. She had blonde hair that hung down to her waist that was beautiful, thick, long, and shiny. By the time she completed Aveda, her hair was short. She hung out with guys from her school who were gay. They partied and danced at the Roaring 20s or the Gay 90s and did poppers — amyl nitrate — and drank. She became sexually involved with a couple of them. One month, when Becca was short on rent, she called my parents to borrow money. They said no. A couple of days later, Becca received a package from my mother. It was crotchless underwear with a note saying she should start "charging for her favors." Becca was shocked and called me.

My own irresponsibility caught up with me. The last week of August, I didn't feel well, and I had missed a period. I realized I was pregnant. It was that one night with Ricardo. I couldn't believe it. That day I went to Karen's, who now lived on the West Bank by the University of Minnesota. I was so nauseated. She massaged my shoulders and fed me M&M cookies and crackers to comfort me. I was thirty and wanted children, so I was trying to decide what to do. I called Ricardo and told him I was pregnant. But he said he wasn't ready for children because his career was just taking off, and he sent me money for an abortion.

I talked to Bill and jokingly said, "If I don't have this baby, and I'm not married by the time I am thirty-five, would you be my baby daddy?" He laughed and said, yes.

I wanted children. My head was yelling yes to an abortion, while my heart was yelling no. I had babies in my dreams. After a couple of sleepless nights, Karen brought me to Meadowbrook Clinic. When I left the clinic, I felt empty and raw; I couldn't think about what I'd just done. I spent the weekend alone, listening to music, playing guitar, singing, and crying. I swore I'd never be in this situation again. That weekend, my life caught up with me again. I lived my life running on adrenaline, trying to keep a step ahead of some sadness I was aware lived deep inside me. Like when I was younger, I'd call friends to have a sleep over or do something to distract me from my life with my parents. Sometimes, it was hard to face those feelings inside me. Feeling like a motherless child with no sense of connection to a family, I ran to my friends, like Karen who fed me cookies, and comforted me with nurturing words. I had to live with the consequences of wanting so much to be loved.

Becca was running wild with her friends from Aveda and getting involved with men who were into men became unfulfilling to her. She found an outpatient drug treatment program on the top two floors of a house and asked me to come as her family support system. After treatment, she changed from doing poppers and drinking to becoming a body builder. She went on a strict diet to lose body fat and took workout classes at the Sweatshop. I went to her first competition as her assistant to rub her down with oil to bring out the muscle definition. When she posed for the judges, she was scored on her muscle development, muscle symmetry, muscle shape and balance, and how she moved. She didn't win, but she got a decent score for a first competition. Afterward, she was offered a job at the Sweatshop as a full-time instructor.

Becca started seeing James, a tall, slender, good-looking, light skinned black man. He was fast-talking, and eventually, she moved in with him. He cheated on her, and one day, she called me crying because he kicked her out. She stayed with me for a while. Then, one night, she went to a party at his house, and he whispered to her to meet him upstairs in the bedroom. She went up, crawled in bed, and waited. Eventually the, door opened, he came in, crawled in bed with her, and started to have sex. It wasn't James—he sent someone else. That finally ended it with James.

Sherrie was in town in August and had a party at her mother's house to see all her friends. I talked about wanting another part-time job. I wasn't in school anymore and needed money. A friend of hers, Pam, who worked at Golden Valley Hospital, mentioned they were looking for a clinical associate to work in the locked adolescent psych unit. She thought it would be nice if I worked there, so I could find out why the nurses in that unit were so negative. I applied and got the job.

Since moving to Minneapolis and exploring my creative outlets in photography, sculpting, and creative writing, I was finding myself and ways to express who I was, but I wasn't making any real money. I hadn't set good limits with men, and there were consequences. With Bill, I had finally learned how to have a male friend with no sex involved. That felt good. I had close girl friends, but I still felt lost. I loved singing, photography, writing, and performing singing telegrams, but those endeavors don't bring in a lot of money. I was apprehensive about starting my new job in the psych unit and dealing with all those issues again, but I would have money again because working at Integral wasn't enough.

Chapter 37
It Was 3 O'clock in the
Morning When I Got Your Call

I started working part-time in September, as a clinical associate on the adolescent unit, at the psychiatric hospital. I ran groups, conducted one-to-ones with patients, and worked with doctors on patient care plans. I worked closely with the nurses who helped in the groups. I became friends with Noreen, a tall, pretty nurse with reddish blonde hair and freckles across her nose. She was newly married and pregnant. I met an interesting nurse, Caitlin, who had lived in India and saw auras. She said mine was orange; an orange aura was the aura of a guru, a spiritual leader and guide. She told me that I gave away too much of myself without replenishing my energy. Katee Kranz, our head nurse, was short, stocky, and had a strong personality to keep us in line.

I soon realized working in a psych unit was very different from working in corrections. The adolescents on the unit had very different issues. One patient came from a family fraught with denial. She literally did not know she was pregnant until she had a baby. She told me she went to bed one night, had a dream that she had a baby in an alley, and cut the cord with a comb. When she got up the next morning, she went outside to look and found her baby lying in the place she had left him in her dream. We worked with her and her family.

We had a patient from Rochester who came from a family of well-known doctors. He wanted to be an artist. The family pressure caused a psychotic break and he was always drawing pictures of a bus. He was driving a bus that didn't go anywhere.

Another patient was a catatonic schizophrenic who stood in a single posture for long time periods of time, and then, suddenly, changed his posture. When he talked, he always talked about clocks and the time. He babbled about being the clock, and clocks weren't his friends.

Some adolescents were there because of addiction issues. One patient was addicted to mentholated cough drops. He always had one in his mouth, and his teeth were rotting away. He had burns around his lips from the menthol. One girl was there for obsessive/compulsive disorder; her hands were cracked and bleeding from washing her hands all the time.

Adolescents with drug problems or habitual runaways were also committed to our locked unit. So, we had a variety of issues and a whole spectrum of personality and mental disorders. There were timeout rooms for patients whose anger was out of control. If a patient totally lost it, the nurses called the orderlies who came and restrained the patient by tying them to their bed. I tried to work with staff to allow for some expression of anger in the groups because it was healthy to work through the feelings. I knew from living with my own father to not be afraid of anger.

The staff on the unit had a lot of unresolved issues. For example, if there was a complaint, the staff on the unit got the brunt of it. I had a doctor complain because of something he ordered me to do. I did exactly what he asked, but the parents complained, and so I was at fault, even though that's what he'd ordered. There were scheduling issues; one day I'd work a three to eleven p.m. and was scheduled to work the next day at seven a.m. to three, meaning I got very little sleep between shifts. There was a hierarchy where the doctor was always right. The unit staff were the ones dealing with the day-to-day issues of our patients. Nurses handed out medication and backed up the clinical associates like me during group sessions. We dealt with the behavioral issues and felt the need to advocate for our patients. Doctors and administration were out of touch with what was really needed in the locked unit. I understood why Pam said there was staff unrest when she talked about the job. The unit staff started talking about unionizing and meeting at Katee's house.

Our unit staff was close. We ate at Byerly's after our shifts and had potlucks on our days off. We had a baby shower for Noreen when she was eight months pregnant.

Noreen and I were charting one day and started talking about cameras, so I told her about my photography classes. She got excited and asked me if I'd photograph her birth. I said I'd be honored.

**

A month later there was talk at Integral about a group of people coming to the U.S. from Norway. They were CEOs from a new company, and the Integral bosses wanted something special. I offered to do a singing telegram. I wrote the telegram with fun details about members of the group. The day the Norwegians were coming, I got up and rehearsed the telegram. Then my phone rang, and it was Noreen. Her water had just broken, so I needed to get to the hospital soon. I called Barb at Integral and told her I couldn't do the telegram, but I recorded a copy for them to play for the overseas guests, with a copy of the lyrics. I brought the singing telegram to Barb and headed to the hospital. My bosses were not happy with me.

I got to the hospital in plenty of time. My camera was fully loaded. I took photos over a period of time. I snapped the crown peeking out with each push. Eventually, the head came out farther, and I could see the hair on the baby's head. I took a picture of the eyes peeking their way out, and then the nose, then the mouth. Suddenly, there was a head. I kept snapping pictures. I ran out of film and quickly put in a new roll. Then came the shoulders, and the body quickly followed, all slippery. Cries filled the delivery room. I gave the rolls of film to Noreen's husband. I was in awe of what I watched through my lens: a human birth, a baby making its way out of its mother's womb. My feelings about vaginas changed. Vaginas gave birth to tiny human beings from deep inside our wombs. Vaginas were beautiful, sacred places, a gift women were given to produce life. I walked out of that hospital a changed person with my feet barely touching the ground.

The day after the birth, I went to Integral and gave my notice because it was too hard to juggle both part-time jobs. My last day was the week before Thanksgiving.

I continued working at the psych hospital with all its chaos. In March, I got sick and went to the doctor. I had strep throat and went home with antibiotics. Work was busy, and the unpredictable schedule was hard on my system because of lack of sleep, so I was back in the doctor's office a couple of weeks later. I still had strep throat, so he prescribed a different antibiotic. When I went back two weeks later and my strep was still there, the doctor put me in the hospital to run tests. While I was in the hospital, I got a call from the head of our unit at Golden Valley. She told me I didn't have any sick days left. I explained I was in the hospital because I had a strep infection that wasn't clearing up. She told me if I wasn't at work the next day, I'd lose my job. The doctor came back with a diagnosis of borderline diabetes. I took classes in the hospital where I learned how to eat balanced meals and no sugar. I even learned how to make my own salad dressing. I lost my job as a result. I couldn't believe a hospital didn't support its employees when they were hospitalized.

Looking back, I realized that what I had was exhaustion and a strep infection. When my life and feelings overwhelmed me, I didn't know how to relax. Not ever slowing down, I often got my energy from adrenaline. I liked to keep things a little exciting. But eventually, it would wear me out.

I was glad to move on. I saw Katee a couple of weeks later, and they still hadn't unionized. After what happened to me, people seemed to lose interest and feared for their jobs.

I continued performing telegrams, writing astrology charts, and reading Tarot cards. Karen and I, or Bill and I, still sang at the Malt Shop once a month. I did a photo shoot for Derek at an abandoned farm. Derek brought a couple clothes changes, and I took photos of him doing a side jump over the pasture fence and him chewing on hay as he looked out over the pasture. Derek made a great model; he resembled Robert Redford. A week later, I did a photo shoot for Becca who needed head shots of her hair and make-up models for her portfolio, and I photographed the wedding of a friend's, daughter. I also started looking for a full-time job.

**

That spring, my parents called because they were concerned with Derek's drinking. I knew about AID (Assessment, Intake, and Diagnosis), and I scheduled my brother for an assessment. My parents drove up with Derek, and when he completed an assessment, he was admitted to a three-week chemical dependency program. When family day came, everyone called me concerned about my parents' drinking, and what we should say. I woke up that morning with a severe stiff neck. I called Karen, told her I couldn't turn my head, and talked about the family session that day. She calmed me down and said everyone had to take responsibility for what they wanted to say. It wasn't up to me. Suddenly, I could turn my head again. Our family session went great. AID had groups for family members with someone in treatment. The one thing I remember from those groups was watching the black women who were unmarried with multiple children. I felt envious of them because they seemed happy just living in the moment, not worried about what people thought of them. When Derek got out of treatment, he lived with Patty and Paul. Paul was also in recovery.

Later that spring, Karen and I discovered The Restaurant on Lake Street by Lake Calhoun, and we went in for supper one night. There was a band performing on stage, and when they went on break, I asked one of the guys if I could use his guitar to sing a song I wrote while they were on break. He said, sure. I performed "Young Boy." Karen loved it and so did the band. A month later, Karen and I brought Peg, and her friend, Penny. The same band was performing and saw me walk in. When they went on break, they announced that I was going to sing a bawdy song about a man. I got up and sang again. Penny was running for the state legislator and needed entertainment for her fundraiser at Harriet Island, so she asked if I would be a wandering minstrel.

I said, "Sure, I could wear my top hat and tails."

I continued writing songs about the life around me. I wrote "Alcohol" that was inspired by my girlfriend's relationships with alcoholic men and of course my experience with my family members going through treatment. I found that music turned my pain into something that was beautiful and healing for me.

This year, I turned thirty and had resigned myself to the fact I might never get married. I had no love interests, and I was enjoying my own life and realizing it would be OK if I never got married. Early in my life, I learned love with men meant taking care of them and giving them what they needed. That I didn't really count. As I got older, I thought I enjoyed all the men and sexual adventures I encountered until I realized how lonely it felt, how empty it was when there was no commitment. I fantasized at times of being a call girl always in control, independent and earning money. But then the feeling came back of wanting a family, commitment, and to be loved. My brother Derek told me he couldn't see me as a wife or mother because I was too much of a free spirit. My mother told me I was a bachelorette. I wrestled with these thoughts. Then, I met someone.

Chapter 38
I Met Him on a Touring Ship

On June 10th, 1980, a Tuesday, my life changed forever. I was hired to wander the tables wearing my top hat and tails, singing and playing my guitar at a picnic fundraiser for Penny on Harriet Island. I saw Peg and Jenny talking to a very handsome man, and Peg introduced me to David as I walked by. He had dark hair, a little on the longish side, a well-trimmed beard, freckles across his suntanned nose, a smile that felt like he was enjoying a private joke, and eyes that twinkled. I said hi and continued to sing. I noticed David watching me.

After dinner, we all boarded the Jonathan Padelford paddleboat for a river cruise. I was done performing, so I took off my top hat and stood at the front of the boat.

Then, I heard a voice just over my left shoulder ask, "So what is this singing telegram business?"

I turned and looked into David's eyes.

I said, "If you want a job, I could always use other singers."

He hesitated and said, "Maybe."

When the music started on the boat, we went in and danced. During the break, he took me back out to the front of the boat and showed me the sights on the river. He told me stories about Lilydale and the yacht club. He showed me the direction of where he grew up in Mendota Heights. St. Paul was an alien place to me, so it was fun learning about the things along the river.

He mentioned he wrote a story for a paper titled, "Are rap parlors really about just rapping?" He talked about sitting in a room to "rap" with a woman while a porn movie was showing on the walls. After talking for ten minutes, she asked him if he was interested in anything else. David said he might be, but what did she have in mind? She told him the prices for a hand job or a blowjob. He purchased the hand job because it was the cheapest, and he wasn't making very much for the article. Then, almost in the same breath, he told me he ran for the state legislature when he was twenty, and he was getting his masters at the U of M in

271

communications. Those three things made we want to go out with him because he was interesting, smart, and he tiptoed a bit on the wild side.

At the end of the night, he shyly asked, "At the risk of being too forward, would you like to go out with me?"

I said yes, and we made a date for Saturday. When David walked in on Saturday carrying a bottle of wine, I was concerned because I found guys who brought their own alcohol were serious drinkers. He said the wine was left over from an end of the year work party he stopped at. I said I wasn't a drinker and put it in the refrigerator for him to bring home. We decided to walk to Lake Harriet before our movie.

As we walked, he said, "How is a girl like you free on a Saturday night?"

I said I wasn't free; I was out with him. A couple minutes later he asked me if I was Jewish or from the East Coast because the way I talked. He laughed when I told him I was from Minnesota.

We walked by the lake, sat on a bench, and looked out over the water. David finally started to relax and talked about living in California for a year with a woman just a block from the ocean. He said he loved the ocean. Pretty soon, it was time to go. We walked back and hopped in his Volkswagen Bug. He sang to me on the way to the movie because the radio didn't work, which I loved. When we got there, the movie was sold out. I mentioned The Artist's Quarter, and we went and listened to music. While we were there, he told me he saw Ricky Lee Jones up close and personal in Malibu. Later, we drove back to my place and made out on my passion pit. He ended up spending the night and left after breakfast.

Later that day, June 14th, Bill came over in the afternoon to play music. We were talking intently about some life event that was happening, and I absentmindedly turned on the light because it was getting dark. It was 3:00 in the afternoon.

Then I said to Bill, "Does that sound like a train to you?"

We looked out the window, yelled, "Tornado!" and ran downstairs to the basement. Jenny joined us on the stairs, and Peg wasn't home. In that moment, the tornado struck. A couple of minutes later, the warning sirens went on. We walked back upstairs when it was light outside again. When I got to my apartment, all my cupboard doors were blown open, and my plastic dishes were on the floor. We looked out my front windows, and the street looked like a bomb had hit. There were toilets and sinks sitting in people's front yards. There were trees thrown on top of parked cars, which were now flattened. The streets were full of branches and random items that didn't belong there, like a kitchen chair and a picnic table. Bill and I went out to look around. Everywhere there was chaos, and a noticeable empty path where all the trees were gone. We walked along Bryant Avenue and saw an apartment building missing its roof, furniture on the front lawn, and in the middle of the street was an abandoned city bus with no windows. Where were the people from the bus? I started crying and told Bill I'd seen enough. I wanted to go back. We had just experienced the longest tornado that ever hit Minneapolis, starting in Edina and traveling seventeen miles to Har Mar Mall, which was demolished, until it ran out of steam. For weeks, my neighborhood looked like a war zone, a constant reminder of the power of nature and our inability to control it. Over the years, Bill and I talked about the day we were in a tornado together.

David called as I was walking back up the stairs. When I answered the phone, he started talking about our date that evening. I interrupted him and said I'd just been in a tornado.

He response was, "No, you weren't. There was nothing on the news and no sirens. I was outside and didn't see any dark clouds over your area."

I couldn't believe it.

I said again, slowly, "David, I was just in a tornado; I have toilets in my front yard, trees sticking through people's windows, a kitchen sink in the middle of the street, and demolished cars."

I told him it looked like a bomb dropped, and if he didn't believe me, he could come and see for himself. Bill left. David drove over, parked a couple of blocks away, and walked to my house.

When I saw him, he said, "You're right; you were in a tornado."

I just laughed.

I discovered over the next few weeks David had been a debater since high school and needed facts to back up statements. Because the sirens weren't blaring where he was and he didn't see black clouds in the sky, then there couldn't possibly have been a tornado. Once he saw my neighborhood, he was convinced. Over the next year, his debate background and my counseling background made for frustrating discussions or arguments. I argued with my heart and feelings; he argued with his head and logic. Eventually, we learned to appreciate our differences. I helped him feel more, and he helped me to calm down and think my emotions through.

A few days later, Karen came over to sit on my back porch and sing. I told her about David and how he was the type of person I would marry. Those words had never come out of my mouth before. I reassured her that I said he was the type of man not *the* man I would marry.

That summer, David and I loved going to the Le Bistro for lunch and having their onion soup covered in cheese with a thick piece of French bread, warm with melting butter or going to W. A. Frost and eating on the outside patio. One morning after making love, out of the blue, David turned to me and asked if Lorenzo had body hair. I had told him the night before about dating Lorenzo because David was a big Twins fan, so he was curious about him. I laughed so hard I had trouble answering him.

A couple of days later, David called to change our plans; he'd forgotten about his work softball game that night. He still wanted to go to dinner, but instead of the movie he wanted go to the softball game and thought I could come and watch.

I said, "Sure."

When we got there, everyone was warming up.

David and I played catch, and after I threw a few softballs, David said, "You throw like a boy."

When it was time for the game to start, David's team was short a catcher, and they asked me if I'd catch. David loved that I played softball.

Later that week, I found out David liked to play racquetball, and I challenged him to a game. We went to my racquetball club. The first game was very competitive, and he won two out of three games. When he lost one, it wasn't a fun thing to experience. This gentle, caring man surprised me with his frustrated anger. He had to walk away for a while and calm down before we could start another game. But we started playing racquetball almost every week.

David talked about his mother Toni often. She was a powerful lobbyist, who served on different commissions and was very well known in the political world. When David was in college, his father passed away during heart bypass surgery. It was a shock to his family. He brought me to his house later that summer, and I met Toni. She was a typical Jewish mother, watchful of her son and giving me the once over. One time, when we went to visit her, I got her talking about David's dad, Victor. She shed a few tears and told me about her life as a widow. David was amazed I got his mother to open up and share her feelings.

Toni had a big beautiful backyard with a charcoal pit made of bricks for outdoor cooking. David said his father did all the grilling growing up, and his family hardly ever used the backyard anymore. I asked him if he wanted to have a 4th of July party in his mom's backyard and said his mom would probably love seeing it get used again. When his mom said we could, we invited our family and friends. We grilled, played volleyball, and talked. Bill, Karen, and I brought our guitars and sang. His mother joined us in the festivities, and it was a really big success. I think David and his mom were happy to see all the activity again in the backyard.

David started to become a tether for my circling boat that had been caught floating loose in many currents. With him, my boat started facing in a forward direction. He gave me a sense of stability, like a pilot light on my stove. I felt relaxed and safe with him. He became my tour guide around St. Paul, a place I didn't know much about. We explored restaurants and shops on Grand Ave, and walked along Summit Ave. and the River Road. He shared stories of his childhood, his grandparents, and what it was like having parents involved in politics. He shared how it felt to lose his father in college, a dad he shared the den with, each at their own desks, listening to classical music, his dad working and David doing his homework.

My relationship with David was a perfect summer romance. I am not a person who likes to shop; I hated grocery shopping and only went to get whatever I needed for supper that night. I had garlic salt, salt, pepper, and maybe onion powder in my kitchen cupboard. When I opened my refrigerator, there was a bottle of ketchup, pickles in a jar, a half of an old onion, and a couple of dried up carrots and celery. David was a good cook. and he knew about seasonings like dill weed, curry, marjoram, basil, and oregano. Within the first couple of days of our dating, David couldn't believe what the inside of my refrigerator looked like. He also discovered, to his chagrin, that I had maggots in my garbage—little white squiggly worms on an old piece of cheese. He dumped my wastebasket outside, and I washed it out. He brought me to the grocery store and bought seasonings for my kitchen, some eggs, bread, mayonnaise, and cheese for breakfast the next morning. He fixed a delicious meal, which we ate, sitting at a card table covered with a colorful tablecloth I placed in front of my living room windows.

He was silly in the morning, and I liked the way his voice sounded when he first woke up because it was deep and resonant. He would sing me "Old Man River" in his rich, baritone voice. Sometimes at the breakfast table when I turned and smiled at him, he smiled back with an orange mouth. He had stuck an orange peel over his teeth. I loved the simple things. To my surprise, I even liked to grocery shop when I was with him. We spent a lot of time at the lakes, walking around them, riding bikes around them, and hanging at the beach.

David's co-workers planned a day of floating down the Apple River in July. David and I went, and we tied our seven tubes together and floated as a group. Sometimes, the current was fast and sometimes it was lazy and slow. When it was slow, I got up and tipped over David's tube. He chased and splashed water at me. One of the women, Shandra, didn't like what she called my "frisky" behavior and kept referring to me as his "little chippy." We ignored her and floated along, laughing. Greg sat on his tube, entertaining us by talking in different accents. First he was a "pimp" from the ghetto, then he was a "man from India," then he became a "southern gentleman." He was hilarious with his vocal impersonations. We had a great time.

David was a vegetarian who sometimes ate seafood or fish. He was down to earth and practical. I was not very practical, so I liked that he was.

One night, I told David I loved to camp and had a Timberline tent. He said he enjoyed camping, too. When I talked to my cousin Mary, who had a cabin on Bay Lake, she said we should camp on Lake Mille Lacs and come over to spend the day. The next Friday, David and I took off and set up my tent by Lake Mille Lacs. Once it was set up, we christened it by having tent sex. Then, we had supper and sat at the end of the dock, cuddling, looking at the lake, and watching the sunset.

David said, "At this moment there are so many different realities happening at once. Someone is watching the sunrise at this moment, someone is sitting outside in the cold, or someone is sitting at a restaurant in Malaysia ordering breakfast."

It was such a profound thought, and we sat there quietly, contemplating. We spent the next day at Mary's cabin exploring the lake in their boat and grilling. It was a nice weekend.

Towards the end of the summer, we camped at the head of the Mississippi River at Lake Itasca State Park. David had been encouraging me to run with him. So, after we drove to Itasca, set up my tent, put in our sleeping bags, "initiated" it, and, we went on my first run. We ran for 30 minutes along a dirt road, and his advice was to keep a slow steady pace. If I felt winded or wanted to stop, I should slow my pace but keep running. When we got back, we showered and made supper. We were warned about bears when we checked in, so we kept all our food locked in the car. After we cleaned up the dinner dishes, we snuggled in our sleeping bag and fell asleep.

I woke up a couple of hours later because I heard growling outside. I had to go to the bathroom but was afraid to leave the tent. I sat up in bed and I heard another growl.

I woke up David, shouting, "There's a bear!"

David startled awake, saw my shadow sitting up next to him, and in his groggy state, he thought *I* was the bear. He jumped. I reassured him that it was me. Suddenly, we heard car doors opening and more growling. Eventually, things quieted down, and David went with me to the bathroom. The next morning, the campers next to us asked if we heard the raccoons the night before. I said we heard growling and I thought it was a bear.

They said, "No, it was raccoons fighting over the food from our car."

One of the raccoons was able to open their unlocked car door and rummage through their bags.

After breakfast, David and I went to where the Mississippi River started. It was a trickle of water flowing out of Lake Itasca and traveled a couple of thousand miles where it emptied into the Gulf of Mexico below New Orleans. Our second night camping, we slept soundly.

In August, I answered an ad in the paper for a Chemical Dependency Specialist for the State Department of Corrections. They wanted someone with a master's degree or at least five years of experience in the field. I sent a resume, figuring I'd never hear from them.

**

On September 1st, David ran a 10K race sponsored by the Twins, which included two free tickets to the game. The race started and ended at Met Stadium. After I watched him cross the finish line, we sat in the outfield bleachers and watched the game.

As we sat there, I turned to David and said, "Let's drive to Winnipeg tomorrow and go to the racetrack."

He started to say he didn't think he could, but I interrupted and said, "Sure you can."

The next day, we left early in the morning. When we drove through North Dakota, the interstate was flat, boring, and went on for miles, so I decided to entertain David. I reached over and fondled his private area. A short time later, David had a big smile and said driving through North Dakota had never been so enjoyable.

We got to Winnipeg that night and checked into a hotel downtown. We went out for dinner and to a nice club where there was music and dancing, and the next day, we went to the racetrack, Assiniboia Downs, and made a little money on bets. We found another club that night, and the next morning, we headed to northern Minnesota and found a cabin on a lake for a night. It was romantic, waking up the next morning, sitting on the front porch having breakfast, and looking at the blue lake rippling in the morning light. I loved that David could be spontaneous and had a sense of adventure in him.

Chapter 39
White Powder, Under Your Nose

When I got home from our trip, there was an envelope waiting for me from the State Department of Corrections. I was invited to participate in a group interview for the Chemical Dependency Specialist job, scheduled on Friday. I went to the group interview, dressed for success, and ready to impress. There were forty of us interviewing. We were put into random groups of five. Each group was given a behavior problem to solve. Through discussion, the members had to come up with a creative answer to the problem. Afterward, we filled out a form stating: who we thought became a leader in our group, who organized the group, who we liked the most in the group, and who provided the most creative answers. There were three facilitators who also filled out the same form. Afterwards, they thanked us for coming and said they would be in contact.

I was one of six people who were asked back for an interview. I interviewed with Ray and James and then with their boss, Vince. I got the job, which I found out was located in Red Stone at the Red Stone correctional facility. My job was training the staff that worked with the adolescent offenders in the cottages, on: how to do a chemical use assessment, how to educate the inmates about their addiction, and to write a training manual, so after my one-year contract, a staff person could use it to do trainings. Also, while I was there, I would conduct chemical assessments on inmates.

I started work in September and was scheduled to work in the St. Paul office on Wednesdays and the rest of the week in Red Stone. I commuted back and forth to Red Stone, whose population was male adolescents incarcerated for serious offenses. For example, there were two brothers who burglarized the homes of elderly women, tied them to their beds, and raped them. Another offender had stolen an arsenal of guns. Assaults, armed robberies, and home invasions made up the majority of the offenses. I didn't deal directly with the offenders, except for doing chemical assessments. I was there to train the staff and write a training manual.

I had my own office in the "school building," and I worked closely with James Hardy, the head of the institution. He was nice, but I could tell he'd worked in corrections a while. One of the first issues I had to deal with was how I dressed. Because of my hippie background, I quit wearing bras. My chest dimensions were modest, so there was no bouncing when I walked, and I wore two layers of shirts, so nothing poked through. During my two-day orientation, I visited cottages to meet the staff and observe the inmates. One of the cottage staff complained to James about my lack of a bra. I really couldn't figure out how he knew, but I had to wear a bra. The staff trainings went well. I started to attract male staff admirers who would find excuses to stop by my office. Other men seemed threatened to have a "bossy female" training them.

I became friends with Arlene, who taught home economics classes in the school, and one night, when there was a bad snowstorm, she offered me her guest room for the night. I took her up on it. Her husband wasn't very friendly, and couple of months later, I heard they got a divorce.

There was a negative vibe in the institution about chemical use and that they couldn't treat the issue themselves. They didn't like outsiders, especially ones from the St. Paul office. But they tolerated me, allowing me to train them and do assessments on the inmates. I held two-day workshops periodically, teaching the "use continuum" for diagnosing chemical use. I taught how addiction affected the family and what needed to be done to intervene in the system. I developed a role-play called "The Balancing Act" where people are stuck on a life raft with no control. I developed a version of "Star Power" that limited social mobility and made them feel helplessness. In a chemically dependent system, no one is in control: drugs control the addict, the addict controls the family, and the result is chaos.

In November, the weather was getting worse, so driving back and forth every day to Red Stone was hazardous. There was a fatal accident one snowy day; a car was driving out of town and was run over by a semi when it jack knifed. The person was decapitated.

That Friday, I attended a morning breakfast with the town officials who met every week. I met Melanie there, and we started talking. She had an eating disorder, was OCD, and wanted a roommate to help with rent, but she didn't want to share her space. So, I came up with an idea. I asked if I could rent a bedroom in her apartment two nights a week. I'd only be there to sleep. She liked that idea. So, I rented a room on Monday and Thursday nights. It worked well.

**

Meanwhile, David was working as a TA at the University of Minnesota where he was getting his master's degree, and he was suddenly very busy. Summertime David was now professor and student David. David was very social, and he liked to come to the Malt Shop when I sang with Karen or Bill. He was supportive of my creative, quirky side. I felt good around him. He calmed me down somehow and made me feel connected.

My relationship with David continued to grow and deepen with his subtle romantic gestures. Christmas and New Years were approaching, and snow was on the ground. The temperatures dipped below zero, and David and I were riding around in his Volkswagen bug, with no heater. He had blankets in the car, but I didn't really dress for winter. I wore short jackets with tight jeans and high heel boots. One night, he brought me out and bought me a thick down jacket so I would be warm in his car. It was so sweet and caring that I let him do it, though I hated down jackets because I found them to be ugly. My friends commented that I dressed differently after I met David: not as sexy.

My neighbors had their first caroling party. It was ten days before Christmas, and the houses were aglow with lights and decorations for the season. There was a nice powdery snow that had fallen that day, and the temperatures were in the thirties — great caroling weather. David, Peg, Jenny, and I went to their house around five o'clock, where they had snacks laid out. They handed out books of carols, and we rehearsed and warmed up our voices. At six o'clock, we started down the street, knocking on doors, ringing doorbells, and singing carols to people who answered their doors. We got lots of smiles and people calling to other members in their household to come listen. At the end of our block, we went into an apartment building and knocked on the first apartment. A nun answered the door and welcomed us in to sing for their Christmas party. There were tables of food and people sitting everywhere. They loved having us there. About three blocks down, at one of the corner houses, a man invited all twenty of us into his living room. There were two grand pianos, and we gathered around them while they accompanied us. When we headed down the other side of the street to sing our way back to the house for hot chocolate, we all agreed to do it again next year.

On Christmas day, David got a large dose of my family. We spent Christmas Eve with his family, which was quiet with just his mom, brother, and his brother's wife. There weren't many decorations as David's mother was raised Jewish. My family's event was just the opposite. They loved Christmas, and the house was decorated from roof to basement with every room lit up with lights. My family was just getting to know David, and were relieved that he wasn't a hippie, he wasn't black, he didn't look like a biker, he was handsome, and he was getting his master's degree. I was relieved they liked him. They didn't know his mother was Jewish, and all my life, Jews were in the same categories as people of color. I was glad I wasn't like them. I liked David and felt like I'd always known him, like we were meant to be together.

In February, David and I headed up north for the weekend to try cross-country skiing. We got a room at Chateau LeVeaux on Lake Superior and rented cross country skis and boots. We skied a different trail through the woods each day. It was beautiful with the pristine snow and the absolute quiet in the woods. We had perfect temperatures for skiing and had a great time. It was our first time cross-country skiing, and we loved it.

**

Things got complicated at my job. One day in early April, I was doing an assessment with an inmate, a sixteen-year-old boy, Lance, who was taller than me, blonde, thin, and very quiet. He was incarcerated for burglary and sexual assault. Red Wing was a minimum-security facility, and the inmates traveled in pairs. When Lance came to my office, because of assessment confidentiality, I had the door partly closed. I conducted the interview, and when we were finished, I got up from behind my desk to escort him to the door. Suddenly, he was behind me, and he put me in a headlock, holding something at my throat.

I asked him, "What are you doing?"

He didn't say anything. He just stood there staring at me. My mind was racing. My first thought was I could take him because I weighed more than him, and I was stronger. But I couldn't see what he held at my throat. The night before, I'd watched a movie where someone was slitting throats with a razor blade, so I was hoping it wasn't that. I couldn't figure out what he was intending to do.

I asked him again, "What are you doing?"

Again, he just stood there, holding me in the headlock. I talked calmly to him, and eventually, he took his arm from around my neck and handed me the pointed scissors he had been holding at my throat. I walked him into the office next door and reported the episode. The receptionist called security. I sat down next to Lance and asked him what he was trying to accomplish. He finally said that he wanted to get my car keys and make a run for it Then, security came and took him to a secure building.

Afterwards, I sat in my office and thought about the incident. I wondered if I had acted scared and screamed, would he have tried to overpower me or if I'd gotten angry, would he have stabbed me? I think he was confused at my reaction, so he didn't know what to do. Years later, as an adult, Lance wasn't happy with his attorney, so he broke into his house, locked his attorney's dog in the closet, and burned his house down.

As I drove home that night, it suddenly hit me what could have happened in my office, and I started to shake. I was glad it was Friday. On Sunday, David was at my house, and we were relaxing and reading the Sunday paper. David reached across me to get a section of the paper, and the sudden movement of his arm, freaked me out and I started to shake. David held me, and then, made me breakfast while I sat on my back porch and played guitar. It took me a while not to jump at sudden movements.

**

In May, I started running 10K races with David. My first was the "Get in Gear," which started at Minnehaha Falls and went along both sides of the river, crossing at Lake street and ending up at Minnehaha Falls. It was exciting to cross the finish line. In Wisconsin, we ran another race that went through flat open areas, wooded lots, and at the very end was "heartbreak hill," which was very steep and long. But we did it. I averaged a ten-minute mile. I wasn't fast, but I was steady. We also raced in Stillwater and again at Minnehaha Falls. I enjoyed the races, even though I felt like a skittish racehorse with a combination of nerves and excitement, just raring to go.

At the beginning of June, my one-year grant was done. I left the Red Stone staff with a thick training manual to help them deal with chemical use education and assessment in their own facility. Now that it was summer, I was free, and I got summertime David back. During the school year, he had papers to write and tests to score, so I didn't see him much during the week. But when summer came, he was back.

In June, he had surprises lined up for the anniversary of when we met, June 10th. One night, it was a dinner at W. A. Frost, our first restaurant, and one afternoon, we rode on the Jonathan Padelford, where we met Then, there was a picnic by Lake Harriet and a lunch at the LeBistro. I think there was a Twins game thrown in there, too. It was a great week with unexpected little gifts along the way. I was in love.

In July, we decided to find a resort up north. We looked in the paper and found a resort on Long Lake. We booked it for a weekend. I hadn't been to a resort for a long time. When we finally found the dirt road leading to our resort, the sign said, "Long Lake Inn, a good place to eat, swim, and pray."

We looked at each other and said, "This can't be good."

We drove into the resort, which consisted of a lodge and one big building with four apartments, two on the bottom and two on top. The walls were so thin we heard the people next to us popping popcorn, and at night, we heard the husband snoring. They had one rowboat, which we took out the first morning. Later, we hopped in the car and looked for other lakes and resorts because we knew there had to be something better than this. We found Woman Lake Lodge on Woman Lake. The lake was huge with four good size bays. The cabins were nice and clean. So, we got information for the next summer. Then, we drove back to our resort on the puddle they called Long Lake and enjoyed being together.

**

Midsummer, I started getting phone calls for consulting jobs. The Minnesota Jail Association hired me to do a series of workshops on chemical dependency and the use continuum, unhealthy versus healthy families, and how to understand and work with inmates who are incarcerated. I did trainings for the staff at the workhouse and jail staff throughout the state of Minnesota, which means I traveled.

At the end of August, I got a call from PGLD, Peer Group, Leadership, and Development, an organization that did peer training in Catholic and private schools to develop positive peer cultures, leadership skills, and taught a week-long chemical dependency and drug use class in the health classes. We also ran sexuality groups in schools. One school system was in a nearby small town, where there had been an investigation of child sexual abuse. The fifth-grade boys called girls either sluts or prudes. We ran two groups and talked about how to treat each other respectfully and how it felt to be disrespected. The students opened up, and we talked about appropriate ways to treat each other.

I worked with some talented people, and one was Eric, a tall, thin, black man, with a short afro. His eyes sparkled with humor. He was smart and creative, and he had a quick mind that dealt with sudden issues that came up. He knew how to get the kids' attention and keep it. He was a brilliant group leader. I trained a lot with Eric and was very attracted to him. He often came over to work up lesson plans for the schools we worked in. He started flirting with me, and one night we made out for a while. But I stopped and told him that I was in a committed relationship, and that we could be friends. We were a great training team and worked together at a lot of schools. Our relationship stayed platonic, and we became close friends.

One day, I was at David's and saw something typed on a cover of a manuscript, "Polygamy vs Monogamy." I asked David what it was. He told me that he and his friend had an ongoing written debate which they'd been writing for years. David made a case for polygamy and his friend chose monogamy. I got a knot in my stomach thinking that David thought it was natural to have many relationships with women. He seemed so loyal in our relationship. I really trusted him, but his viewpoint shook my foundation. I thought he felt the same, and we ended up having an argument. We had reservations at a restaurant and a nice night planned, but I couldn't shake the feeling.

David, in his gentle voice, said, "Can we take this argument and put it on the shelf for later?"

I wasn't sure I was ready to let it go, but reluctantly I agreed and we "put it on the shelf." We went out and had a great night of dinner, movie, and a walk by the lake. When we got back to his apartment, we talked, and David reassured me it was just a philosophical debate.

After David and I had been dating for over a year, we talked about our relationship and where it was going. I told him that I wanted children, and at 31, my biological clock was ticking. I said I'd give our relationship another year, but if we weren't headed to the same goal, I needed to break it off to find someone who wanted what I did. He said he basically wanted what I wanted, and during the summer, we talked about living together. David suggested we live in the same apartment building, but in two separate apartments. I said I wasn't interested in that. Then he said that if we lived together, he needed to have his own office space. I said that was fine with me. It bothered me a little that he seemed afraid of living together or maybe it was the commitment, which I understood.

Chapter 40
Here Is My Light, I'll Share it With You

In the fall of 1981, David's mother had a two-bedroom apartment available in her Grand Avenue apartments in St. Paul. We decided it was time to move in together, and we rented the apartment.

I was excited about moving in with him, but also nervous, anxious, and ambivalent. It felt like a huge change and commitment. I loved my apartment and my freedom and felt an underlying anxiety about giving it all up. I trusted David more than I'd ever trusted anyone else; he felt like home to me. My ambivalence showed when Karen and her boyfriend came to help me move. Karen laughed when she saw all my shoes still lined up on the closet floor and all my clothes still hanging in my closet; nothing was packed.

She looked at me and said, "Are you sure you're ready for this?"

I handed her a garbage bag and said, "Yes, let's just throw things in here."

So, we dumped all the shoes in one bag and the clothes in another. A couple hours later, the furniture was loaded on the U haul truck with my kitchen dishes, pots and pans, and my garbage bags full of clothes and shoes. And we drove to my new home in St. Paul.

Our new place was across the street from a grocery store, a Kentucky Fried Chicken, and an Arthur Treacher's restaurant. The first thing we did was paint the apartment white, and Karen came to help. As we painted, I felt like I was coming down with a cold and had trouble breathing. When I went to work the next day, it cleared, but it came back when I returned home. I realized I was allergic to paint. Anytime anyone painted in our building, and I was in the hallway, my nose became congested.

Our apartment was long. There was a three-season porch in the front, then a living room, then a long hall, and the first door on the right was the first bedroom and the second door on the right was the second bedroom. A little further down the hall was the dining room, and then the kitchen, where we had a small kitchen table. David's grandparents lived in our apartment when David was growing up. So, it brought back good memories for him because he was close to his Grandpa Joe. David's grandmother was Jewish and attended a synagogue, and his grandfather was Muslim.

We lived in a trendy area of St. Paul. There were shops a block away with ice cream, gourmet chocolates, fresh pastries, and specialty restaurants we walked to every night. The pastries and the chocolates were our favorites.

In September, my work with PGDL started up again for the school year. One of the first assignments was a team-building workshop for seventh graders in a Catholic school. We did trust exercises, and we talked about who we went to when we were upset. One girl said she went to her father because he was honest and a good listener. Her last name was Aldy. I suddenly flashed back to when I was twenty-two, and I had just moved back to Minneapolis from Milwaukee. A man had brought me to his apartment in St. Paul, and told me to take off my dress, threatening me with a knife. His name was Frank Aldy. Later that day, I asked the girl if her dad's name was by any chance Frank.

With a big smile on her face, she said, "Yes, do you know him?"

I said I'd met him a few years back.

We both smiled and said, "What a coincidence."

Inside, I had a knot in my stomach, and didn't feel like smiling. My mind was still working on the new reality. Frank was married with a two-year-old daughter when he brought me to that apartment eleven years ago. I wondered what he would think if he knew I was teaching his daughter.

My own singing telegram business was doing well, and I received calls every week to perform for a variety of venues and celebrations: birthdays, weddings, graduations, expression of love, funny, and poignant ones. I mostly wore my top hat and tails, but every once in a while, I was a gorilla or a cat, or danced on a table with a rose between my teeth before I began singing. It was fun, and I made some good money.

**

A couple of months after we moved into our apartment, we discovered we had mice. I convinced David to get a cat; he OK'd it with his mother because it was her building, and we got a golden long-haired rescue kitten. We named him Rocco. Rocco became our first "child." When we got home from work or after dinner, we had kitty playtime. Down our long hallway we threw jingle balls to each other. Rocco chased the ball, or if he got tricky, he hid in a bedroom and attacked the ball as it went by. We played every day. I think we had as much fun as Rocco.

Our cat had this one endearing quality. When I walked in the door and made eye contact, he jumped into my arms, putting one paw on each shoulder, and laid his head next to my neck purring loudly. It was his greeting to let me know he missed me. One time, I got mad at him for getting into the flour when I was making cookies and picked him up to put him in the next room. After the cookies were in the oven, I went into the next room; Rocco jumped into my arms and gave me the biggest kitty hug like he was saying he was sorry. His nickname was Kitty Witter Fitter Bitters.

There was a lull in my work schedule in the fall, so I took a trip out East to visit Marty in New York and Sherrie at Purdue University. I traveled by train and stayed with Sherrie for two nights. On the second day there, Sherrie invited friends over for lunch and to read a play. She had five copies, and after lunch, we each took one, decided who would read which part, and spent the next hour reading the play. I enjoyed it and her friends.

That evening, we went to a co-worker's for dinner. When we arrived, I noticed a picture on the wall of a young boy riding a white rocking horse. It seemed like a happy picture, celebrating children and their toys. But I felt an undercurrent of darkness and obsession when I looked at it. It was a story I read years ago, about a young child wanting to help his poverty-stricken family by riding a rocking horse. The child discovered if he rode his rocking horse long enough, a winner of the horse race would come to him. In the end, the child died from exhaustion, leaving his family with money from his predictions, but sad at their loss. The image of that boy followed me into the living room, where I sat surrounded by two couples.

The picture began to haunt me, and I suddenly blurted out, "Do you know what the picture in the hallway is about?"

They all looked at me puzzled. I explained the story of the *Rocking Horse Winner*. The hosts for the evening had two young children, and they were shocked at the story and the picture's meaning.

Later, when we were at the dinner table eating, Sherrie mentioned that I read palms and did astrology charts. After we cleared the table, and their children were in bed, the couples asked if I'd read their palms. We went upstairs to the third floor, and I read everyone's palms individually, mixed in with my astrology insights. It was quite an interesting evening, and I enjoyed the two couples. When we got ready to leave, I noticed the picture across from the front door was no longer hanging there. A couple months later, I received a letter from the couple who hosted the dinner, saying they were going to be in the Twin Cities and wanted to know if they could have another "psychic" reading. They said the one I did for them was so accurate, and I was the best psychic they had ever been to. I'd never really thought of myself as a psychic.

The next morning, Sherry brought me to the train depot to continue on my trip to New York where I was staying with Marty for three nights. Marty had given me instructions for when I took a cab to her place in the village. She said to suggest the route to the driver, so I didn't get scammed for more money. After the cab dropped me off, I got a key from her neighbor, dropped off my luggage, and I walked to her workplace. I was wearing high heel boots, tight jeans, and a waist jacket, and I got whistles and comments all the way there.

When she saw me, she asked, "You came dressed like that?"

I said, "Yes, and I was harassed all the way."

Then she explained the appropriate walk-down-the-street outfit in New York was bumper tennis shoes, baggy jeans, and a long sweater or sweatshirt. I enjoyed my visit with Marty. We went shopping in the village, and I tried to get in touch with Ricardo. But he was unlisted. We visited with her friend Leann that lived with us on 1st avenue when she was pregnant. Her daughter was now ten, and Leanne was an artist, a painter, in the village.

When I returned home from New York, I walked into my apartment, and was surprised because David had bought fancy toys for Rocco. He bought him a triple-decker, carpeted kitty perch with three apartments the kitten could hide or sleep in. David, who wasn't sure he wanted a cat, and a man who doesn't like to spend money, fell in love with our cat while I was gone. I knew then that he was a man I could marry and have children with.

In December, David and I continued the caroling tradition, and two weeks before Christmas, we invited thirty people over to go caroling. Just about everyone came, and at 5:00 p.m., we handed out singing books, gathered in the living room with a cup of hot cider, and rehearsed the carols. When our voices were warmed up, we put on our jackets, mittens, and hats, and walked a block down Grand turning right into the Crocus Hill area, where the houses were big with beautiful front porches to sing on. The first house threw open their doors after a couple of songs and invited us in for cookies. We piled in, had a cookie, and continued on down the street. Every house was inviting with their Christmas lights twinkling, the people's faces full of warm smiles, singing along with us. Some houses offered us cups of hot cider or hot chocolate. At every house, the occupants joined in. Afterwards, we went back to our apartment for homemade chili, cookies, and hot cider. Everyone loved David's homemade vegetarian chili, and it became a must at our caroling parties. Our faces glowed with Christmas spirit and our cheeks and the tips of our noses were pink from the cold, but our smiles were warm with the joy of the season.

In January, David and I decided to go cross-country skiing up north. We brought Rocco with us and put him in the back seat of the car in a warm blanket. We packed our cross-country ski clothes, two copies of the play Othello, kitty litter, and toys for Rocco. When we got to our cabin, we unpacked, left Rocco at the cabin, and drove into Nisswa to rent cross-country skis and boots and look in the gift shops lining the street. An hour later, we drove back to the cabin, made dinner, fed Rocco, and went to bed. Each morning, we got up, had breakfast, played with Rocco, and then took off mid-morning to ski the amazing ski trails through the woods. There were big, tall, beautiful trees, dusted with a nice light snow, and a gentle wind we could hear coming for miles. It seemed like the trees were whispering a secret to us as we skied. It felt like we were the only ones out there. Then, we went back for afternoon sex and a shower, and later sat with our books on the couch with Rocco snuggled in between us, and read the play Othello out loud, each of us taking parts to read.

The last night at the resort, I noticed David and I were finishing each other's sentences and he'd ask me something just as I was going to ask him.

So, I said at dinner, "Let's see if we can read each other's minds."

I told him to think of one person in the restaurant and focus on what they were wearing. I guessed who the person was. Then he tried to guess what I was thinking and couldn't do it. I kept doing it and got five out of five correct and with the sixth one, I was half right because all I could read from his mind was purple and there were two people with purple on. I was getting goose bumps because I would get a rushing noise in my ears and then I'd "know" the answer. I'd never done this before. I asked him to think of a number from 1 to 10, and I got the number.

Then I said, "Think of any letter in the alphabet," and I got it.

Then I said, "Just think of any number there is."

My body got the rushing feeling, and all I got was the number nine. He said the number was ninety-nine. I got serious goose bumps because I was reading his mind. I realized later that because I was so relaxed, my mind free of worry, and I trusted David completely and felt safe with him, I was really open and able to read his mind.

**

289

May, that year, David took me to dinner at the Willows Restaurant in the Hyatt Regency, a very nice, white-tablecloth-with-candle restaurant, and known for its great service.

He turned to me after the waiter took our order and left, and said, "I think it's time to talk about this marriage thing."

I said, "What?"

He said, "I think we should set a date to get married."

I looked at him and asked, "Are you proposing?"

He said, "Yes, I guess I am."

Then, he reached over and kissed me. Inside I was excited, I didn't feel like I wanted to run away like I had with other proposals, and I really wanted to marry him. We had a superb dinner, and when David and I got in the car, I smiled to myself. We drove home, looked at the calendar, and decided to get married that year on October 10th, 1982. We liked how that number felt, and I liked a Libra wedding because Libras were about balance, fairness, and partnership. We talked about going to a justice of the peace and having a potluck supper at someone's house after. But when I told my mother, she suggested a reception at the Decathlon Club and then David said we should get married at Macalester chapel with a Unitarian minister.

In the summer, we went to Woman Lake Lodge, the resort we found last summer. It was a nice cabin, until the shower drain backed up with sewage. We ended up with a backhoe outside our windows digging and fixing it for almost a week. For a couple of days, we had to use the bathroom at the lodge across the road. But the lake was beautiful, and we had a fishing boat with a small motor to explore the lake. David's friend, Mark, and his girlfriend, Jill, came up for a couple of days. David was training to run his first marathon in the fall. I ran six miles with him, Jill said she could run the next six miles, and Mark ran the last six miles with him. It was a nice week. When the week ended, though, the owners didn't acknowledge our inconvenience or give an apology. We decided to find another resort on the lake for the next year.

**

In August, I started feeling anxious about getting married. I called Keith, my past therapist, and made an appointment. As we talked, he said it wasn't a fear of commitment, but it was the fear of abandonment and trusting and depending on anyone completely. It was a fear I learned in my early childhood. I told Keith that if I felt someone distancing, or pulling away, I would break up with him first, and I always had someone waiting in the wings just in case. I was afraid of depending on one person. My other fear was being trapped in a marriage like my parents.

Keith soothed my fears and helped me see David and I were nothing like my parents. David drank alcohol occasionally, maybe a glass a wine or a snifter of brandy late at night while he graded papers. I never saw him drunk, and the times he drank were few and far between. Also, David didn't yell, and we could talk through our arguments and resolve issues together. He was never abusive. We talked about how David wasn't perfect, but he was perfect for me. Keith helped me realize David was nothing like the family I grew up in. I felt lighter as I left Keith's office and realized I *wanted* to love David with all my heart, to jump in with both feet and trust.

The next day, David and I mailed out fifty invitations to our wedding, and one hundred and fifty invitations for our reception.

I wanted a small wedding, and I didn't want a fancy wedding dress. I bought a nice white dress that was short with a couple of little ruffles. We kept it simple. I didn't want to feel like a princess walking down the aisle; I wanted to be a real person committing myself to another real person. I didn't want to spend a lot of money or ask my parents for anything. I wanted it small, intimate, and low-key. My best friend Karen sang with my best friend Bill. Bill performed a song he wrote "Ode To My Women Friends" as I walked down the aisle. It was perfect. During the ceremony I looked up at David, with tears in my eyes and thought, *I found the college professor, who wears patches on his corduroy sport coat, the one I said I'd marry one day.* I was finally trusting someone enough to let my boat be tethered to theirs. As we sailed along on a current together, I knew sometimes a wave would hit, and it would change our direction. But I knew I'd look over and see the other boat still tethered to mine. I was no longer alone on my journey down the changing river of life.

Epilogue

At the end of my one-woman-show, Merica's Story, people stood up and gave me a standing ovation. They approached me after with tears in their eyes and told me parts of their own story. I received so many hugs and smiles. I had requests from many venues to perform my story for them: churches, theatres, schools, "Y" programs, and treatment centers. My story brought up many tears for people, but everyone felt better at the end. As I said in the beginning, you have to go through the pain, not around it, not avoiding it. You must feel to heal, and there *is* a light at the end of the journey.

David and I have been married for 36 years now with two children and two grandchildren, a third on the way. Life has had its ups and downs because that is what life does. David is still a little like an absent-minded professor, a man with good intentions, who tries hard to do what's right, but doesn't necessarily see what's right under his nose: me. Our family grew up with yearly trips up north to a resort, frequent road trips all over the country, family game nights once a week, and frequent camping trips with friends. Life was calm, happy, and I felt like I had found a placed I belonged and was loved.

My mother, father, and mother-in-law passed away, my daughter at four was diagnosed with a Kawasaki's disease and hospitalized, and my eight-year-old son had hernia surgery all over a ten-month period of time. My hyper vigilance kicked in. My survivor's need to be in control caused "battle fatigue," my doctor said. But I had David to support me through those times and other times as the years went on.

I am good at juggling many balls. I have two children and two grandchildren who I've taken care of for two to three days a week for the last six years. Meanwhile, I have a music studio where I teach voice, piano, and guitar. I perform periodically in cafes and coffee shops. I've written plays and hired actors to perform them around the city, and I put a band together and produced CD's of original music. I've written a book of short stories. I always have multiple projects going on at once.

The survivor in me still lives on, trying to stay ahead of things, creating more and more songs and stories. I guess I will always be a recovering survivor, trying to not be an adrenaline junky and enjoy each moment of each day. Appreciating what I can out of each moment. My grandchildren teach me that every day as I watch them grow. I try to take the time to see me. I will always be recovering from my adrenaline addiction. Analyzing things keeps my feelings of inadequacy at bay. Being a survivor has its cost: a sense of loneliness. I have been fighting so hard all my life to survive what is thrown at me. I get lost in the battles and the quiet, sensitive child in me gets lost, too. At times I am still haunted by the thought: can anyone see me?

I love my family of origin, but we are not close. We have tried over the years, but there is too much pain hidden in the walls of our childhood no one wants to talk about.

My older brother William is very involved in his church, and his older daughter is a missionary, his son a youth minister, and his youngest daughter died at seventeen from a complex blood disorder. He is very much a family man and devoted to his wife and his church. He is not comfortable with anything that is too different.

My older sister Patty is married to her second husband, who is an alcoholic but has been in recovery for many years. She has taken anti-depressants over the years. She is an artist and makes incredible decorations and arts and crafts for home décor. They have two sons.

My younger sister Becca is married with two children. As she got older, she started having memories of inappropriate touching by my father, my sister's boyfriend, and my brother, William. She has a horse ranch and rides in rodeos. Her ministry uses horses as therapy for children with issues. She calls it Mount up for the Lord.

Derek is married to his second wife and has two sons. He has his own company in the hospitality field and travels all over the world visiting incredible resorts. He has three daughters by his first wife, who he met in treatment for his alcoholism. She was a pathological liar with eating disorders who eventually divorced him. She ended up murdering her third husband and then killing herself, all on the 10:00 news in a southern state.

My younger brother and sister found strength in a born-again religion, and God is helping them heal.

All my family members are intense and driven in the way they live their lives.

**

I know I am broken, and I know the family I grew up in is broken. Over the years, I hid all the ugliness because I wanted to be normal, fit in, and belong. People came to me with their problems because I looked like I had it together. I was a survivor, and I couldn't let my brokenness show for fear of rejection. All my life, I've kept a smile on my face and soldiered on.

The energy from my brokenness seeps out in the songs, books, and plays I write. I'm always trying to understand my brokenness and how to heal it. I have a private relationship with God that's just between Him and I. I still want to belong and fit in but know I won't. I am unique with a deep ability to feel my feelings and the compassion and empathy to feel the feelings of others. I'm not afraid of their stories. A psychic once told me I was a Shaman because I had visited the underworld and brought my knowledge back to help people heal.

This book reveals to the world my brokenness for the first time. I have found beauty in my dark places.

In writing this book, I had to face those places and memories I hid deep inside myself and didn't want to acknowledge. I now know who I am. I have learned to love and accept myself. I will always be a survivor. I know there are others like me, and I hope we all have the strength to tell our stories. I hope we all find the beauty in our own brokenness.